To V

I hope you get well soon — here's a little something to read. I hope you enjoy it!

signature
Aug 2010

When Free Markets Fail

When Free Markets Fail

*Saving the Market
When It Can't Save Itself*

SCOTT McCLESKEY

John Wiley & Sons, Inc.

Copyright © 2010 by John Wiley & Sons, Inc. All rights reserved.

Published by John Wiley & Sons, Inc., Hoboken, New Jersey.
Published simultaneously in Canada.

No part of this publication may be reproduced, stored in a retrieval system, or transmitted in any form or by any means, electronic, mechanical, photocopying, recording, scanning, or otherwise, except as permitted under Section 107 or 108 of the 1976 United States Copyright Act, without either the prior written permission of the Publisher, or authorization through payment of the appropriate per-copy fee to the Copyright Clearance Center, Inc., 222 Rosewood Drive, Danvers, MA 01923, 978-750-8400, fax 978-646-8600, or on the Web at www.copyright.com. Requests to the Publisher for permission should be addressed to the Permissions Department, John Wiley & Sons, Inc., 111 River Street, Hoboken, NJ 07030, 201-748-6011, fax 201-748-6008, or online at www.wiley.com/go/permissions.

Limit of Liability/Disclaimer of Warranty: While the publisher and author have used their best efforts in preparing this book, they make no representations or warranties with respect to the accuracy or completeness of the contents of this book and specifically disclaim any implied warranties of merchantability or fitness for a particular purpose. No warranty may be created or extended by sales representatives or written sales materials. The advice and strategies contained herein may not be suitable for your situation. You should consult with a professional where appropriate. Neither the publisher nor author shall be liable for any loss of profit or any other commercial damages, including but not limited to special, incidental, consequential, or other damages.

For general information on our other products and services, or technical support, please contact our Customer Care Department within the United States at 800-762-2974, outside the United States at 317-572-3993 or fax 317-572-4002.

Wiley also publishes its books in a variety of electronic formats. Some content that appears in print may not be available in electronic books.

For more information about Wiley products, visit our Web site at www.wiley.com.

Library of Congress Cataloging-in-Publication Data:

McCleskey, Scott.
   Financial regulation and the markets : a guide to understanding today's environment / Scott McCleskey.
      p. cm.
   Includes index.
   Summary: "Authoritative guidance for navigating inevitable financial market regulation. The reform of this country's financial regulation will be one of the most significant legislative programs in a generation. *When Free Markets Fail: Saving the Market When It Can't Save Itself* outlines everything you need to know to stay abreast of these changes. Written by Scott McCleskey, a Managing Editor at Complinet, the leading provider of risk and compliance solutions for the global financial services industry. Looks at the intended result of these regulations so that institutions and individuals will have a greater understanding of the new regulatory environment. Offers a realistic look at how these regulations will affect anyone who has a bank account, a car loan, a mortgage or a credit card. Covers the reforms that have been enacted and looks forward to future reforms. Both theoretical and practical in approach, Financial Regulation and the Markets provides a strong overview of coming regulation laws with insightful analysis into various aspects not easily understood."
–Provided by publisher.
   ISBN 978-0-470-60336-9 (hardback); ISBN 978-0-470-64954-1 (ebk); ISBN 978-0-470-64955-8 (ebk); ISBN 978-0-470-64956-5 (ebk)
   1. Financial institutions–State supervision–United States.   2. Financial institutions–Government policy–United States. I. Title.
   HG181.U5M33 2010
   332.10973–dc22   2010018648

Printed in the United States of America

10 9 8 7 6 5 4 3 2 1

To my wife Ester and daughter Nicole,
the two ladies who keep me going

Contents

Acknowledgments   xi

About the Author   xiii

Preface: In Defense of Regulation (and of Free Markets)   xv

In the Beginning, There Was Adam	xvi
The Shift from Philosophy to Math	xvii
Can Markets Regulate Themselves?	xix
Regulation versus Justice	xx
Conclusion	xx

Introduction: Why Regulatory Reform Matters to You   xxiii

The Structure of the Book	xxv

Chapter 1: Meltdown in the Markets: Systemic Risk   1

How Systemic Risk Works	2
The Case for Government Intervention	9
Why Hasn't the System Collapsed Before?	10
Conclusion	12

Chapter 2: Can an Institution Be Too Big to Fail?   15

Policy Options	17
Conclusion	22

Chapter 3: Moral Hazard   24

The Theory	25
The Reality	26
Punish the Leaders, Not the Organization	27

viii ■ Contents

The Other Moral Hazard	28
Conclusion	30

Chapter 4: Toxic Assets — 31

What Are Toxic Assets, and Why Are They Toxic?	32
Building Low-Risk Assets Out of High-Risk Ones	33
Credit Rating Agencies and Structured Finance Products	35
Credit Default Swaps	37
Conclusion	40

Chapter 5: Should Regulation Stifle Innovation? — 41

Policy Implications	44
Conclusion	45

Chapter 6: Rewarding Success, Rewarding Failure: Incentives and Compensation — 46

Big Brother is Paying You	47
Regulating the Level of Pay	47
Performance Goals and Risk	49
Methods of Aligning Reward with Risk	50
Who Matters?	53
The 2009 Federal Reserve Guidance	53
Was Adam Smith Right?	56

Chapter 7: Who Protects the Consumer? — 57

Were Existing Regulations Effective?	59
Is a Separate Consumer Regulator the Right Answer?	61
What Powers Would the Agency Have?	65
A Word about Consumer Protection and Systemic Risk	67
Conclusion	68

Chapter 8: Transparency: Letting the Sun Shine In, or Sipping Water from a Firehose? — 69

Transparency as Regulation	69
Degrees of Transparency	71
What to Consider When Transparency Is the Proposed Remedy	73

Chapter 9: Rebuilding the Regulatory Structure — 75

Why So Many Regulatory Agencies?	76
The SEC and the Investment Banks	77
The Federal Reserve	78
Other Proposed Changes	79
Consumer Protection	80
Do We Need a Systemic Regulator?	80
To Concentrate or Not to Concentrate	81

Chapter 10: Rating the Raters: The Role of Credit Rating Agencies — 83

NRSRO Status	84
How Ratings Are Made	89
What Really Keeps the Rating Agencies Up at Night (And It Is Not Your Mortgage)	92
The End of the NRSRO?	94
Conflicts in the Rating Agency Business Model	97
Are Rating Agencies Utilities?	97
Conclusion	98

Chapter 11: The Politics of Regulation — 100

The Political Process	101

Chapter 12: Nice Law, Now Go Do It: Regulators and Compliance Officers — 106

The SEC	107
Examinations and Inspections	108
Conduct of Examinations	110
FINRA	112
Compliance Departments	113
Conclusion	119

Chapter 13: Cost-Benefit Analysis — 121

Basics of Cost-Benefit Analysis	122
The Benefits of Cost-Benefit Analysis	128
Government Use of Cost-Benefit Analysis	129
Cost-Benefit Analysis as a Negotiating Tactic	130
Conclusion	132

x ■ Contents

Chapter 14: It's a Small World, After All — 133

Sunday Is the New Monday — 133
Overseas Regulators — 135
International Organizations — 139
Conclusion — 141

Chapter 15: Where Do We Go from Here? Conclusions, Observations, and Recommendations — 142

Modern Markets Are Too Complex to Regulate Themselves — 143
Planning for the Next Crisis — 144
The Need for a Professionalized Regulatory Service — 146
Creating a Federal Regulatory Service — 148
Elevating the Compliance Profession — 151
Decisions Are Made by Individuals, Not Organizations — 152
Keep the Rating Agencies—But on a Short Leash — 153
Put Down the Pitchforks — 154
Conclusion — 154

Chapter 16: Judging for Yourself — 156

Conclusion — 161

Appendix 1: Summaries of Regulatory Concepts and Issues — 163

Moral Hazard, Too Big to Fail, Systemic Risk — 163
Unlevel Playing Fields — 165
Unintended Consequences — 166
Self-Regulation — 168
Regulatory Capture — 169
Information Asymmetries — 172
Conflicts of Interest — 173
One Size Fits All — 174

Appendix 2: Excerpt from Obama Administration's Reform Proposal, "Financial Regulatory Reform: A New Foundation" — 177

Index — 187

Acknowledgments

ALTHOUGH THERE IS ONLY one name on the cover of this book, in one sense it is the product of the combined experience of a number of people with whom I have had the pleasure of discussing regulatory reform since, and even before, the onset of the financial crisis. In some cases, their contributions came in the form of the normal debates and interactions around which my work revolves, and in other cases through more focused discussion and guidance. The colleagues with whom I have discussed and debated the issues include market professionals, regulators, journalists, and academics in the United States and overseas.

A few individuals and organizations in particular stand out for their support and guidance. First among these are my colleagues at Complinet, where I serve as Managing Editor for the New York office. In many ways, this is my dream job because it lets me talk all day long with people smarter than I am about issues I believe are important and interesting. Whether in London or New York, and whether journalists, compliance officers, or salespeople by trade, I have learned a great deal from them and I am grateful for that.

Additionally, I have sought the guidance of a handful of individuals whom I regard as experts in particular areas in order to inform, amplify, or verify the views reflected in these pages. Lisa Roth has an incredible breadth and depth of knowledge regarding the role and responsibilities of compliance officers, and she was very helpful in helping me make sure that my depiction of the world of Compliance was not limited to my own, possibly unrepresentative, experience. Likewise, you can stop Nick Paraskeva in the hallway and ask him what is the current status of any regulatory issue in the market, and he'll be able to tell you, along with the practical implications for the firms involved. Suffice it to say I spent a lot of time stopping Nick in the hallway.

Eric Kolchinsky was a respected colleague at Moody's, and was kind enough to review my description of the rating process in Chapter 10. Similarly, Jerome Fons, another former Moody's colleague (and also well respected), gave

xii ■ Acknowledgments

me valuable insight into the challenges of regulating the rating agencies in the course of several discussions and professional interactions. Genevievette Walker-Lightfoot, a former SEC attorney and one of the very few who raised concerns about Bernie Madoff, walked me through the SEC examination and investigation process to provide the kind of insight that comes only from experience. Additionally, each of these three, in their own capacities, raised alarms about practices and abuses that lie at the center of the financial crisis and its aftermath. We all owe them a debt of gratitude for that service as well. They are not alone, and I hope the historians who will write the story of the crisis recognize that the ranks of financial professionals, regulators, journalists, and academics who worked to prevent or address the crisis far outnumbered the greedy and incompetent few who caused it.

Manuscripts don't become books by themselves, it turns out. I am grateful to the professionals at Wiley who believed in this book and worked hard to get it out where it could, hopefully, do some good. I am particularly grateful to David Pugh, Brandon Dust, and Dexter Gasque, but there are many others all along the way from manuscript to book who helped make this happen.

Finally, I am deeply grateful to Ester. Being married to me is probably never all that easy, but when I committed myself to writing this book I committed her, too. Thanks for the patience and toleration.

About the Author

SCOTT McCLESKEY IS A New York-based financial journalist and is the US Managing Editor for Complinet. Specializing in financial regulation and reform, he has two decades of industry experience including roles in New York, Washington, Brussels and London. His background includes a range of roles, including retail stockbroker, stock market surveillance analyst, stock market policy director participating in the drafting of new European Union legislation, and working in and managing global compliance departments.

His publications include books and articles examining the financial markets with an eye to making regulatory issues understandable for everyone, in outlets ranging from professional journals to The New York Times. He has testified to Congress and worked with a number of agencies involved in reviewing the events that led to the financial crisis.

Scott holds a Master's degree in International Relations from Cambridge and a Bachelor's degree in Government from William and Mary. He lives near Philadelphia with his wife and daughter.

Preface: In Defense of Regulation (and of Free Markets)

REGULATION IS NOT SEPARATE from "the market," a concept foreign and antithetical to capitalism. It is in fact an integral part of a free market, as necessary as such widely accepted notions as competition or transparency. This is because free markets in the real world operate differently than in Economics textbooks, where models are distilled in an attempt to illustrate the *principles* of how real-life markets work. It is too often forgotten that markets came first, and market theory later arose to explain them. Much of the recent debate seems to take the view that the models came first and markets should be constructed to reflect the (largely regulation-free) models to which the commentator subscribes. In other words, it is all too easy to fall into the ideological trap of trying to make reality fit the model rather than the other way around.

This may not seem an especially provocative argument, but in some circles it is regarded as heresy to acknowledge the ideological legitimacy of regulation. During a time of turbocharged markets in everything from stocks to real estate to esoteric new financial instruments, there was an almost reflex reaction to regard regulation as a socialist corruption of the pure model of free markets. Though this mindset was not universal, it was widespread enough to cast any new regulatory proposal under a pall of suspicion. It didn't help that the booming markets coincided with an enthusiasm for deregulation that began in the early days of the Reagan Administration and endured for over two decades, regardless of which party held power.

The most glaring and tragic example was the resistance to efforts by the Commodities Futures Trading Commission to bring transparency to the credit derivatives market nearly a decade before that market collapsed. The very thought of imposing mere transparency—to say nothing of actual restrictions—on this market was greeted ferociously not only from the industry but by other government agencies as well.[1] The lineage of the notion that regulation reduces the freedom of the market can be traced back through the history of economic thought at least to the Scottish Enlightenment and the birth of modern capitalism, though the connection is actually a bit tenuous.

IN THE BEGINNING, THERE WAS ADAM

Capitalism existed long before Adam Smith, just as gravity existed long before Isaac Newton. There were even attempts to describe what we now regard as markets and market behavior before *The Wealth of Nations* was published in 1776. But *The Wealth of Nations* gave the world an *aha!* moment when it described, in a mere thousand pages or so, the way that markets worked at that time. And so, we rightly attribute the birth of the theory of free markets to Adam Smith and *The Wealth of Nations*.

Don't try to read the book, unless you enjoy spending five hours with Smith's unhealthy fascination with how nails are made. The good news is that people have read the book over the last two centuries and distilled from it the essence of Smith's economic theory. The bad news is that they overdid it and boiled it down to two words: *invisible hand.* For the ensuing 200-odd years, economic practitioners then reversed the process and expanded those two words into an economic dogma faithful to the original, they think. A lot of nuance was lost in the process.

The Wealth of Nations was written at a time when government intervention in the markets didn't mean pesky regulations here and paperwork there. This was the time of the British East India Company, an absolute government-imposed monopoly with no legal competitors (unless you count the *Dutch* East India Company). Smith's book was written as a repudiation of the prevailing mercantilist system, in which decisions were made by governments rather than by a dispassionate market. Given the state of governments in 1776, it is no wonder that Smith held little faith in the competence of government officials. His acceptance of government regulation was grudging and limited, but three points remain: He wrote at a theoretical level; his theories were grounded in

---

[1] For an excellent summary of this battle, see the PBS *Frontline* documentary, "The Warning".

reference to a far simpler economic and market environment than exists today; and, in spite of it all, his rejection of regulation was not absolute.

So when Smith talked about freeing markets from government intervention, he was writing about simpler markets operating in a completely different context from that in which we live. Of course, his basic premise still holds true in a general sense, but not in an absolute one.

Finally, Smith was an academic writing a treatise on the theoretical principles under which markets operate. Like other theories, it assumed away practical matters that complicate the actual operation of the theory (just as Newton's laws of motion assume no friction) in order to illustrate the guiding principles of free markets. Inefficiencies and imbalances distorted markets then, and they do now. Some participants seeking their own self-interest will have more market power (Smith loathed monopolies), or more information than others. People sometimes act dishonestly to distort prices. Do markets automatically correct these frictions? Not always, and not in the short run. Rules and regulations are meant to address these "market failures" and ensure a more fair and efficient market. When used this way, regulations actually make the market *more* efficient, not less. Of course, there are bad regulations as well, such as the one that said you had to buy all your tea from the government monopoly. The point, however, is that regulations are not inherently antithetical to free markets, and that good ones are as necessary to the operation of markets in the real world as traffic signs are necessary to free travel.

Smith's arguments in *The Wealth of Nations* center on three issues, only one of which is really related directly to markets: the division of labor, the pursuit of self-interest, and free trade. The markets he discusses, it should be remembered, were not specifically capital markets and certainly not capital markets as we understand them today. The market mechanism he described was as much a reference to 18th-century markets in corn as it was to anything else. Moreover, Smith and other political economists of his day were attempting to do for economics what Newton had done for nature—create a model system that could describe universal and therefore general phenomena. His models were meant to be *descriptive* of how markets work in principle, not prescriptive as an absolute blueprint of how they should be constructed.

 ## THE SHIFT FROM PHILOSOPHY TO MATH

If you do crack open Smith, or for that matter Ricardo, Malthus, Mill, or most other economists of the 18th and 19th centuries, you won't see many graphs, symbols, or arrows. Throughout its first century, Economics—*political economy*, as it tellingly was called back in the day—was philosophy. Indeed, many economists like Smith and John Stuart Mill had already established reputations through philosophical works before they tackled Economics (Smith with his *Theory of Moral Sentiments*, for example). Even the concepts of supply and demand, equilibrium price, and marginal cost were largely creations of the very late 19th century and the 20th century. The disadvantage to treating Economics as philosophy was that it wasn't very precise and therefore not of much practical use to those buying and selling in the market. The good thing was that everyone knew that was the case, and economists didn't try to measure things that defied accurate measurement. It was enough that free market theory told you in which direction prices or your profits would move as you produced more or less of your product.

The shift of Economics from applied philosophy to applied mathematics both reflected and propelled a desire to predict outcomes in the market. Later in the 20th century, a parallel development occurred in the field of risk management. In both cases, the ability to make outcomes more predictable and easily measured had great benefits. Policymakers could determine with greater certainty whether their measures were having the desired effect and when those measures could be stopped or reversed (think of the Federal Reserve and interest rates).

But the race for ever-more-precise measures runs the risk of forgetting that there are limits to the precision of measurements and that not all things are measureable and predictable—in other words, treating an art like a science. But when something is regarded as progress, it is difficult to argue that further progress is not achievable or desirable. No one ever got a patent, promotion, or Nobel prize for saying, "We've taken this as far as we can." Conventional notions of progress assume that there is always one more degree of exactitude that can be reached. But in a world of chaos and uncertainty driven as much by human whim and error as by the forces of mathematics, there is not always an nth degree. You may be able to measure only up to a certain point and then the rest is unpredictable. When it comes to risk, in particular, we should understand that our models are useful ways to group information and put it in context, but the equations can't tell us what to do and not to do.

A second danger arises with respect to the creation of mathematical models. Too often, their validity is tested by reviewing how accurate they have been in the past. That's all well and good as long as the future looks roughly the same as the past. Rating agencies were confident of their models used to assess the credit risk of subprime-loan pools because their methodologies had worked well in the (stable and benevolent) past.

And here's where regulation comes in. If you think that regulation in the form of "transparency" is sufficient on the grounds that the market can regulate itself as long as it has sufficient information, you place more faith in our ability to measure and predict market behavior than can reasonably be done. In a complex financial system, it's difficult enough just to know who has sold credit default swaps to whom, let alone the consequences of their deterioration under specific market circumstances. Reforming the credit default swap market by making their trading and ownership transparent may help to solve the first problem (though even this premise is somewhat doubtful, as one chapter in this book discusses), but it won't do anything to solve the second.

 ## CAN MARKETS REGULATE THEMSELVES?

One of the powerful things in favor of free markets is their ability to "regulate" themselves. While it is true that they do tend to self-correct with respect to prices, supply, and demand, that falls far short of saying that regulation is unnecessary. Regulation operates on other goals and characteristics of markets, for instance, to protect investors, to avert systemic risk, or to prevent unfair competition. In other words, they are meant to correct the parts of the market that it can't inherently correct itself. Regulation aims to make real-world markets look more like the ideal free market model, and that is why it is illogical to argue that regulation has no place in a free market.

So the argument in favor of free markets is that market mechanisms work automatically to set prices and allocate resources, *not* that they will automatically identify and neutralize their own failures. Some would grudgingly concede the need for the odd regulation here and there, but say that they should be as few and as limited as possible. I would agree. But as the markets have grown more complex, and hence more uncertain, the need for regulation grows. We need more regulatory oversight than we did 20 years ago, and less than we will need 20 years from now.

This book will also touch on the Efficient Market Theory, which holds that markets perfectly absorb information and translate it into changes in the price of a good (this is an oversimplification of a concept that could fill volumes). Implicit in the Efficient Market Theory is the assumption that regulation is superfluous. But, as I argue in the following chapters, we have reached the point where markets are too complex to absorb and process all of the relevant information. The market collapsed in 2008 in spite of all of its efficiency.

The problem with invisible hands, then, is that they are invisible. If we simply assume that the markets are invisibly regulating themselves, we abdicate our responsibility to confirm that they are in fact doing so. That is the story of the last decade, and how the Great Recession began.

REGULATION VERSUS JUSTICE

A recurrent theme in this book, and indeed in the regulatory reform debate, is that the financial crisis has left us with a sense of failed justice as well as failed markets. It doesn't help matters that so few individuals have been held accountable for their roles. There are logical and historical reasons for this. Building a criminal case takes a long time given the higher burden of proof required compared to a civil case, and historically regulators have found it more cost effective to settle a case than to go to court with it.[2] But the problem facing policymakers now is how to prevent a future crisis, not how high to hang the executives responsible for the last one. Although there are regulations against fraudulent activity, punishment is more properly the domain of the civil and criminal justice systems. Regulation should focus on preventing systemic failure and on protecting customers. The distinction between regulation and retribution is an important one, and one which policymakers and voters alike should bear in mind.

CONCLUSION

Perfect markets regulate themselves perfectly; all others require some level of regulation. And perfect markets don't really exist.

Given the very real calamities for the many caused by the excesses of the few, regulation should be viewed no longer as a necessary evil, but as necessary, period. All this supposes, of course, that the regulations in question are appropriately crafted, intelligently implemented, and effectively enforced by knowledgeable regulators.

---

[2] Kevin G. Hall, "Why Haven't Any Wall Street Tycoons Been Sent to the Slammer?," *McClatchy Newspapers*, September 20, 2009.

While the pursuit of self-interest may be the driving force that makes markets work, it did nothing to prevent homebuyers from applying for mortgages they patently could not afford, investment bankers from churning out billions of dollars' worth of instruments based on shaky sub-prime mortgages, rating agencies from diluting the meaning of AAA, or Bernie Madoff from stealing money on the order of a small country's gross domestic product. Self-interest can drive markets, but selfish interest can drive irresponsibility, inordinate risk-taking, short-termism, and outright fraud.

If you believe in free markets, you believe that they should be efficient and fair. You believe that they should be regulated.

January 2010
New York

Introduction: Why Regulatory Reform Matters to You

A DISHONEST MORTGAGE BROKER persuades an unwitting homeowner to sign paperwork transferring ownership in her house to him. A high school senior learns that he has no money for college because the trust fund established by his grandparents invested with Bernie Madoff. The Secretary of the Treasury calls the heads of the largest financial institutions into an emergency meeting to tell them that the government is going to take an ownership stake in their firms in order to save the world's largest economy, whether they like it or not.

These (true) stories have become typical and almost mundane, highlighting both the human cost of the recent financial crisis and the frightening scale of a crisis that sent the world to the edge of an economic abyss. Yet the stories are all about what happens when regulation *fails*. When regulation works, it is no more newsworthy than a traffic accident that doesn't happen. As the dust begins to settle on the financial crisis, people want to understand what happened and how we can avoid a future crisis. To do that, they need to become familiar with how financial regulation is made and how it works.

It seems strange that we don't take more interest in a process that has such a direct effect on our lives. We grow up learning that every good citizen should know the basics of how government works. We vote for the people who will best represent our interests in Congress—it seems we should know what those interests are. We follow, and sometimes participate in, active debate on somewhat esoteric subjects such as separation of Church and State or the meaning of the right to bear arms, but we have no idea how our credit card rates can be determined, whether a broker is required to give us the best

xxiii

xxiv ■ Introduction

available price when we buy or sell a stock, and whether our financial system will be steered off a cliff. We tend to close our eyes and assume that the development of financial rules is too complicated to be grasped by the layperson. We assume regulation is the domain of faceless lawyers, bankers, and civil servants with specialized knowledge and a high tolerance for tedium. It does seem strange that we ignore the rules that govern our financial health.

But there's something about the collapse of an entire global financial system that focuses the mind. The reform of financial regulation has become a popular, not to mention populist, issue. More and more people are concerned about how we got to the brink in the first place, and whether the laws being written to change the market will work. To do so, though, they need to be brought up to speed in the discussion. Terms like *credit default swap* and concepts like *moral hazard* aren't self-explanatory but they are swung around in the debate with abandon. But you don't need to be fluent in the lingo to understand what's being discussed—you just need to be conversant.

That's what this book is for. It is written for the outsider. It presumes little or no knowledge of regulation and is meant to be clearly written so that it is accessible to nonspecialists. It doesn't aim to provide an exhaustive examination of each issue, but rather to provide sufficient background for the reader to understand the debate and the policy alternatives and their potential impact. If you wish to explore a particular issue in greater depth, there is a long and expanding list of sources from which to draw and you are encouraged to do so.

When Free Markets Fail is meant to be objective in its analysis and descriptions, but like any book of this nature it rests on certain practical assumptions. Among these are that free markets are best for society and that that the goal of policymakers should be that the markets operate as efficiently as possible. Importantly, it also assumes that markets left to themselves will be inefficient and even fail, which good regulation can prevent or moderate.

The book also recognizes that regulation is a political process, subject to ideological filtering and to the give-and-take of Beltway negotiation. Lastly, the book assumes that bad regulation (whether poorly written or poorly implemented) can also damage the market and cause harm to individuals, and so regulation for regulation's sake is not always the answer.

It would be disingenuous to represent that the author of any book does not have his or her own views, experiences, and theoretical framework that form the foundation of its content. So here are mine: I support free markets, and have worked in a number of them for some 20 years, both on the business side and the compliance/regulation side. This experience has led me to see the markets as they really are, warts and all. And that is why you will see reflected in these pages an acknowledgment of the need for regulation as part of a free market.

The reader may not agree. If this book is like good regulation, there will be something in it for everyone to disagree with. And so the book also aims to assist readers in making their own judgments about regulatory proposals. In addition to the explanations in the body of the text, it offers at the end a series of questions to ask about any piece of regulation, to serve as the framework for deciding whether the proposal is or is not "good" regulation. Armed with this reasoned opinion, readers can then have a say on the subject through the same channels as they exercise civic responsibility—by writing members of Congress, through the media, or by the ballot box.

THE STRUCTURE OF THE BOOK

The book is divided into three sections. Chapters 1 through 10 discuss a wide range of issues that underlie the debate on how to reform the markets. The topics of some of these primers may ring a bell: systemic risk, "too big to fail," and the question of compensation. Others may be less familiar but are nonetheless important to the reform of the markets. The debate over the very structure of financial regulation and the roles of the various agencies is also discussed, with the caveat that the outcome of the debate is still up in the air as this book goes to press. The section also includes a chapter on the role of credit rating agencies, because they play a central role in the markets in good times and bad, but their function and processes are not particularly well understood. By way of full disclosure, I was responsible for compliance at one of the major rating agencies for two years (which might make me biased in their favor), but I have also provided testimony in Congress critical of some of that agency's practices (which might make me biased against them).

Chapters 11 through 14 shed light on the way regulation is made. It addresses the political drivers at the beginning of the process as well as how the regulators and compliance officers at the pointy end of the sword make sure that firms and individuals comply with the rules. There is also a discussion of how regulators and others weigh the costs associated with proposed regulation against the benefits to be gained.

These first two sections are meant to be reasonably objective in outlook, except where they identify arguments in the debate that are not well founded. The final two chapters are about opinions. This section starts by considering various regulatory alternatives and offers recommendations based on my own conclusions and experience. Lastly, I offer the questions that might form the basis for the reader to form his or her own opinions about what they read or hear regarding financial reform.

Together, the three sections are meant to build a coherent picture that will help lift the veil of jargon and complexity from the ongoing debate, and perhaps provide a persuasive argument in favor of particular policy proposals. At the same time, the chapters can be read as more-or-less standalone essays for those who have an interest in a particular subject. They do not presume that previous chapters have been read although they do on occasion point to other parts of the book for deeper discussion of particular topics. The inevitable consequence of such an approach is a certain degree of repetition, which is hopefully restricted to reinforcing concepts previously discussed or putting them in a different context.

For better or worse, the entire concept of financial regulation is up for grabs in a way it has not been since the Depression and in a way that is not likely to recur in our generation. This book is about why that matters, and why it matters to you, whatever your connection to the world of finance.

CHAPTER ONE

Meltdown in the Markets: Systemic Risk

THE ONE THING EVERYONE should know when trying to understand Economics is that the economy is about connections; this is all the more the case with respect to the financial system at the core of the economy. This seems both simplistic and obvious, but it is often overlooked as analysts, academics, and commentators agonize over individual firms—the trees—rather than how these firms are connected to and dependent on each other—the forest. An economy is not the sum total of its parts, but rather the sum total of the interactions among the parts.

This lesson was relearned as we watched the financial system crumble before our eyes. We were all busy watching the individual firms and not looking at how the interactions could turn the system upside down. The notion that one or two failures could endanger the whole system is known as *systemic risk*.

HOW SYSTEMIC RISK WORKS

The whole idea behind an institution being too big to fail is that its collapse would lead to the collapse of other firms (what has been called *micro* systemic risk), or of virtually the entire financial system (*macro* systemic risk). In connection with the financial crisis, the term *systemic risk* has been bandied about rather widely, and in policy debates the concept is often swallowed whole without substantial critical thought. This is troubling, given that the most important and wide-ranging regulatory reform proposals have been premised on the notion of systemic risk.

So, exactly how does the collapse of one firm risk the collapse of others? To understand this, it is important to understand how big firms operate and fund themselves, and how the markets they engage in lead them to be more, or less, deeply entangled with other firms large and small. It is also important to understand the importance of the most elusive and difficult-to-price commodity in the market: confidence.

Day-to-Day Funding

The collapse of Bear Stearns provides an instructive example of how firms fund their operations. The important point to understand is that, although they are competitors, they fund each other. This is one of the main reasons why they are so exposed to each other and why it is as important to see the connections in the financial system as it is to see the individual firms.

The fact that financial institutions fund each other is logical and perhaps inevitable. They are not in the business of keeping money hanging around in vaults doing nothing, so they like to keep it invested. But they don't necessarily want to tie up their spare cash for long periods of time, and so they lend it out for periods as short as overnight. They will make a far smaller interest rate than if they had loaned it out for a year or more, but when you are talking hundreds of millions or even billions of dollars, a small interest rate still means a nice little pile of cash; by loaning the money out for a short period of time the firm retains the flexibility to deploy the money elsewhere as soon as the opportunity arises. This is a far more efficient use of the money than leaving it uninvested.

On the other side of the transaction are firms that borrow money over a short duration to avoid long-term commitments that reduce their flexibility. When they borrow in this way, they do so by pledging securities or other collateral they don't need in the short term.

This type of overnight arrangement is known as a *repurchase agreement* or *repo.* The advantage of overnight repo financing is that it gives both sides the flexibility of short-term commitments and still allows the efficient use of otherwise idle funds and securities. The disadvantage is that it results in a financial system that needs to refinance itself every day. As long as things go well, or even reasonably well, there is no problem. There is very little credit risk (risk that the money will not be repaid) since the securities held as collateral are being held only over a very short term—how likely, after all, is it that the collateral will fail in one day?

How a Problem Goes Systemic

But things can go wrong, as they did during the financial crisis that led to the Great Recession. Some of the assets held at Bear Stearns, for instance, were linked to mortgage-backed securities or other difficult-to-price assets. When confidence drops on securities like these, it can fall right off the map and take their market price with it. No one wants to be holding the bomb when it goes off, and so the pressure to sell the securities turns into pressure to dump them and a rush for the exits. And since no one is committed for long periods of time, they can rush to the exits at the first sign of a panic. Thus, the trigger for a systemic problem is the uncertainty that arises as the result of one firm's collapse, not merely the financial difficulties of that firm itself. As one commentator put it, "Runs occur on solvent banks during panics because there is insufficient information in the public domain . . . to discriminate between the strong and the weak."[1]

A decline based on a loss of confidence isn't usually a straight line, but looks much like a downward-sloping curve that gets steeper as it goes. This reflects panic. The risk of fluctuations in the overnight price of an asset used as collateral in the repo market is normally accounted for by requiring slightly higher value of the collateral than the value of the money loaned. But steep drops are a different matter, and if a large proportion of a firm's ready assets are of questionable value, it will face a situation where some firms will ask ever-increasing amounts of collateral for each dollar loaned (effectively anticipating a larger and larger drop in the value of the collateral) or simply refuse to engage in overnight repos with that firm. The latter makes a lot of sense, since there are plenty of other firms to do business with instead. The failing firm finds that it has to pay higher and higher interest rates and post more and more collateral to

---

[1] Christopher T. Mahoney, "Market Discipline Is Not the Answer," *Barron's*, November 30, 2009.

4 ■ Meltdown in the Markets: Systemic Risk

entice other firms to keep doing business with it—just as any individual with credit problems must do. This reinforces the vicious downward spiral that could ultimately lead to collapse.

"At the Mercy of Rumors"

In the uncertain environment that builds around the potential failure of a big financial institution, rumors start to swirl. In the eyes of many, the rumors are what cause a crisis. In December 2008, nine months after the implosion of Bear Stearns, its former Chairman Ace Greenberg said in an interview that the investment banking model is now dead, that "that model just doesn't work because it's at the mercy of rumors,"[2] and later added that

> a rumor can put any of these firms at peril. . . . (Even Goldman Sachs and Merrill Lynch) had to convert over the weekend to banks, had to have infusions of capital because they couldn't withstand the self-fulfilling prophecies of the rumors.[3]

Bank runs and rumors—underlying it all is the crucial, though somewhat slippery, issue of confidence. Once a firm's ability to raise money and to meet its obligations is questioned, its entire business can seize up almost literally overnight. The downward spiral picks up speed when those responsible for assessing the firm's value or its ability to pay its debts—research analysts and credit rating agencies, respectively—downgrade the firm's stock and credit ratings. Doing so may be an entirely accurate reflection of the state of things: Counterparties are reducing overnight funding to the failing firm or demanding increased collateral, and so the firm's ability to meet its obligations is in fact shrinking. But when the downgrades are announced, the failing firm is hit with a double whammy. First, the downgrade lends an air of objective confirmation that the firm is indeed having liquidity problems and gives thus credence to the rumors. Second, the firm's problems are no longer merely a matter of rumor control and market psychology, since many of its counterparties' risk management controls prohibit or restrict dealing with a counterparty that has a "speculative" (junk) bond status. They have no choice but to pull away from the failing firm and its debt, given the legal covenants governing their investment practices in order to protect them. These measures have the ironic

---

[2] Elizabeth Hester and Peter Cook, "Greenberg Says Death of Bear, Lehman Means Wall Street Finished," Bloomberg.com, December 9, 2008.

[3] Interview, *Frontline*, "Inside the Meltdown," PBS, February 17, 2009, transcript available at www.pbs.org/wgbh/pages/frontline/meltdown/interviews/greenberg.html.

unintended consequence of spreading the panic, and, as was the case with Bear Stearns, a rating agency downgrade can easily turn into the tipping point from which there is no return.

One of the lessons of the financial crisis is that avoiding this tipping point is crucially important.

This is how a firm can find itself falling from the top of the heap to the bottom of the pile with dizzying speed. Still, in many cases the problem corrects itself eventually when an investor with a higher risk tolerance sees the value of the collateral as undervalued, or the higher interest rates extorted from the failing firm as a good investment. The market creates a floor at which point investors come in, and the market stabilizes. Of course, if all else fails, the government could step in and play this supporting role—in other words, give a bailout. Either way, once the market sees that the firm is not on the verge of collapsing overnight, the process tends to reverse slowly. But in rare cases, the uncertainty as to the value of the assets prevents the floor from being created, and the firm goes *poof.*

Discussions among policymakers regarding systemic risk have focused largely on one factor, and that is the size of the firm. A big firm tends to owe big debts to a lot of other firms, so undoubtedly the failure of a large institution is likely to cause other firms to fail. But "big" is merely shorthand for a number of factors that are really more important, and that happen to be common among big firms. The better notion is captured in the term used in recent legislation, *systemically important.* This term pulls off the feat of being ambiguous in a way that only bureaucratic terms can be, and at the same time usefully capturing the concepts that make a firm a potential threat to the financial system.

Many firms are important to the system but are not big. Stock exchanges, the clearing houses that administer and settle the trades, the rating agencies, and firms that are small but hold an important segment of an important market (such as AIG and its dominance in credit default swaps) are examples.

It is important to know why a particular firm is important because this should help determine which tools would be used in case the firm finds itself in crisis. The potential failure of the Depository Trust Clearing Corporation (DTCC), for example, would have severe consequences for the markets but such a failure is more likely to be technological in nature than a matter of credit and liquidity, since DTCC does not trade or invest. It could be argued that the failure of the rating agencies had already occurred when they failed to perform adequately their role in assessing the risks inherent in various complex structured instruments. In neither of these two examples would a financial intervention have helped. So, while it might make sense to increase capital

Collateral Damage

Another factor that can turn a firm from big money-maker to big money-loser is leverage. *Leverage* simply means borrowing money to invest, on the assumption that you will make more money from the investment than you will owe on the loan. A firm's leverage is customarily expressed as a ratio of borrowed money to hard assets (that is, loan to collateral). It makes winning bets into huge winning bets, but can work just as powerfully in the other direction in case of a loss. Of course, losses happen all the time and so a mechanism is built into the process in order to protect the parties loaning the money. This is the *margin call.* A margin call requires the borrowing party to pony up more cash or other collateral to back up the loan if the investment bought with the borrowed money has dropped significantly in value (the investment is the initial collateral).

So now view the Bear Stearns collapse from the point of view of the rest of the market. For some, the use of risky and difficult-to-price toxic assets will mean that you demand higher collateral, or that you simply cease to loan money to Bear Stearns at all. Others may not have accepted toxic assets as collateral, but they start to feel exposed nonetheless because the firm is so highly leveraged (say $30 of loans for every $1 of collateral), they fear the firm will head for bankruptcy, and all forms of collateral will be at risk.

When a run like this starts, the impact is not limited to the repo market. The repo market is used to fund the day-to-day requirements to buy and sell shares for customers, to meet mutual fund or hedge fund redemption, and to settle derivatives and other trades done for its own account. If the firm's ability to raise cash in the repo market is constricted, so are many of its other activities that touch other firms and investors. Even those firms that do not loan money to the failing firm in the repo market may well be reluctant to engage in any business at all with it, fearing that the firm will not be able to meet its obligations. It's a kind of institutional run on the bank, where the other firms may know that it is bad for the financial system for everyone to pull out and it may not even be warranted, but no one wants to be the last one left when all the money has been taken. The people at the other firms making the decision as to whether they should continue doing business with the failing firm owe no duty to the failing firm and not even an explicit duty to "the system." Their duty is to their own firm and so it is easy to see why the reluctance to deal would grow.

Money Market Funds: From Safe Harbor to Live Wire

Beyond repo agreements, financial institutions need a stable place to keep their cash that is not invested in the market. They don't open a checking account at the local bank, however. In order to achieve a slightly higher interest rate than they could with a normal bank account, they keep their funds in what is called a *money market fund* (as do other big institutions). The attraction of these funds is that they have virtually the same liquidity as a bank account (meaning immediate access to your money) while paying a higher interest rate. Money market funds have become the principal means by which large institutions hold their ready cash, and its importance is reflected in the fact that some *$3.5 trillion* moves through this market every business day.

Some of these funds are available to retail investors and some only to institutions, but they share essentially the same characteristics: safety of principal, high liquidity, and higher interest rates. Retail money market funds should not be confused with money market *accounts* at banks, which are simply a way of paying interest on what would otherwise be a checking account (by law, actual checking accounts are not permitted to pay interest). These accounts are general obligations of the bank and as such are not backed by assets in the way that a money market fund is.

SEC regulations restrict what a money market fund may invest in. These restrictions specify that the investment must meet specific standards with respect to quality (the law requires that the fund invest only in something that is deemed to present "minimal risk," as evidenced by its credit rating among other things), and maturity (13 months or less, with a weighted average of 90 days or less). The funds must also diversify their holdings, with no more than 5 percent of the holdings having been issued from any single issuer. The two exceptions to the 5 percent concentration rule are government securities and, as fate would have it, repo agreements. Thus, money market funds had no statutory limit to prevent them from loading up on repo agreements from one or two investment banks. Since money market funds are one of the main places for financial firms to place their funds, their ability to load up on repo agreements from a small number of banks is one of the main mechanisms of interdependency in the financial industry. It is also one of the least transparent,

8 ■ Meltdown in the Markets: Systemic Risk

since it is hard to know in which funds a particular firm is holding its cash, and what those funds are buying.

Money market funds have been the norm for decades as a means through which financial institutions and other large firms have managed their cash. This phenomenon was driven in good part by their reputation as a safe place to put funds. They are constructed to ensure that the share price stays stable at $1 per share: If you invest $100,000, you know you will get back $100,000 when you need it, plus whatever interest has accrued. If the price were to fall below a dollar per share—"breaking the buck," in financial parlance—the depositor would lose some of its invested principle. For this reason, breaking the buck was the ultimate taboo and it had happened only once since the early 1970s—until Lehman Brothers went belly-up.

What happened then illustrates why and how these funds can transmit and amplify financial shock and turn one firm's failure into a potential economic disaster. The restrictions on the investments available to money market funds, meant to ensure that the funds are stable and conservative, induce them to invest in highly rated repo agreements, and since the 5 percent rule does not apply to repos a fund can become disproportionately exposed to the repos of a single financial institution. The fund has an incentive to invest in particular in the repos of the institution paying the highest interest, and that is likely to be the one that is weakest. So, when things start to go wrong they can go very wrong, very quickly. If a failing firm's credit rating is reduced from investment grade to junk—often falling several levels at once—it is difficult to justify calling the debt a "minimal risk," and so it is no longer eligible to be held by money market funds. And things can get worse. When Lehman Brothers filed for bankruptcy on September 15, 2008, its repo agreements and other debts were essentially worthless and had to be written down to zero by the funds holding them. Among those holding a large proportion of Lehman debt was Reserve Primary Fund, the oldest money market fund in the United States and at $62 billion one of the largest. Writing down such a large chunk of its assets meant that its net asset value (price) fell below $1 per share. Now, Lehman Brothers' problem became a problem for any firm that held its money in Reserve Primary Fund.

Moreover, since no one knew which other money market funds held Lehman repos, it was anyone's guess whether another fund would break the buck, by how much, or when. The prudent thing for a company treasurer to do in such a situation is to start pulling the company's money out of money market funds at least until the situation becomes clear. Indeed, by the end of the week more than $200 billion had been withdrawn from money market funds—some $40 billion more than the estimated cost of the entire savings and loan crisis.[4] If enough companies pull out of a fund, it has to sell its holdings in order to pay cash to the customers pulling their funds out, and this could create a downward spiral on the assets of that fund (causing it to break the buck). This can also cause a run on the assets being sold by the failing fund into the market, and this in turn could cause the panic to spread to other funds holding the assets being dumped into the market at ever lower prices. In this scenario, money market funds become the conduit though which the crisis spreads far beyond those firms directly exposed to the failing bank's obligations. The analogy is no longer falling dominoes but a live wire that spreads the shock to all who touch it.

In the end, there was no run on the bank in money market funds, partly because the Treasury announced three days later that it would offer to insure money market funds to keep them from falling below $1. Whether this intervention was appropriate will be the subject of debate for some time, but whatever prevented the panic from spreading was crucial to bringing the financial system back from the edge and avoiding a catastrophe of far greater proportions than the severe one we did endure. If the money market system had shut down, the entire financial industry would have had an immediate liquidity crisis and would have frozen in place, cutting off lending to the entire economy.

As scary as this near-miss was, it is not an indictment of the money market system as a way of funding the economy. Overnight lending and money market funding worked without a hitch day in and day out for decades and will continue to do so, most of the time. As long as events and circumstances stay in the fat, "normal" part of the bell curve everything works perfectly. Like so many other causes and effects of the financial crisis, the problem lies in ignoring the tails of the bell curve as if they never occur. The lesson is to recognize that systemic risk acts through panic and uncertainty, and that the key to avoiding future crises is to plan for measures that give comfort that it's safe to keep trading and investing even if one or more firms are failing.

THE CASE FOR GOVERNMENT INTERVENTION

Clearly, one of the principal contributing factors of the financial crisis, and perhaps the main trigger of the systemic collapse, was the absolute dependence of the market on confidence, and the self-fulfilling nature of negative rumors

---

[4] "The Lehman Legacy: Catalyst of the Crisis," *Financial Times*, October 12, 2008.

when a firm is already in a weakened and vulnerable condition. This leads some to the conclusion that a clear, even explicit, expectation of government support in such situations is critically important to avoid the rush for the exits that turns the problems of one firm into an economic crisis. This implies that some sort of formal government policy regarding support for failing systemically important firms, or at least a plan for the orderly resolution of a firm that will be allowed to fail, is not just appropriate but necessary. Bear Stearns Chairman Ace Greenberg made the point by comparing the vulnerability of investment banks, which did not have explicit government support, with commercial banks, which do:

> (I)f a bank is solid, the Fed will just say, "The bank is solid; we'll give them money to pay off the crazy people that are running on the bank." If the bank isn't solid, the Fed will say, "Let it go," like they [did] in many instances in the past year. So there is security in being a bank.[5]

An established government process for supporting a failing institution or for ensuring its orderly resolution through bankruptcy makes sense for the simple reason that it addresses the real causes of systemic risk: uncertainty, lack of confidence, and panic. Having *no* such process is bad policy, and so any plan that seeks either to leave failing firms to the wolves, or to eliminate the problem by limiting the size of institutions, places the financial system in danger. Plan B should also include stiff sanctions against the individuals at the firm responsible for its predicament. The policy implications of government support are discussed in Chapter 15.

 ## WHY HASN'T THE SYSTEM COLLAPSED BEFORE?

Given the closely interconnected nature of the financial system, one might easily wonder why we did not have a huge financial collapse earlier, at least not since the 1930s. It almost seems inevitable that a bad day on the market for one firm, or the rumor of a bad day, would lead to financial Armageddon within days. So, why have we been so lucky? The answer is probably precisely that— we have been lucky—but there are two points worth raising.

---

[5] Interview, *Frontline*, "Inside the Meltdown," PBS, February 17, 2009, transcript available at www.pbs.org/wgbh/pages/frontline/meltdown/interviews/greenberg.html.

One is that the financial system has become more complex than it was 5, 10, or 25 years ago. It is complex in that there are more institutions with more points of connection with each other, whether as counterparties in loans and transactions or by investing in each others' commercial paper, swaps, and other securities. And the financial instruments that have been summoned into existence such as credit default swaps and collateralized debt obligations have made the connections more volatile and powerful. It is also complex because no one really sees all of the connections or the size of the exposures they create, and because they change from day to day (think of money market funds, for instance). At the same time, the number of connections and exposures has brought firms into closer proximity to each other. It used to be said that no actor was more than six degrees of separation from Kevin Bacon, but in the markets today it is likely that no firm is more than two or three degrees of separation away from any other firm. As a result, failure does not move linearly like a set of dominoes, but in all directions like a flu epidemic in a crowded city. This is a fundamental reason why the last financial crisis was different from the Savings and Loan crisis of the 1980s and 1990s. That crisis shut down nearly 750 savings and loan institutions, but the sector was not as intimately entangled with the rest of the financial system as were the investment banks of the recent crisis.

This opacity resulting from the complexity of the system means that uncertainty, fear, and rumor are part of the market. In earlier crises, it was indeed fear itself, or at least uncertainty, that was our greatest enemy. And like it or not, it has often been the government that has stepped in, directly or indirectly, to restore confidence and stop the panic. When the Long Term Capital hedge fund collapsed, threatening to take the big banks down with it, the government arranged a bailout of the fund, though it did so by using moral suasion to get the banks to fund the bailout themselves. And so the role of government intervention in its various forms should not be overlooked when considering why we had been lucky for so long.

The second point is that we will be unlucky again. The financial crisis has taught valuable lessons, but it was not The Crisis to End All Crises any more than the First World War was the War to End All Wars. We have learned of the need to view risk from a systemic point of view rather than on a firm-by-firm basis—but as we pulled away from the brink we quickly started to forget how close a near-death experience we had had, and this sense of denial may force us to miss important opportunities to reform elements of the system.

Even if we did learn all of the lessons, though, crises would still be inevitable. The system is already too complex to be fully understood and reliably monitored by people or by computer systems, and the resulting uncertainty and unpredictability make it inevitable that things will get ahead of us again. This is one of the more ironic features of post-crisis reform: We all seem to agree that some financial instruments were too complex to understand, but we have not recognized that this means the markets themselves have become too complex for market participants to understand. We still believe that markets can comprehend these steroid-enhanced instruments and correctly price them, and that the markets can therefore look after themselves. What is needed instead is a plan to prevent crises as best as possible and to mitigate them when they do occur, so the world is not dependent on a handful of bankers and bureaucrats, looking like Jack Bauer around hour number 22, working over a weekend to prevent a global catastrophe.

CONCLUSION

The threat of systemic risk has gone from an academic hypothetical to the central theme of regulatory reform. It is now as likely to be heard from a politician on an afternoon cable show as from a professor at a conference. It has become a familiar topic because it has become a reality, and one that has had a direct effect on everyone. But the fact that it is commonly mentioned does not mean that it is commonly explained, and one can form an informed opinion of how it should be addressed without understanding how it works. This chapter has aimed to provide such an explanation, albeit a simplified one, so that the reader has a better picture of what exactly is meant by "systemic risk" when the term next pops up in the media or on the campaign trail. The most important things to remember are:

1. Regulation that focuses on the firm and ignores the system as a whole is doomed to fail.
2. The system is complex and therefore prone to uncertainty and rumor, especially when the financial environment moves into uncharted territory.
3. In a period of increased uncertainty, the general attitude toward risk can turn on a dime as individuals and firms become defensive, either by instinct or, once the tipping point has been achieved, by covenant, policy, or even law.
4. Unchecked uncertainty can build on itself and trigger panic, and so the government's ability to intervene on behalf of a firm can help stem a systemic panic before it begins.

Conclusion ■ **13**

EXAMPLE

Bear Stearns and Systemic Risk

Like other investment banks, Bear Stearns was so profitable because it did not limit itself to its own money when it went to the market. It borrowed from other firms. When an investment bank invests borrows money in this way, it enters into an obligation with someone to pay the borrowed money back and it does so on two assumptions: (1) that it will make money on the investment and thus have money available for repayment of the loan when it is due, and (2) that not everyone will demand repayment of the bank's outstanding loans at the same time. If assumption number two holds, assumption number one does not need to hold all the time. There will be enough money at hand from the firm's existing capital, or the firm can borrow money to make good its payment.

The market for this kind of short-term financing—the "repo market"-is usually very liquid, meaning that there is plenty of money available and it is relatively cheap to borrow. This is because there is much less chance of a firm reneging on its obligation to pay a loan in the space of one day; it is a relatively low-risk way to get a little bit of interest on funds that would otherwise be earning nothing. This all works well, and has done so for decades, as long as overnight lending is considered low risk. And it needs to work well, since this overnight funding is how the big banks finance their operations.

When questions started to arise as to the creditworthiness of Bear Stearns, it became more and more difficult for the firm to borrow the billions of dollars it needed in the overnight market. If firms begin to question whether another firm can meet its obligations, they will either refuse to extend credit in the overnight market or demand more collateral for the funding. Since collateral can be pledged to only one counterparty at a time, a firm experiencing this vote of no confidence rapidly runs out of collateral, runs out of funding when it can no longer secure overnight loans, and ultimately goes bankrupt.

The ball started rolling against Bear Stearns when the housing market collapse led to the equally precipitous fall in the value of residential-mortgage-backed securities (RMBSs; see Chapter 4). Bear Stearns had borrowed heavily to invest in these securities and had done very well while the securities did well. The market knew that Bear Stearns was heavily invested in (that is, exposed to) the RMBS market. Of course, the market did not know exactly how exposed the firm was, and that uncertainty served only to exaggerate fears. As the value of these investments plummeted, so did the level of Bear Stearns' reserves (since the notional value of how much money

(continued)

14 ■ Meltdown in the Markets: Systemic Risk

(*continued*)

the firm could raise by selling them—if it could sell them—was reduced). Their value as collateral in the overnight loan market also fell. As rumors spread about Bear Stearns' liquidity, a run on the bank began. No firm wanted to be left holding the bag as a creditor to Bear Stearns the morning they went bankrupt. Unlike depositors covered by FDIC insurance, creditors to Bear Stearns would have to wait in line, possibly for years, to see whether they would get repaid from any remaining assets. Given their fiduciary responsibility to their investors and their own personal interest in trading profitably, decision makers at many, then most, firms became reluctant to do business with Bear. Some reduced their exposure, some demanded more or better collateral, and some simply stopped doing business with them.

Once this type of run on the bank begins, it is as difficult to stop as a runaway train. The market reached a tipping point when it collectively lost confidence in the firm and as a result funding vanished, literally overnight. Perhaps the final shove over the edge came from the rating agencies, who (rightly) downgraded the rating of Bear Stearns debt, including its repos, in recognition of its increasingly shaky position.

Of course, investment banks have been exposed to bad asset classes before without bringing the capital markets to the abyss. Why was this different? For one thing, few asset classes had been so highly inflated and had such a large market as RMBSs. For another, Bear Stearns not only created many of the RMBS securities that were sold into the system, but it also bought more and more of them. The decision to eat their own cooking turned out to be a fatal one when it became clear it had been cooking with toxic ingredients. ■

In the end, the fate of Bear Stearns and others shows that firms can grow to the point that they are systemically important because their size brings large exposures to a large number of firms in the financial system, making them too big to fail. But the financial system isn't vulnerable to these firms simply because they're big. Their size makes them too interconnected to fail, so that the opacity of the market means that no one knows who is exposed to the failing firm. A lack of confidence in one firm becomes a lack of confidence in all firms. Having institutions that are too big to fail may not sit well with everyone in the policy debate, but good policy would recognize this fact and consider why they pose a threat in the first place.

CHAPTER TWO

Can an Institution Be Too Big to Fail?

T O A GREAT EXTENT, the debate over how to fix the financial system has boiled down to an argument over how to handle institutions that are "too big to fail." Do you ban a firm from getting that big? Do you penalize it for its size in order to create an incentive to remain small? Do you guarantee it against failure?

This section delves into the nature of firms that are "too big to fail" and how policymakers have proposed to address the issues they raise. It begins by considering how these firms are identified in the first place and the complications that arise in doing so. It also looks at some of the proposals for dealing with these firms, and the potential impact of the proposals on the financial system. But (*spoiler alert*) it will also conclude that a fixation on the size of a firm is misleading and an exercise in self-deception, which can result in overlooking other systemically important institutions.

The first problem with the *too-big-to-fail* concept is the phrase itself. The term was too catchy not to catch on, but it is an unfortunate choice of words since it implies a narrow focus on size. Because of the complexity of the markets, size is not the only factor that makes a firm important (as discussed in other chapters). Though the more accurate term *systemically important* is used in official documents, the nature of many policy proposals reflects an obsession

15

with the size of the firm. Overlooking "unimportant" firms simply because they aren't behemoths is courting disaster: As one market expert has put it, "The history of financial crises is the history of the threatened failure and default of financial institutions previously considered unimportant."[1]

What really matters is the magnitude of the impact an institution's failure would have on the system, by which we mean on a large number of other firms. Clearly, a big firm has the capacity to take down a number of other firms because it has positions or other exposures to a large number of firms. But a medium-size firm that is highly leveraged (borrows a great deal of money and then invests it) can easily punch above its weight in the market, and its failure can thus also be magnified. It is doubtful, for instance, that regulators would have identified Long Term Capital Management (LTCM) as too big to fail until it failed, its size having increased dramatically but away from the eyes of the regulators as it bet, ultimately the wrong way, on arbitrage between the prices of bonds. It was only after the Asian and Russian financial crises led to huge losses at LTCM that it became apparent how exposed the large investment banks were to LTCM, and how its failure could have systemic consequences.

Perhaps the vulnerability of and to LTCM would have been spotted if the concept *too-big-to-fail* were based simply on a threshold of assets rather than a somewhat arbitrary *"I-know-it-when-I-see-it"* list of big firms, as proposed in the days after the recent financial crisis, and if LTCM had been required to report the size of its positions to the SEC—a task not required at the time for hedge funds like LTCM.

While this approach is more objective and presumably more effective than an arbitrary list of well-known large banks, it presents its own problems and limitations. First, the threshold number itself would be arbitrary, and there would of course be considerable back-and-forth among lawmakers and the industry as to whether a particular level is too high, too low, or just right (that is, politically convenient). There would also need to be agreement on how to measure size (total assets, assets weighted by level of risk, market capitalization, or a combination of the above, for example). Second, setting a threshold means establishing a process for monitoring the size of firms to see which has crossed or is approaching the threshold—and even which has fallen back below it.

That's just the first step. Once the list of firms that are too big to fail has been created, the process would also have to include identifying those other (smaller) firms to which the big firms are exposed—for instance, the LTCMs of the world. This only makes sense: If you are worried about Bank of America

---

[1] Christopher T. Mahoney, "Market Discipline Is Not the Answer," *Barron's*, November 30, 2009.

failing, you had better figure out to whom Bank of America is exposed and by how much. Of course, this is easier said than done: information will change from month to month and day to day. Moreover, the truly large institutions enter into deals around the globe, not just with those firms within the jurisdiction of the U.S. regulators. So, what do you do when you see that Goldman Sachs or Morgan Stanley has a large exposure to a Russian fund, into which even the Russian authorities don't have much transparency? The process gets more and more complex because it is not enough simply to identify the Big Banks of the world.

So identifying systemically important institutions is more than a matter of finding the biggest banks. Other factors discussed in Chapter 1 on systemic risk should also be considered by the authorities responsible for monitoring systemic risk and systemically important institutions. But saying that size isn't everything is not the same thing as saying that size does not matter. It does, and so the big institutions should be addressed—but as part of an approach that includes other factors as well.

 POLICY OPTIONS

How, then, should regulators deal with the too-big-to-fail banks once they have identified them? Three principal approaches, which are not necessarily mutually exclusive, have dominated the debate in terms of preventing firms from becoming too big to fail: don't let them get too big in the first place (and break up those that already are); separate the banking from the investing and trading activities; and impose higher capital cushion requirements.

Keep the Banks Small(ish)

If you want to prevent the financial system from being vulnerable to the fortunes of a few Superfirms, it seems logical simply to keep firms small (or at least below a particular size). That would mean breaking up the existing big firms, and setting limits on the size of any firm in the future. Such direct intervention—even interference—in the market by the government goes against all the principles of free market theory, but it is hardly without precedent. In 1982, AT&T settled a years-long battle with the Anti-Trust Division of the Department of Justice over its dominance of the local phone market, leading to the breakup of AT&T and the creation of the "Baby Bell"

18 ■ Can an Institution Be Too Big to Fail?

regional operating companies. Of course, this was not the first use of anti-trust powers to break up big companies, and in fact the original anti-trust legislation, the Sherman Anti-Trust Act, has been on the books since 1890 and has been used to break up big companies in everything from railroads to linseed oil. Since the government already has this well-established prerogative to break up big companies in order to protect the markets from abuse, it is not a terribly large leap to give the same power in order to protect the markets from collapse.

Which brings us back to the question of how to decide which firms are too big to fail. Is there an absolute number above which a firm is too big (and if so, does this number need to be adjusted for inflation?). In reality, the vulnerability does not come from whether a bank is above some arbitrary size threshold, but rather from its relative size. If you break up the big banks into their component parts you may not do much to relative market share. Take Citigroup, for example. If you decide it's too big and so you order it broken up, you are likely to come up with plan that spins off its banking, insurance, and investment activities into separate subsidiaries, but any of those three subsidiaries may continue to dominate in their respective sectors. Anti-trust concerns are, after all, all about market share, a relative term, rather than size, an absolute term. Some firms that were subject to anti-trust litigation were not all that big, but they dominated their markets. Others were big, but their size may be a result of their market domination as much as a cause of it. Since breaking up a firm on anti-trust grounds is about reducing the firm's relative power, not its absolute size, this approach doesn't help determine the magic threshold above which firms should not be allowed to grow.

Even with Sherman Act–like powers to break up firms, would the markets be less vulnerable if there were no firms above a given size? Researchers will likely build careers on this question, but the short and unscientific answer is, "Who knows?" By reducing the size of the firm, the risk is probably somewhat dispersed. But remembering the point that vulnerability is a function of interconnectedness as well as size, the system is likely to remain vulnerable since the new, smaller descendants of the big firms continue to do business as before. In other words, breaking up the big firms may reduce systemic risk but it will not eliminate it and it would be dangerous to believe otherwise.

Bring Back Glass-Steagall

The second approach is to separate commercial banking activities from investment banking activities, an approach advocated by Senator John McCain and former Fed Chairman Paul Volcker in the United States and Bank of

England Governor Mervyn King in the UK. The main concern in mixing the two activities in the same firm is that investment banking is all about the bank risking its own money but its failure risks everyone's money. As the biggest banks saw their prospects turn around in 2009, their mandatory financial disclosures showed that many of these "bank holding companies" had made most of their money from trading activities. The risk had not changed, it was just operating under a new label. And so advocates of a return to separating commercial and investment banking activities worry that commercial banks will become vulnerable every time a trader rolls the dice. While individuals' deposits are insured, paying off thousands of accounts is still a government bailout of excessive risk if the accounts were at a bank destroyed by bad bets in the market.

Some aspects of functional separation—loosely called "the Volcker Rule" by the Administration in an effort to lend it the respectability of its main proponent—are fairly straightforward and easy to implement. For example, prohibiting banks from owning hedge funds is not all that confusing. But other aspects—and critical ones at that—are more problematic. Chief among these is the proposed prohibition against "proprietary trading" by commercial banks. Proprietary trading is generally the activity in which a firm bets its own money rather than that of its client. But laws have to be precisely written, and proprietary trading is a lot more difficult to define when looked at with a regulatory microscope. For example, some firms use proprietary trading to acquire stock which they will later sell to their clients, or will buy from a client when there isn't sufficient demand to sell the client's stock at a good price. Proprietary trading, it turns out, is another one of those *"know-it-when-I-see-it"* things. Not surprisingly, the Volcker rule has not met with an easy fate in the debate.

Increase Capital Requirements

The third approach is to raise the capital requirements for those firms that are deemed to be systemically important, whether by virtue of size or some other factor. What this means in simple terms is that they must have a higher proportion of cash and other liquid assets to support their riskier activities, so that you do not have $1 of collateral for every $30 risked in the market. This approach serves two purposes at the same time: It discourages banks from getting too big by making it more expensive to be that big, while at the same time providing for an extra level of safety in case everything does go south for the firm.

This approach has the virtue of letting the market do the dirty work. The downside to the approach is that it is, in the end, voluntary. If a firm decides that it wants to be big, and that the cost associated with the punitive capital requirements is inconsequential, then that firm will grow to whatever size it desires (and it may then be chased up the scale by others).

A fiendishly subtle but effective addendum to this approach would be to limit the pay of officers at firms which cross the threshold. Remember what happened to the largest TARP recipients. After the Treasury Department announced that pay would be capped on top executives until their firms had paid back all the TARP money they received, the rush to repay the money was breathtaking. Of course, the firms involved would not connect the dots in exactly that way, but it is hard to ignore the phenomenon as real-world evidence of the deterrent effect of pay caps.

These three approaches demonstrate the range of options available to prevent banks from getting too big or too important to fail. But what if we find ourselves up against the wall again, either because a bank skirted the regulatory restrictions or because the restrictions themselves overlooked factors which made a firm systemically important? Two basic approaches are available—bail or fail.

Create a Resolution Authority

It would be negligent for policymakers to assume that establishing one or more of the preventive approaches, together with the unblinking eye of the systemic risk authority, will absolutely prevent the failure of one or two firms from threatening the whole financial system.

It is necessary therefore for policymakers to establish a Plan B for the one that gets through the net. The most frequently discussed proposal of this nature has been a "resolution authority," which would have the power to wind down a failing financial firm in an orderly way, in the same way that the FDIC wound down hundreds of small banks in the wake of the crisis. Several variations on this were proposed, largely limited in scope to systemically important institutions however they are defined.

The question then is the nature of the pool of money from which resolutions are funded (to pay existing obligations, pay staff during the transition period, etc.). One option is for all the systemically important institutions to pay into the pool so that the money is ready and available when needed. This is not a crowd-pleaser with the firms that suspect they might be regarded as systemically important, because it means tying up money they could put to more profitable use elsewhere (though the pool might earn interest, the firms are no doubt convinced they could do better). The alternative would be to leave the fund empty and pass the hat when a firm is judged to be failing. The problems in this case are not only administrative and logistical, but practical: If one firm is about to fail, particularly because of external economic forces or due to its exposure to a particular type of instrument or a particular counterparty, then it is entirely likely other systemically important institutions are exposed as well. So when the fire bell rings, all the banks may claim to be too poor or too exposed to be able to pony up.

The lessons of the financial crisis teach us another potential flaw in the resolution authority approach, and it is perhaps a fatal one. In the very short period of time in which firms like Bear Stearns were on the brink of collapse, the traders and bankers in the other firms had to decide whether it was worth the risk to expose themselves to the collapsing giant either by loaning money, buying repos, or engaging in other transactions. Knowing that a resolution authority would be able to wind down Bear Stearns in an "orderly" way would probably not have convinced anyone that it was safe to go swimming in the Bear Stearns pool. Traders, risk managers, treasurers and other decision makers in the market think in terms of what their balance sheet will look like hours and days from now. Knowing that the failing firm will be wound down in an orderly way means that the resolution authority will, after due deliberation, provide an as-of-yet undetermined portion of the obligation back to the firm that dealt with it. So they could risk trading with the failing firm on the assumption that they will eventually get some or all of the money back, or they can just avoid trading with the failing firm at all.

Thus, a resolution authority replaces the risk of total loss with the risk of unknown loss to be repaid at some unknown point in time. Since the cause of systemic risk, as discussed in Chapter 1, is this very uncertainty, establishing a legal bankruptcy process is not likely to succeed in averting a crisis.

That leaves the distasteful but unavoidable alternative of direct government intervention that will promptly step in to support those firms which agree to act as counterparty to the failing firm. In some cases, simply stepping in as guarantor may succeed in calming the market and getting the funds flowing again, without costing the taxpayer any money. But to succeed, the government would need to be able to back up its claims, and so a variation of the resolution authority in which the funds are used to guarantee counterparties is arguably the best alternative.

Government intervention of this nature need not be a painless free ticket for failing firms. While it is important that the money be available quickly to reassure markets, it should be structured as an interest-bearing loan, not a grant. And the deal should come with the provision that the government has the authority to fire senior management and dismiss or appoint board members.

Does this create "moral hazard," encouraging firms to take inordinate risk because they can't fail? As discussed in the next chapter, the answer is "no," as long as senior management and boards of the failing companies—those who actually decide to take those risks—are held personally accountable.

Do Nothing

The final option is to do nothing, or more precisely, to leave it to the market and have the government do nothing. Subscribers to the traditional notion of moral hazard are likely to sympathize with this approach, since a clear warning to the market that failing banks will be allowed to fail would, according to the theory, cause them to act more prudently. While the failure of Lehman caused disruption that many now say could have destroyed the financial system if the government had not intervened, adherents to this approach would say that Lehman would have acted more prudently if the government had not already bailed out Bear Stearns.

CONCLUSION

The moral to this story is that it is foolish to believe that lawmakers, regulators, the market, or anyone else can come up with a way to identify systemically risky institutions and render them un-risky. The complexity of the market and the speed with which exposures change make it impossible to do so. We should try; arrangements to monitor systemic risk and to prevent firms from becoming systemically risky are in general a good idea. But there needs to be a Plan B, for the same reason skydivers carry two parachutes. As Chapter 1 argues, the way to prevent systemic risk is to keep one firm's problems from causing uncertainty and panic among the firms that are or may be exposed to that firm. As much as we may regret it on a philosophical level, providing a mechanism for the government to support an institution at least temporarily is the Plan B that must be available to regulators. The individuals at the firm who are responsible should indeed be held accountable at a personal level, but that is another matter.

Nobody likes the thought of a firm getting reckless, threatening not only itself but everyone else, and then getting a free pass from its rich Uncle Sam. But we would be merely hurting ourselves if we let our offended sense of justice drive economic policy. The complexity of the markets is what leads to fear and uncertainty and it is those factors, not justice, which will require immediate action. Government support is the swiftest, the best, and perhaps the only way to assure the markets that they will not go down with the ship. Justice can be served in due course, and it should be served on the individuals responsible for the failure of the firm, not on the firm itself.

CHAPTER THREE

Moral Hazard

THE ULTIMATE QUESTION FOR policymakers as they rethink financial regulation is whether the government should bail out failing financial institutions. The debate has taken on a fairly ideological complexion, particularly among those who believe that any government intervention to save a failing firm would be against the most fundamental principles of a free market. More to the point, some observers fear that institutions that know they would be bailed out by the government would act irresponsibly, taking risks they would not take if they were walking the high wire without a safety net. This argument, known in intellectual circles as *moral hazard*, is another of the largely academic notions that have been thrust into the light of day as a result of the financial crisis.

Until the crisis, the best course of action for a government was to remain silent on what action it would take in the case of a failing, systemically important institution (aside from the federally insured deposits of individuals). Doing so meant that firms were not able to rely on a bailout but did not box in the government by ruling out intervention entirely. The financial crisis forced the government's hand in the United States, but the actions taken—bailing out AIG and Bear Stearns but not Lehman Brothers—only served to lend an air of inconsistency and confusion to the markets.

As policymakers sat down after the crisis to draft new rules to address systemic risk, they no longer had the option to remain silent. All eyes were on them and so the debate as to whether the government should have the option or even obligation to intervene rose to the top of the public debate. And because it lies at the very heart of the regulatory reform, it is important to understand moral hazard and even to question whether it really does exist.

THE THEORY

The theory of moral hazard is fairly straightforward. Risks are really only risky if there are negative consequences to them. Remove the consequence of failure, and you have turned a risk into a one-sided bet. The potential rewards are concrete and often immediate—for instance, revenues generated in the present quarter that will improve the firm's earnings. If a firm knows that the ultimate negative consequence—the firm's failure and dissolution—is not going to happen, its appetite for risk increases because it is really just an appetite for reward.

Evidence of this effect lies in the interest rate paid on bonds issued by *government-sponsored enterprises* (GSEs) such as Fannie Mae and Freddie Mac before their bailout, or even on Treasury bonds issued directly by the government itself. For years, the market assumed that the GSEs benefited from an implicit government guarantee. Since they were set up by the government for the purpose of advancing government policy (affordable homeownership), government sponsorship was assumed to imply that the firms would not be allowed to fail. Because of this implied level of safety, the interest rate on bonds issued by Fannie Mae and Freddie Mac were lower than for riskier corporate bonds. If the market did not believe the government would bail out the GSEs, they would be viewed to be riskier investments and so they would have to pay higher interest in order to attract investors. The interest rates on GSEs were higher, though, than U.S. Treasury bonds issued by the government, whose safety is more explicitly guaranteed by the people who print the money. The three prevailing interest rates—on government bonds, on GSEs, and on corporate bonds—reflect the different levels of government backing. As discussed in the following, however, this reflects moral hazard as viewed by a firm's creditors, not by the firm's managers.

THE REALITY

Beyond the theory, the practice of moral hazard is far less straightforward. One way to look at it is to consider those practices that encouraged risk in the years leading up to the financial crisis and ask whether firms had engaged in them because they assumed the government would bail them out if everything went south. A detailed answer to that question is beyond the scope of this work, but the instinctive answer is probably "no," since the risky activities were engaged in by all sorts and sizes of firms and not just those that could consider themselves too big to fail. Another way to look at it is that such an assumption implies that people understood the risks they were taking. Most observers agree that the risk was actually little understood because the instruments and the financial system were so complex (and because some of the riskiest assets had AAA ratings). Finally, moral hazard addresses only the Armageddon scenario, where the firm is on the brink of going out of business. It addresses total collapse and bankruptcy; it does not serve as insurance against losses, even big ones that result from a poorly judged business decision. So, moral hazard might theoretically encourage risky behavior if there are only two possible outcomes of a risk: that it will make money or bankrupt the business, and nothing in between. But if the outcome includes losses short of bankruptcy, the government would tell the firm to take its losses and deal with the consequences. So moral hazard is about life insurance, not health insurance, for a financial firm.

For moral hazard to be a deciding factor in the risk decisions of financial firms, all of the following would have to be true: (1) The risky behavior is exclusively engaged in by firms that are too big to fail and thus candidates for a bailout (doubtful); (2) the risks are fully understood to be risky and the magnitude of the risk is also fully comprehended (not a valid assumption, given the failure to anticipate the losses that led to the financial crisis); and (3) the downside risk is financial ruin and nothing short of that (never really the case).

PUNISH THE LEADERS, NOT THE ORGANIZATION

The most important point, though, is that decisions are not made by organizations, they are made by people.[1] The distinction is not merely a semantic one, because it changes the focus of the consequences from the firm onto the decision makers. In the real world, CEOs or other executives are more likely to be concerned with their own fate than whether the firm will survive after they have been fired. Put differently, it is unlikely that a decision maker would think, "If it all goes wrong, I'll be fired and disgraced but the firm would be bailed out. Let's do it." Even when the decision is made by a group of individuals, responsibility will lie with one person (or a small number of people) who can be held personally responsible.

This implies that regulatory policy should not be driven by notions of moral hazard that punish or reward the *firm*, but rather should focus on the *individual*. If the government wishes to discourage excessive risk taking, it should provide specific sanctions against the individuals responsible for making the risk-taking decisions. If they know that a bad risk that forces a government bailout will result in the end of their livelihoods, and potentially civil liability, there will be far fewer bailouts than if we simply decided to let failing institutions fail. This is especially so given the fact that many directors of institutions that failed in the crisis moved right over into seats on the boards of other companies,[2] and from these lifeboats they are able to view the wreckage they caused without getting wet.

Put differently, it might be said that the government creates moral hazard when it fails to punish the leaders who made the decisions that sank a firm and threatened the financial system. This is not the same as caving in to craven demands for "justice" against those seen by the public to be responsible for the crisis. Instead, it should be a matter of policy that government intervention and the use of the emergency pool of funds would trigger the government's authority to dismiss any or all members of senior management or the Board, with those subject to dismissal also being subject to a bar from similar positions

---

[1] The importance of understanding the factors that drive the decisions of individuals in the financial markets is the focus of the field of "behavioral finance." This field has gained increasing interest among academics and policymakers, and there are a number of excellent books and articles that provide further discussion on the topic. See also the "Your Mind and Your Money" feature on the website of the PBS Nightly Business Report, http://www.pbs.org/nbr/site/features/special/mind_and_money/

[2] Gretchen Morgenson, "What Iceberg? Just Glide to the Next Boardroom," *New York Times*, December 26, 2009.

in the future, clawbacks in compensation and civil liability. In conclusion, it is hard to imagine that the presumption of a government bailout encourages greater risk taking in the real world. It just does not happen, and it flies in the face of common sense. But moral hazard does have the potential to encourage risk from another quarter: those who lend to the firm.

THE OTHER MORAL HAZARD

Other than the failing firm, its employees, and owners (shareholders), those who are most exposed to the failure of a financial firm are its creditors. Firms that buy bonds, repo agreements, or other debt or that extend credit to the irresponsible firm stand to lose some or all of their investment if that firm were to collapse. That should be enough to make the decision maker at the lending firm think twice. But if there is the explicit or assumed promise that the government will bail out the irresponsible firm and assume its debt should it fail, there is no need to exercise the normal level of prudence. If the market assumes that a failing firm will be bailed out by the government (either because of an explicit government policy or because of previous bailouts), it may view loaning money to that firm as a one-sided bet. With no risk of loss, traders would pile in on the guaranteed investment and neglect more pedestrian market opportunities that have some level of risk. Moral hazard operates not on the irresponsible firm but indirectly on those doing business with it, effectively reducing or removing the market discipline that would normally move the rest of the market to shun the irresponsible firm.

It is argued elsewhere in this book that the government should have the clear authority to support failing banks in order to prevent uncertainty and panic from creating a systemic shutdown. The assurance of government intervention such a policy implies would create the third-party moral hazard just described, making it necessary to ensure that creditors do in fact assume some risk even if there is a bailout. The key task is to structure the intervention so that creditors are at risk of a moderate loss, and so dealing with the failing firm provides neither the risk of total write-off nor a guarantee against loss. One approach that has been suggested by policymakers is to require creditors of a bailed out firm to take a write-down (called a "haircut" in the market) on their investments in the firm's securities. Fixed at the right level (perhaps 15% or 20% below face value) this would create a loss and therefore instill some level of market discipline in the process while still reassuring the market that the failure of the firm will not ruin them all. Short-term funding contracts such as repos might be exempted from the haircut in order to keep overnight funding flowing to the firm. Importantly, the government support, even with the haircut, should be paid within or close to the normal settlement period rather than the months or years that could be required in the case of a bankruptcy or resolution authority. That means that the pool of money from which such interventions are made must be pre-funded.

This power should be clearly and explicitly in the government's remit when dealing with a failing firm, since experience in the financial crisis has demonstrated that moral suasion alone will not carry the day. When dealing with the failure of AIG, the Federal Reserve had to make things up as it went along, putting it under pressure to agree to terms it might not have had it had the time to consider other approaches and marshal support for them. Such was the case with respect to paying off AIG's counterparties at the full face value of their investments: According to Benjamin Bernanke, the Fed did not have the power to force a haircut on the creditors and so the creditors got the government to pay full value for its obligations. He testified that:

> UBS offered a 2% discount if and only if all the other counterparties would accept one. That was not the case. We did our best to get a reduction there. But given that AIG was not bankrupt, and given that we were not going to abuse our supervisory power, we really had no way to create a substantial discount.[3]

So moral hazard does exist, but it does not precisely fit the role customarily assigned to it in the regulatory debate. It is most powerful among a firm's creditors, not its own managers. The distinctions made in this chapter have serious policy implications, especially when coupled with those raised in Chapter 1 on systemic risk. These implications are discussed in greater detail in Chapter 15. Briefly, they are that provisions with respect to failures should include:

1. Sanctions against senior management. As mentioned in the discussion on systemic risk, it may be wise for the government to support institutions in order to prevent systemic failure, but that does not mean that the individuals taking the risk should be bailed out. Potential sanctions should include forfeiture of pending salary and incentive compensation, "claw-back" of previous compensation, and fines. A ban on serving as an officer or board director on any publicly traded company in the future is an

---

[3] Testimony of Benjamin Bernanke to the Senate Banking Committee, December 3, 2009.

important sanction, as is potential civil liability. Put differently, have a bailout process in place, make it clear, and make it bad for the managers.
2. Creditors will not be made whole, but neither will they be left holding the bag, and so a haircut of the failing firms' obligations, other than overnight repos, should be imposed as part of a bailout.

The preventive measures like keeping banks small are good and wise, but it is neither good nor wise to neglect the need for a Plan B in case something does happen. If there is an explicit policy of *no* intervention as some have suggested, regulators will have a difficult time restoring confidence, since the one thing that worked the last time (government bailout) would already have been ruled out.

CONCLUSION

Moral hazard is a hot topic in the regulatory debate, but it presumes that decision makers will make wanton decisions and take inordinate risks based on the assumption that the organization will survive. If financial firms were run by nuns, perhaps we could make policy decisions based on such altruistic behavior. But because firms are run by businesspeople concerns over their own self-interest are likely to act as a check on their behavior as long as they have reason to believe that if the government steps in, they step out. The markets are better protected by the ability of the government to support systemically important institutions, and to avoid the third-party moral hazard that arises from government support.

CHAPTER FOUR

Toxic Assets

THERE CAN BE LITTLE doubt that the collapse of residential mortgage-backed securities (RMBSs) and similarly complex products played a central role in triggering the financial crisis. Securities constructed from pools of assets, commonly referred to as *structured* or *securitized* products, are not new, having been around in one form or another since the early 1970s. But over time they became more widespread and more complex, as did the use of derivative products that do not confer ownership in an asset but whose price is linked to the value of the asset or index from which it is derived. In the course of the debate over financial reform, terms like *CDO, CLO, CDS,* and *CMBS* (just to take the *C*s) have populated the discussion even though the meaning of the terms and the nature of the instruments were not well understood. This chapter aims to provide a summary view of structured instruments and derivatives, how they turned into toxic assets, and the role of rating agencies in assessing the risk presented by them.

31

WHAT ARE TOXIC ASSETS, AND WHY ARE THEY TOXIC?

The term *toxic asset* has come to be used in the wake of the financial crisis to describe a number of instruments, primarily structured investments or derivatives, whose value has plunged catastrophically and that were so widely held that their failure took on systemic proportions. But they are not new and they are not inherently "toxic." What they are is high-risk, and like all such investments they are cash machines when things go right but disastrous when things go wrong.

The idea behind structured finance is to take an asset that produces an income stream, such as payments on mortgages, aircraft leases, or credit cards, and bundle a very large number of them into one big pool with a very large combined income stream (both interest and principal). The owner of the pool, normally a standalone entity created specifically for the pool being created, then issues bonds that entitle the bondholder to receive a share of that income stream.

If you have a mortgage that was created in the past few years, there's a very good chance that your payments no longer go to the bank that gave you the loan. Within months, or even before you made your first payment, the bank sold the mortgage to an "arranger" and eventually to a standalone entity (often called a *special-purpose vehicle*—SPV). The SPV then issued bonds backed by your mortgage and all the other mortgages in the pool, and ultimately the SPV acts as a conduit for the mortgage payments to pay the interest on the bonds. This is what is called a *residential mortgage-backed security* (RMBS); similar instruments are made for commercial real estate (*commercial mortgage-backed securities*—CMBSs). Indeed, the same arrangement can be done with any asset that creates a stream of income and these are collectively called *asset-backed securities* (ABSs).

Now comes the interesting part. Since the bank knows it is going to sell a mortgage to an arranger virtually as soon as it closes, it has very little risk in making the loan to the home buyer. After all, who defaults on a mortgage within a few months? That means that the bank can extend loans to people less creditworthy than it had in the past. It has been pointed out that the banking industry was in fact encouraged and mandated to do so by federal laws passed to broaden homeownership to those traditionally left out of the market. In the eyes of the bank, its risk to this *subprime* mortgage is eliminated as soon as it sells it to the arranger. In reality, though—and this is a critical point in understanding the crisis—the risk has *not* been eliminated; it has simply been moved elsewhere in the financial system. And though it could be argued that putting it in a pool with a lot of other mortgages dilutes the risk, the fact is that over time so many subprime mortgages were created and then sold into these pools that risk never really disappeared. Moreover, the economic conditions that increase the likelihood of default by the mortgage payer have the same negative impact on everyone, so that many mortgages in a single pool start to default all at once. The result is that the actual creditworthiness of the mortgage backed securities plummeted faster than their ratings could be downgraded.

BUILDING LOW-RISK ASSETS OUT OF HIGH-RISK ONES

And so the question has been asked: How could pools of subprime mortgages be considered safe investments, and even receive AAA ratings? The answer lies in how structured investments are actually structured. The SPV arranges the pool into several *tranches*, each with its own bonds backed by mortgages in the investment pool. The tranches are arranged in order of seniority with the most senior tranche being the lowest risk because it is first in line to be paid, and therefore its bonds get the highest rating (AAA) and pay the lowest interest rate. It is wrong to assume, as many do, that this means that the most secure mortgages go into the AAA tranche and the subprime go into the junior tranche. Tranches are not specific groups of mortgages; rather they represent where the bondholder stands in line when payments are made. The senior tranche gets paid first, the lowest tranche gets paid last.

Why would anyone want to buy bonds from a junior tranche? The fact is that investors have a wide range of investment needs and risk appetites, and so some will be seeking a higher interest rate while being able to stomach the additional risk entailed in standing last in line for the money. In the case of RMBSs and other ABSs, the investor is usually a large institution.

In spite of recent history, this structure is actually very useful and beneficial as long as the risks are understood. Over the past 35 years, structured investments have given investors a better opportunity to find investments that provide them with the rate of return they seek that matches their risk appetite. If all had gone well, the RMBS pools could have absorbed the subprime mortgages into the market without incident, since a senior tranche composed even *entirely* of subprime loans might never lose money: Suppose the top tranche represented 25 percent of the payments. Now suppose that the default rate for the loans in the pool rises from the assumed rate of, say, 3 percent, and spikes to 10 percent. That means that

90 percent are still making their regular payments, and so everyone in the senior tranche, being among the first 25 percent to get paid, will get their regular payments.

But mortgage payments are sensitive to economic conditions, and subprime mortgages are even more so. Recent experience had lulled homeowners, banks, and investors into believing that real estate was the unburstable bubble. Even the rating agencies based their ratings on historical data that did not account for the bottom falling out of the housing market, allowing them to give out AAA ratings even as economists gave warnings that the end was nigh. And so investment banks continued to create RMBS securities and even invest in them for themselves, happy that the AAA ratings put them on the same footing as U.S. Treasury bonds—but at a much higher interest rate.

And here's where things started to run off the rails. Spreading the risk did not eliminate it from the system. It eliminated it from the bank approving the loan—the people best positioned to judge whether the loan was sound—and so removed any incentive to exercise prudence. All that was left at the bank was a financial incentive to approve as many mortgages as possible. No one, in fact, had any incentive to ensure that the loans were sound except the people left holding the bag—the RMBS investors—and they had the assurance of the rating agencies that the investments were as sound as Treasury bonds. As a result, more and more subprime loans were created and spread throughout the financial system. And while spreading the risk may sound like a good way to dilute it to the point where it is inconsequential, creating more and more risk to be spread has the opposite effect—the market became a septic tank of bad loans. Risk was never eliminated, it was in fact increased.

It should be evident that the role played by rating agencies was critical to the entire process of turning subprime debt into AAA investments. The process is dependent on the assignment of accurate ratings to the tranches so that prospective investors can select which bonds if any they wish to purchase. Given their perch astride the entire credit market and their deep analysis of economic trends in all industries, they could have been the heroes who saw the coming decline in the housing market, connected the dots, and reflected the bad news in their RMBS ratings. But rating structured products came to be very big business, ultimately comprising over half the revenues of some agencies. And though senior managers in the structured finance departments undoubtedly ascribed the growth of revenues to their own business savvy and analytical prowess, the fact is that the structured finance business fell into their collective lap as the securitization sector took off. The gatekeepers simply left the gate open so the money could pile in.

CREDIT RATING AGENCIES AND STRUCTURED FINANCE PRODUCTS

The business of issuing credit ratings and the conflicts of interest inherent in the industry are discussed in greater detail in Chapter 10. What is important here is to understand that structured finance ratings are, like those of plain-vanilla bonds, given by committees of specially trained analysts following prescribed procedures. A rating is not merely the output of a single analyst looking over a spreadsheet and giving a reasoned guess. Ratings are based on methodologies developed within the firm by senior, experienced analysts; these methodologies tell the analyst what information to review, how to review it, and which rating would be appropriate based on the result of the analysis. Accompanying the methodologies are specific models, which are statistical data that help indicate the probability that a given mortgage or other debt will default.

Analysts rating structured finance tranches generally did not see the actual mortgages on which the entire investment was based. In fact, the SPV normally had not even purchased any mortgages yet. Instead, it provided to the rating agency information regarding the characteristics of the mortgages it would buy for the pool. These characteristics reflected four- or five-dozen relevant factors—the mix of maturities, interest rates, credit score of the mortgagee, geographic diversity, loan-to-value ratio, and so on. Once the SPV had received the preliminary ratings for the tranches, it would purchase mortgages reflecting the characteristics it had represented to the rating agency.

Importantly, the statistical data are based on probabilities, best visualized as the typical bell curve we all learned in high school math. The most probable outcomes lie in the fat middle of the curve; the further out into the tails one goes the less likely the event is to occur. But "less likely" does not mean "never," especially when the bell curve is based on historical data that is by its nature backward-looking. To put it simply, the ratings for many of the structured finance bonds were based on data in the middle of the bell curve, but economic conditions then occurred that were historically rare and therefore in the tail (such as housing prices declining, let alone crashing). So important data assumptions were wrong, and the AAA ratings were very, very wrong. In giving senior tranches AAA ratings, the rating agencies equated their risk of default with that of Treasury bonds issued and guaranteed by the federal government.

A point of ongoing controversy is the role of the rating agencies in the structuring of the tranches. In practice, arrangers always wanted the senior tranche to receive the highest possible rating, AAA, in order to be able to sell at the most lucrative price, since a lower rating would mean that it had to pay a higher interest rate to bondholders. But given the complexity of structuring the pool with mortgages with dozens of variables, it could be anyone's guess whether a tranche with particular characteristics would in fact qualify for the coveted AAA rating. Consequently, there often developed a back-and-forth dialogue with the rating analyst as different structures were tried or were backed with different (but costly) "credit enhancements" such as buying bond insurance or setting aside cash reserves.

The issue is whether this back-and-forth discussion degenerated into an outright advisory process in which the rating agencies told the arranger what to do in order for the tranche to qualify for a AAA rating, either by changing the characteristics of the pool (i.e., reduce the concentration on Florida mortgages) or credit enhancement (overcollateralize the pool). The rating agencies have passionately denied that they perform an advisory role. The truth is probably a bit murky, but the implications of performing such a role would be quite serious from a legal point of view. It would mean that they had *helped create* the investment rather than merely providing an objective analysis of its credit characteristics, and as such they could be equally liable in civil court for the ultimate failure of the instrument. The question of whether the rating process for structured finance instruments constitutes an advisory service is an area of contention between the rating agencies and regulators (and courts) worldwide, and is not likely to be definitively settled any time soon.

As bad as the collapse of the housing market was, it probably would not have led to the near collapse of the financial system if the market for securitized products had not taken off in the way that it did. The explosion in the growth of asset-backed securities, and especially RMBSs, reflected their popularity among big institutions. Many financial institutions, large and small, gobbled up the securities as fast as they could be created—faster, in fact, given that a secondary market developed for trading the securities. Some institutions invested so heavily in them that their value became a large part of their risk exposure—including Bear Stearns and Lehman. And as described in an earlier chapter, when one firm is highly exposed to the risk of a particular type of security, so are all of the firm's market counterparties. So, when the rate of defaults skyrocketed and the cash flow through the RMBSs failed to match the expectations implied by their ratings, there was a big problem for the system. The securities had become toxic, because no one knew the real quality of the RMBS pools and no one knew who else was exposed and by how much. Firms continued to value the toxic securities on their books at their original value instead of the market value—whatever that was, it was certainly dramatically lower—and so even the publicly released financial figures for the institutions holding them could not be trusted.

Structured investments, and particularly those backed by subprime mortgages, became toxic because of three factors: (1) The risk of default was fatally misjudged; (2) the appetite for high returns with ostensibly low risk spread them throughout the financial system; and (3) no one quite knew who was exposed to them and by how much. If any one of these factors had been absent, the damage wrought by them would likely have been much smaller or at least localized among a few firms.

 CREDIT DEFAULT SWAPS

What really makes a systemic crisis systemic is when failures in one instrument lead to the failure of others. When mortgage-backed securities started to fail and to take firms with them, the contagion spread to, and through, a number of instruments, but the biggest of all was the market for *credit default swaps* (CDSs). Put simply, a credit default swap is insurance against the default of an issuer's bonds and other debt obligations. CDSs were written against RMBS securities and against the bonds of financial institutions and all other kinds of debt issuers.

The firm "writing" (selling) the CDS receives a premium from the firm buying it; this fee takes the form of a onetime payment and then periodic payments over the life of the swap. Prices are determined by the market, so that a higher premium reflects the writer's view that the issuer's debt is riskier. In most periods, default rates have been low and so the business of writing CDSs has been quite lucrative—a sizeable, stable flow of income that seemed to hold less risk than other investments (who would have bet a few years ago that Lehman Brothers would implode?).

CDSs also make sense for buyers, and for the market as a whole, most of the time. For a firm holding RMBS debt, a CDS provides an extra layer of protection by protecting against the risk of default. Even if the triple-A tranche you hold as an investment goes into default, the CDS acts as insurance and pays you to cover your loss. From the market's point of view, CDSs looked like a great idea, since they were an additional risk management tool. Theoretically, they took a situation in which risk was spread among RMBS buyers, and turned it into one in which risk was effectively *offset* through the CDSs.

But as the market grew, something important happened: First, because the buyer of a CDS does not need to own the underlying security or have any other kind of exposure to it, people started buying them for speculative purposes. This

38 ■ Toxic Assets

is tantamount to buying life insurance on people you haven't even met. As the CDS market shifted from risk management to speculation, the market grew—and grew and grew. According to the Bank for International Settlements, the estimated size of the market in 2007 was $600 trillion.[1] If you win $600 million in the lottery, then do it again a million more times, you will have a stash the size of the CDS market before it went bust.

All of this money was changing hands "over the counter" (which means it was not done on any exchange) and so there was no transparency to it. Neither the regulators nor anyone in the market knew how many contracts were written against any particular issuer, who held which CDS and who had written them, or what anyone's total exposure was. It wasn't just playing in a casino; it was playing in a casino with the lights turned out—there was no telling how many were playing at the same table, who they were, or what they were betting.

What became clear is that the firms on the hook to pay in case of default took on more CDS liability than they could pay. This is because firms that sold CDSs were not required to maintain cash reserves to fully cover the potential losses, and instead generally held a lower level of reserves based on the historical likelihood of default. But those to whom the money was owed did not realize that the money might not be paid. One former CFTC official interviewed on PBS's *Nightly Business Report* indicated that nobody, including those holding the CDSs, really understood that there was not enough money set aside to actually pay the insurance in the event of default.[2] As a result, the firms exposed to the risk did not understand how exposed they were, and the regulators could not address a risk they could not see.

In normal conditions (the middle of the bell curve), that would have been okay. But when the defaults started to escalate, the CDSs became toxic and rocked the firms like AIG that had written them. The market lost confidence in CDSs as it came to question whether the underwriting firms would be able to pay them. That meant that their value plummeted and the financial statements of firms that owned them became questionable. Worse still, no one was sure how exposed anyone else was to CDSs, casting doubt by everyone on everyone else.

This is another way that the collapse of Bear Stearns and Lehman Brothers turned systemic. A large number of firms held CDSs insuring against default by Bear Stearns or Lehman Brothers, either because they owned debt issued by them

---

[1] Bank for International Settlements, *BIS Quarterly Review*, September 2008, Annex 1, p. 103.

[2] Michael Greenberger, former Director of Trading and Markets, CFTC, interviewed on *Nightly Business Report*, aired on PBS on October 29, 2008.

or for speculative purposes. When the firms collapsed, no one knew whether the firms that sold the CDSs had sufficient reserves to pay the amount due, rendering the value of the CDSs themselves questionable. And so the CDSs themselves served as another medium through which the crisis spread. The same problem arose across the market for CDSs written to cover RMBSs as RMBS defaults rose and the validity of the CDSs covering them began to look iffy.

Of course, there were a few firms that everybody knew wrote a tremendous amount of CDSs. The most notorious among these was AIG. And this brings us to another problem that changed the face of the CDS market. As the market for CDSs came to be dominated by a few firms, risk was actually *re-concentrated* rather than offset. This is perhaps the most important phenomenon in turning CDSs from a risk management tool to a risk multiplier—the Typhoid Mary of the financial crisis. Since AIG had written so many CDS contracts, it was no secret to the market that it had significant exposure to the rising number of defaults. Even worse, its tenuous position led the rating agencies to lower its credit rating. This was a particularly deadly blow because market practice had allowed a firm with a high credit rating like AIG to write CDSs without depositing collateral with the counterparty in the full amount of the CDS exposure. The lowered credit rating therefore led to demands from AIG's counterparties to deposit more reserves—cash and liquid assets—to cover the outstanding CDSs. This created a liquidity crisis for AIG and was the tipping point for the firm, leading ultimately to the Federal Reserve's unprecedented step of establishing a credit facility for AIG, in which taxpayers' funds were collateralized by AIG's now dodgy assets.

As policymakers began to comb through the wreckage of the financial system and consider regulatory reform, one of the earliest areas of consensus was that the CDS market had to be made more transparent and more stable. But this was not the first time a regulator had called for more control over the market. In 1998, the Commodity Futures Trading Commission (CFTC) under Brooksley Born issued a concept release proposing that over-the-counter derivatives, and particularly swaps, lose their existing exemption from federal regulation and be subject to transparency and other regulatory requirements. The CFTC's analysis proved to be right on the mark with events as they transpired ten years later, but its efforts to bring regulation to the market ultimately came to nothing.[3]

---

[3] For an excellent summary of the CFTC's efforts to regulate the OTC derivatives market and why these efforts failed, see PBS's *Frontline* episode, "The Warning," originally aired on October 20, 2009 and available at www.pbs.org/wgbh/pages/frontline/.

CONCLUSION

As head-spinning as the story of mortgage-backed securities and credit default swaps is, it provides only a snapshot of how the normal operation of asset markets started a chain reaction that nearly pushed the financial markets off a cliff. When risk is viewed as the road to higher returns, the market forgets that it is subject to the laws of gravity, and it is easy to forget which end of the snake they are holding.

Rather than diluting risk, securitization concentrated the risk into mortgage backed securities that then infected the entire financial system as they were sold to financial institutions and investors everywhere. Some have argued that securitization is a product we would have been better off without. This brings us in the next chapter to the question of whether regulation should act as the gatekeeper to financial innovation.

CHAPTER FIVE

Should Regulation Stifle Innovation?

A COMMON COMPLAINT ABOUT proposed regulations is that they would have the consequence, unintended or otherwise, of "stifling" innovation in the financial services industry—the creation and growth of new financial products. The charge is routinely rolled out in opposition to regulations of any sort, and had been for years before the financial crisis. It was no surprise, then, that the charge would arise with respect to major pieces of legislation aimed at reforming the markets in the wake of the near-collapse of the financial system.

In the U.S. market, the idea of stifling innovation is akin to censorship in the arts—by limiting creativity you limit genius and progress. The notion that financial innovation is at the heart of economic growth is so deep-seated among free marketers that it has become nearly unchallengeable. And it is true, up to a point. But while the logic of expanding the frontier of financial engineering is compelling on the surface, the financial crisis has challenged the underlying assumption that all innovation is good.

Without a doubt, innovation has increased choice, efficiency, and the management of risk in the markets for as long as there have been economies. The recent crisis aside, the beneficiaries of innovation have not only been the big financial firms: We have all benefited directly or indirectly from

41

innovations, even though the expense and risk of developing them has fallen largely on financial firms. Some innovations have been simple—money market accounts that allow you to earn interest on what would otherwise be a checking account—and others have been so complex that few fully understand them. Generally speaking, the simplest innovations have been the most beneficial to the consumer. Those that increase the complexity and decrease the transparency of the market have tended to increase the risk to the markets, and ultimately to the individual consumer.

So innovation is a desirable thing in general, but not all innovations are beneficial. When innovation becomes experimentation, and instruments devised to manage risk become vehicles for speculation, innovation can threaten, and has threatened the financial system itself. And so the task falls on the regulators to identify the dangerous ones and . . . well, stifle them.

But it seems that the argument is never that a regulation would "stifle the wrong innovations"; it is always "stifle (all) innovation"—a sweeping statement echoing the assumption that all innovation is good. Allied with this view is the parallel argument that a regulation would "reduce customer choice," implying either that it would prevent new products and services from being created or that unnecessary restrictions would be placed on their use. In either case, the insinuation is that both innovation and choice should be unlimited. Yes, some people will make bad choices and will pay the price for it, so the argument goes, but that's how markets are supposed to work. The problem with that logic is that complex innovations in complex markets often mean that the price is paid by others, not the person making the bad choice.

An enthusiastic devotion to innovation may be ideologically satisfying but it defies both logic and history, and especially recent history. It is hard to argue that innovations that were at the center of the financial crisis—namely mortgage-backed securities and credit default swaps—were good for anyone. Some distinguished economists and bankers put the case more strongly. Paul Volcker, Alan Greenspan's predecessor as Fed chairman and never a man to express half an opinion, has made clear his views on unrestrained innovation:

> I hear about these wonderful innovations in the financial markets, and. . . . I can tell you of two—credit-default swaps and collateralized debt obligations—which took us right to the brink of disaster. Were they wonderful innovations that we want to create more of?[1]

---

[1] "Paul Volcker: Think More Boldly," *Wall Street Journal*, December 14, 2009.

Should Regulation Stifle Innovation? ■ **43**

Put slightly differently, just because you *can* do something doesn't mean you *should* do it. But the markets themselves impel the drive for innovation because successful ones are moneymakers. In this respect, the financial services industry is no different from the technology or toothpaste industries. But few if any industries are free to innovate entirely free of regulatory restraint. The development of new products in the pharmaceutical industry, for example, is tightly regulated, with the explicit aim of stifling those innovations that are undesirable. While some executives might chafe at the way the process is carried out, few people argue the principle of government restraint over the development of new drugs and devices.

In the end, financial regulators have always had the ability to regulate new products, though they are often well behind the pace of innovation (a concept known as *regulatory lag*). According to one market analyst, the quality of oversight can also be undermined by the regulator's overt or subconscious deference to the presumed superior knowledge of the market, especially when that market is soaring. Interviewed on the *Nightly Business Report*, Karen Petrou expressed the view that the regulators believed that the people creating the new products, and the rest of the market, had an insight into the products that they themselves lacked. As a result, she said, the products that they believed were distributing risk were instead making the market vulnerable to untested models.[2] The need to staff regulatory agencies with a more knowledgeable and experienced corps of professionals who would have been less likely to be hoodwinked by those they regulated is addressed in Chapter 15.

The credit default swap (CDS) market is the most prominent example of an innovation that should have been put in a straightjacket, if not stifled altogether. It is risky, it is widely interconnected, and it is huge. As noted in the chapter on toxic assets, its size is in the neighborhood of $600 trillion[3]— that's $600 million dollars, a million times over. When the market for a product is ten times the gross domestic product of Planet Earth, someone is making one hell of a lot of money. It's hard to argue with people who have a slice of a pie that big that their market should be curtailed.

The real problem for the financial system is that financial innovation pushes the boundary of complexity further and further over time. And as the engineering maxim tells us, the more complexity in a system the greater the

---

[2] Karen Petrou, Managing Partner, Federal Financial Analytics. Interviewed on PBS *Nightly Business Report*, aired October 29, 2008.

[3] Bank for International Settlements, *BIS Quarterly Review*, September 2008, Annex 1, p. 103.

risk of catastrophic failure. There are many reasons for this phenomenon, which should be considered an iron law in the financial markets.

The first is that when a firm creates some new derivative or synthetic instrument, it does not necessarily accompany the innovation with adequate internal risk controls to monitor exposure to the instrument. Indeed, some innovations are so deeply rooted in mathematical modeling and technology that they are too complex for their risk really to be understood at any given time by anyone anyway. The second reason is that many of the new instruments are not regulated and therefore are not transparent to the regulators, the market, or anyone else. This can occur either through regulatory lag, mentioned earlier, or because the innovation has been created specifically to avoid regulation or to move activity off a company's balance sheet. The merits and limits of transparency as a regulatory tool are discussed in a separate chapter, but suffice it to say here that keeping an instrument away from regulatory scrutiny is rarely a good thing and is never good when the instrument is new and complex.

So, the inevitable march of innovation brings a rise in complexity in the markets, and a corresponding rise in risk. The increase in risk is probably exponential rather than a straight line, since the risk is amplified by the fact that so many of these instruments are intentionally or unintentionally linked to each other (for example, credit default swaps providing insurance for residential mortgage-backed securities).

POLICY IMPLICATIONS

This leads to an important point for policymakers to consider: The capacity for increased complexity resulting from innovation is unlimited, but the capacity to monitor, assess, and react to the risk generated by that complexity is limited. At some point the complexity in the market exceeds our ability to manage it, both at the firm level and across the system. Up until the financial crisis, this problem was never explicitly addressed. But it seems apparent now that we didn't just tiptoe across that line years ago, we took a great flying leap over it. The challenge for those working on regulatory reform of the financial system is to get back across that line so that the market, the regulators, and the public can feel confident once again that the market is a market and not a (rigged) casino.

CONCLUSION

Innovation is generally a good thing in financial markets, as it is in other endeavors. But as Paul Volcker pointed out, some innovations we would have been better off without. Whether through greed, recklessness, or the law of unintended consequences, a handful of innovations were at the core of the closest thing we have had to a financial meltdown in two generations. We've earned our experience the hard way, and we should put it to good use by understanding that innovation is not a sacred cow to be kept always and in all ways. In following the back-and-forth of the debate over a proposed financial regulation, then, the sweeping accusation that it would stifle innovation should be viewed with skepticism. There may be other reasons to disagree with the proposal, but merely constraining innovation should not be the basis for rejecting it.

CHAPTER SIX

Rewarding Success, Rewarding Failure: Incentives and Compensation

I N A WORLD OF complex instruments, models, and markets, a little knowledge is a dangerous thing. A lot of knowledge is not much better, it turns out, it's just more expensive.

Across the financial services industry, this lesson became abundantly clear as employees were richly paid for expertise that ultimately failed to prevent, and in some cases caused, serious damage to firms and to the larger economy. The debate on restructuring the way individuals are paid in the industry has been one of the more closely followed aspects of efforts to reform financial services regulation. There are two reasons for this: First, there is something instinctively offensive (and therefore worthy of ink and airtime) when it appears that the only punishment for the culprits is to receive millions, instead of tens of millions, in compensation. The punishment seems like Al Capone's jail cell, stuffed with fine furniture and luxurious comforts—only without the jail cell.

It is in fact outrageous that the only consequence for the greedy and incompetent would be banishment to their ten-acre estates in Greenwich. But only a handful of those who worked in the industry were greedy and culpable. And more importantly, policymakers should not be drawn into issues of justice or revenge—these are the business of judges and mobs, respectively. Allowing such situation-specific considerations to influence long-term policy is a recipe for bad policy even if it does make good politics.

The second reason why compensation reform has been so closely followed is that its outcome could have long-term implications for the safety and the functioning of the economy. This has always been the case, but it is only now being recognized. In contrast to arguments that begin and end with the question of whether it is fair that executives continue to receive huge pay packages, the long-term debate has rightly settled on an examination of pay *structure* rather than pay levels. This chapter will examine some of the considerations from both sides of the debate.

BIG BROTHER IS PAYING YOU

The financial crisis has given the world many spectacles it thought that it would never see—the demise of the investment banking industry, a rush to Keynesian stimulus packages, and the virtual nationalization of the largest U.S. automaker, the largest insurance company, and several banks, for example. Topping the list, though, is government regulation of how people are paid in the financial services industry—the very embodiment of free market forces at work. The change in attitude is neither subtle nor trivial: Almost overnight, compensation has become a regulatory issue. In the financial services industry, at least, the government gets a very big say in how people are paid. The question is what form this role should take—deciding how much people should be paid or how their pay should be structured.

REGULATING THE LEVEL OF PAY

In an early draft of the 2009 Senate bill on financial reform, Senator Chris Dodd proposed a ban on compensation plans for large banking institutions that provide "excessive" compensation. The difficulty of enforcing such a standard is self-evident. "Excessive" is a truly subjective notion. Different people will start with different points of reference (like speeding cars on the highway, anything higher than me is excessive). They will have different ideas as to what is relevant in judging whether a particular level is excessive (it may depend on risk, on levels of experience, on industry benchmarks, on requisite training and education, etc.). Levels of pay will also vary within a firm based on the level of experience and specialism, and will vary from one location to the next.

Of course, common sense tells us that there does come a point where pay is excessive and in this respect the financial services industry is not breaking new ground. Ask anyone what they think of the salary for the centerfielder who missed the pop fly last night, or the pop star with more trips to detox than to the Top Ten. When the pay in question comes from taxpayer money, though, the issue is no longer merely a matter of our offended collective dignity; it is a matter of public policy and the stewardship of public funds. When a firm receives a government bailout and then turns around and passes out $165 million in extra pay (as AIG did), the firm had better be able to give a compelling argument why the bonuses were necessary. In fairness to AIG, this figure represented only a tenth of 1 percent of the government bailout money it received, but this is understandably not a point AIG is likely to stress very strongly. So regulating pay levels does make some sense when the money is coming from the taxpayer.

The argument that such large bonuses are necessary in order to retain key talent gets to the heart of the distinction between pay levels and pay structures: Whereas pay levels are meant to keep people there, pay structure is meant to influence their behavior. Yes, the prospect of more pay may make some of them take more risk, but that is a matter of *how* they are paid—what criteria will trigger higher pay—not *how much.*

The specific culprit in terms of structuring pay is that portion which varies depending on performance, commonly referred to as *incentive compensation.* This term covers a number of different types of pay, including bonuses, stock options (which only make a profit when the stock price rises above a given level), and restricted stock (which, like other stock, is worth the market value once it has been granted to the employee). Pay packages often include a combination of these, in addition to a base salary. What distinguishes incentive compensation from salary is that the amount paid is variable, and this is meant to guide behavior in a specific direction (greater productivity, higher profits, etc.). Meet your targets, get your bonus. In some cases, the amount itself is not variable—you get the bonus if you meet your target, but the amount of the bonus does not vary once the target has been met. In other cases, the incentive compensation may be capped, or it could be completely variable—for example, when you share in a percentage of the profits in your trading account.

The idea that a portion of a person's compensation should vary with performance is not inherently controversial. In most settings, it is actually beneficial because it recognizes good performance and, when it includes department- or firm-wide goals, can promote teamwork. The real questions are twofold: Do the goals by which performance is measured encourage excessive risk-taking or other undesirable behavior, and are the timeframes over which the compensation is paid shorter than the time it takes to determine whether the risks paid off?

 PERFORMANCE GOALS AND RISK

The point behind regulating compensation is really to regulate the behavior encouraged by the compensation, not the compensation itself. Once it is decided to take the leap into regulating compensation, then it would be pointless to ignore the performance goals that determine whether the employee receives incentive compensation. Performance goals are, after all, meant to give specific measures of what the firm wants the employee to achieve. Depending on the role, the goals could include making a certain number of mortgages, increasing trading profits, or increasing market share. Goals are supposed to be measurable, and the problem is that things like profit, market share, and revenues are more easily measured than concepts like risk. Performance goals can also create harmful conflicts of interest, for instance, when a manager's goals include both the approval of mortgage applications and increasing revenues.

When the incentives are skewed all throughout the system, all feet are firmly on the accelerator and no one's foot is on the brake. Continuing the scenario, if the bank's senior management is evaluated and compensated based on increasing revenues, but has no incentive to ensure that those receiving the mortgages are creditworthy since the bank will simply sell them on to an RMBS pool, the culture of excessive risk is promoted further. The same risk culture passes through the entire system: The person buying the mortgages to create the RMBSs is judged by the number and size of RMBS deals successfully created in the course of the year, and since most or all of the RMBSs will be sold into the market it does not matter to him or her whether the mortgagees will still be paying in two years. He or she also works closely with rating agency analysts who provide favorable ratings. While the rating analyst's performance goals generally do not include revenue or market share goals, the managers to whom they ultimately report do. Once put together, the RMBSs are sold to the market by people whose performance goals are based on the volume sold, and they are sold to portfolio managers whose goals are based on the returns they get for their investors. RMBSs consistently paid higher interest rates than safer instruments like Treasury bonds (at least until they stopped paying at all), and so purchasing the RMBS shares helped the portfolio manager meet his or her goals. It is because of these incentives that it was in everyone's *individual* short-term interest to create, package, promote, and sell the mortgages that probably should not have been written in the first place. They were the bottom card in an upside-down house of cards.

This scenario addresses only one aspect of the industry but it illustrates two important points. First, as already noted, the risk posed by incentive compensation comes from what people are paid *for*, not what they are paid. Second, firms don't make decisions, people do. If you want to keep firms from putting the financial system at risk, you have to look at what is influencing the relevant decision makers to act one way or the other.

There's plenty of blame to go around in the scenario, and not just in the banking sector. Not every person who bought a mortgage he or she could not afford was hoodwinked by a slick mortgage broker. Moreover, it can reasonably be argued (and has been) that the permissive mortgage environment that became the first domino in the financial crisis was a product of well-intentioned legislation aimed at increasing homeownership among those traditionally not able to purchase a home. A laudable goal, and one that made good campaign fodder—the performance goal of a lawmaker, of course, being measured in votes.

This last point leads to an important caveat with respect to regulating compensation: Not all incentives are monetary. Employees will wish to increase revenues, profits, or market share because that is what will make them look good within the firm. You can theoretically put everyone on a flat salary and there will still be unwritten incentives for employees, from the nakedly ambitious ladder-climbers to the more altruistic who simply want to do a good job. This imposes a natural limit on how far you can deter excessive risk-taking simply by removing or reengineering incentives. It does not, however, rule out the creation of *disincentives* that discourage excessively risky behavior or "clawback" incentive pay when the risks go sour. Such systems, described later in this chapter, are known as "malus" systems to contrast them with bonus systems.

METHODS OF ALIGNING REWARD WITH RISK

Much of the criticism regarding incentive compensation has centered on the fact that bonuses were often paid annually based on the performance of activities or investments whose risk might not be clear for several years. A simple example would be that loan originator at the bank. If she had a goal to approve 50 mortgages a year, she might approve a number of loans for individuals with marginal credit or poor documentation of income. At the end of the year, the loan officer has produced 50 loans and gets the bonus. But the loan officer has put the bank at risk since there is an increased probability that a number of the homeowners will default. If you award the medals for a marathon at the two-mile marker, you will get some pretty impressive times among the awardees but you may not see them at the head of the pack when the race is done.

In reaction, policymakers and some firms have placed an emphasis on aligning the time horizon for incentive compensation payouts with the risk associated with the employee's activities. This is a variation on the concept of *vesting*, which has already been the standard practice for non-cash components of executive compensation such as restricted stock or stock options. With vesting, the award granted in any given year will be paid out over a period of years, normally in tranches of equal size. Thus, a person may be awarded 3,000 shares of restricted stock, none of which is actually available on the date of the award—it is all "restricted." After one year, one-third of the award vests and is freely available to the employee, in two years a second tranche becomes available, and in the third year the final thousand shares vest. The purpose behind vesting has always been to provide a motive for the employee to stay at the firm, since he would leave any unvested options or shares on the table when he left. It is now seen also as a method to stretch out the payment of the cash component of incentive compensation (i.e., a bonus) in order to avoid rewarding the employee while the jury is still out on the transaction in question.

This approach is not perfect. First, many investments have unclear or open-ended time horizons, for instance, when one firm acquires another. Second, calculating bonuses could become very complex, given both the fact that several investments with differing timelines may well be entered into in the course of a year, and the need to measure actual versus expected performance for each. Finally, this method accounts for risk only to the firm itself, not to the wider system. If an investment banker slaps together a highly risky portfolio of mortgages but passes it on by selling it into the market, the firm will neither care nor know how the security performed years down the road.

A second method, one supported by the Federal Reserve for the banks it regulates, is to lengthen the time horizon of incentive awards. In other words, pay bonuses every two years instead of every year. This approach is likely to be neither popular—who wants to wait an extra year for their big payouts?—

nor effective, since it still assumes all risks will succeed or fail within the newly fixed timeframe.

A third option reduces the rate at which awards increase as an employee achieves higher levels of the performance measure. The idea is to provide rewards for good performance, but to avoid the possibility that the employee pulls out all the stops in order to rake in the bonus money with both hands.

Alternatively, the firm could apply a "risk factor" up front to the bonus. The idea goes like this: Two employees in roughly the same role are eligible for bonuses of 25 percent of base salary. But one engages in riskier transactions to meet his targets, perhaps with a relative risk rating of 1.5 (50% more risky than the other employee). Under this system, the potential bonus for that employee would be reduced to 16.6 percent (25% divided by 1.5).

A more straightforward approach is the *clawback* (the most widely used malus system). With such an arrangement, the employee is bound by contract to pay back any amount of bonus paid for a transaction that subsequently soured (or pay back a proportionate amount reflecting the difference between original assumptions and actual performance). Whenever an employee leaves, any unvested amounts could be paid, with a legal obligation to repay the firm on demand (alternatively, the unvested portion could simply continue to be paid over time and withheld if the transaction deteriorates).

Clawbacks should in fact be used any time cash compensation vests in tranches in order to avoid either the firm or the employee having an incentive to terminate employment early. Consider two situations: In the first, the firm is suffering financially and does not want to be seen by its employees or the public as teetering on the edge of bankruptcy. Instead, it lays off a few well-compensated employees to save the expense of paying the unvested bonus amounts. Clearly it would be unfair to allow a firm the discretion to dismiss employees at will without the obligation to make good the unvested amounts. But a second situation illustrates why it would be unwise simply to pay departing employees all unvested cash compensation without a clawback. Suppose an employee, who is best positioned to know the health of the transactions into which he entered, sees that the investment is likely to fail and sees it before the firm does. The logical course of action would be to quit when he sees the problem, and so the employee receives all of the unvested funds. Adding a clawback provision enables the firm to recover the loot in question when it becomes apparent that it had been had.

Malus schemes are becoming increasingly popular with lawmakers and banks, if not with employees, having been mandated in some countries and adopted by some institutions of their own volition.

WHO MATTERS?

If the purpose of reforming compensation practices is to reduce the creation of incentives that encourage inordinate risk, then it is important to recognize that most employees, even at the riskiest firms, are not in a position to place their firm or the market in danger. Arrangements such as malus schemes should be limited to those whose decisions involve the taking of risk and can endanger the firm. This will vary from firm to firm, and so it will be incumbent upon each firm to identify the individuals specifically. A few broad guidelines are appropriate, however.

First, and obviously, top management would fall within the scope of revised compensation. They are paid to make the big decisions that put a firm at risk, either actively or tacitly through their role in reviewing the decisions of their subordinates. Next, there are the officers and employees in critical functions. While senior managers obviously fall within this description (for instance, the head of a trading desk), so, too, may the worker-bees who carry no management responsibilities but whose actions could lead to the taking of excessive risk. Examples here might include individual traders and research or credit analysts. Employees and managers in control functions such as internal audit, finance, and compliance might also fall within this sphere. There are also classes of employees who do not individually have the ability to place the firm at risk, but who collectively do. For instance, individual loan officers at a bank do not generally have the individual lending authority to take big risks, but as a group their activities create both big rewards and big risks.

THE 2009 FEDERAL RESERVE GUIDANCE

Throughout 2008 and 2009, much of the debate focused on reining in the pay packages and changing the compensation practices at TARP-financed institutions. In October 2009, though, the Federal Reserve issued proposed "supervisory guidance" that had a far more wide-reaching and permanent impact. The guidance applies not just to an unlucky handful of senior executives at TARP-funded firms, but to the thousands of banking institutions regulated by the Federal Reserve System. Although the guidance was issued initially as a proposal and so had not been formalized, the Fed cut right to the chase and told banks that it expected them to begin reviewing their compensation practices immediately to determine the extent to which they conformed to the proposals. In fact, the Fed required the largest banks to report information on their current pay practices by the following February.

The Fed's move was one of a number of initiatives taken by regulators in the United States and abroad. The House had already approved its first bill on pay practices in the summer of 2009, which aimed to limit executive compensation and to give shareholders a nonbinding vote on compensation arrangements. At the international level, the Financial Stability Board issued principles on "sound compensation practices" in April 2009, on which the Fed guidance was based. But in comparison to these other measures, the Fed proposals were distinguished by the breadth of their applicability, their level of detail, and their continuing nature.

Supervisory guidance from the Fed is not a mere suggestion—banks are now required to demonstrate that they conform to the guidance and will be tested in that regard in the course of the examination process. Failure to conform without adequate justification would therefore have real consequences.

The scope of the guidance implies considerable additional work to be performed by affected banks, both initially and on an ongoing basis. The virtual certainty of formal regulatory scrutiny and the unpleasant consequences for failure should raise this issue right up the risk matrix in very short order.

Since the Fed's guidance applies to all institutions under its jurisdiction, it applies to U.S. bank holding companies, state-chartered banks that are members of the Federal Reserve system, and the U.S. operations of foreign banks that have branches or other relevant activities in the United States. That means that the guidance has a far wider reach than those measures adopted only with respect to TARP recipients, which went away when the TARP money was paid back. Throughout 2008 and 2009, the financial services industry found itself searching for something resembling best practice for compensation, putting the Fed's guidance in position to become one of the early standards by which the financial industry (and even nonfinancial firms) measure themselves.

Within Fed-regulated banks, the guidance applies based on whether a particular employee or officer's role places the firm at material risk. This is in marked contrast to TARP-based guidance, which captures individuals based on their relative level of compensation (i.e., the 25 highest-paid executives). The Fed then takes this functional approach a step further, applying the guidance to compensation structures for groups of individuals who *collectively* create material risk for the firm (as discussed earlier). While relatively low-level mortgage origination officers at a bank may not individually create so much exposure that the resulting risk would be material to the bank, they may fall within the remit of the guidance as members of a department that collectively creates large exposure.

When banks' compensation arrangements are reviewed in their examinations, the size and complexity of the institution will be factored into account in determining the depth of the review. Still, all examinations will include a compensation review of some sort, regardless of the size of the institution. As noted in the following, this means that even relatively small and straightforward banking organizations will need to demonstrate that their compensation arrangements are appropriate, even if the burden on them is meant to be lighter than on a large and complex bank.

Importantly, the Fed forgoes placing caps on salary levels, and instead seeks to ensure that incentive compensation schemes do not encourage excessive risk taking. It therefore largely ignores compensation components such as fixed base salaries and profit-sharing plans that are determined based on overall company performance.

The guidance provides three principles for assessing a bank's incentive compensation program. The first is that the program should "balance risk and financial results in a manner that does not provide employees incentives to take excessive risks on behalf of the banking organization." The guidance notice provided extensive discussion on this point, including commentary on the determination of performance measures, the use of quantitative risk metrics, and methods currently used in the industry to align rewards with risk. The guidance outlines four such practices that the Fed expects firms to use individually or in combination.

The second principle concerns risk management processes and internal controls to ensure compliance with the firm's own compensation policies. The guidance includes an explicit expectation that banks will have internal controls specific to the design, implementation, and ongoing monitoring of any relevant incentive compensation arrangements. This includes a process to identify the individuals and units that create a material risk for the bank and how the risk will be measured. Moreover, banks are expected to conduct "regular internal reviews" to ensure compliance with the process, and to ensure that sufficient documentation is created to facilitate such reviews. For many banks, all this will be new.

The third principle requires banks to have "strong and effective corporate governance to help ensure sound compensation practices." An expectation of effective corporate governance is by no means new, but the guidance reflecting this principle requires direct involvement of the board in the incentive compensation process, including the expectation that the board should "monitor the performance, and regularly review the design and function" of the incentive compensation program, and should receive data and analysis from within the organization as well as external sources sufficient to permit this review.

WAS ADAM SMITH RIGHT?

In the end, the mechanism through which incentive compensation operates is self-interest. People will do what their performance measures and bonus programs require them to do. To recognize this is to get to the heart of the issue of compensation. The consequence may be good or bad, intended or unintended, but people will follow the path of self-interest paved by incentive compensation.

And so the same mechanism that drives behavior in the marketplace also drives behavior in the workplace. But there is a critical difference between the two. Smith's "invisible hand" is the operation not just of self-interest, but of *competing* self-interests that act in the long run to balance each other out and move prices toward equilibrium. Office politics aside, interests within an organization are not so efficiently balanced. For every person incentivized to increase profits, there is often no countervailing person with an interest to restrain activities. Indeed, to the extent that there is competing self-interest in the firm, it may act to further increase risk because the employees are in competition to create the largest profits. To the extent there is a countervailing interest in the firm, it would be in the form of compliance or risk management staff. And this is why it is so important, though unfortunately often not the case, that compliance and risk management staff have independence, authority, and equal standing with the business units that are in the business of putting the firm at risk.

Perhaps ironically, the regulation of pay structure is an affirmation of Adam Smith's concept of self-interest, not repudiation. The leap of logic that is necessary to recognize this is that self-interest drives decisions, not just in the marketplace but in the workplace as well. If you want to restrain risk and keep individuals from torpedoing the firm, the best way is to have smart, targeted regulation of incentive compensation structures.

CHAPTER SEVEN

Who Protects the Consumer?

G IVEN THE POLITICAL NATURE of the regulatory process, it is no surprise that there have been several issues that proved contentious as they moved from proposal to debate to law and into implementation. But it was on the issue of creating a consumer protection agency that the daggers truly came out.

When the proposal for a Consumer Financial Protection Agency (CFPA) was first floated by the Obama Administration, seven consumer groups joined to present testimony supporting the move, blaming poorly underwritten mortgage loans and a dysfunctional patchwork of regulators for the financial crisis.[1] The testimony was supported by findings of the Government Accountability Office (GAO), which had previously found that the

> fragmented U.S. regulatory structure contributed to failures by the existing regulators to adequately protect consumers and ensure financial stability. . . . [E]fforts by regulators to respond to the increased risks associated with new mortgage products were sometimes

---

[1] Testimony of Gail Hillebrand, Senior Attorney, Consumers Union, to the House Committee on Energy and Commerce, July 8, 2009.

57

slowed in part because of the need for five federal regulators to coordinate their response.[2]

But create one über-regulator for consumer protection issues in all sectors of the financial services industry? The response from those who would be on the receiving end of the agency was swift and unambiguous. The American Bankers Association decried the creation of a new and powerful agency that would be authorized to create financial products and then require banks to offer them to the public. The chairman of J.P. Morgan reportedly "railed against the plan," and the U.S. Chamber of Commerce got a media blitz going warning that small businesses would lose access to credit.[3] The creation of a separate, powerful agency also drew opposition from Republican lawmakers, and particularly those on the Senate Banking Committee, who proposed instead a system of better coordination among existing agencies.

When we look back on regulatory reform in the coming years, we are likely to see the debate surrounding the creation of a Consumer Financial Protection Agency as one of the most significant of the reform period. Its work not only would touch on the financial wellbeing of virtually every consumer in the country, but would affect the way business is done throughout the banking sector, and other corners of the financial services industry as well. As this book goes to press, it is unclear what the outcome of the debate will be and whether a separate agency will be created. The result is likely to be a compromise that, in the best traditions of representative democracy, will be equally unacceptable to all concerned. But whatever happens, the consumer protection genie is out of the bottle and it is not in a good mood.

The idea of creating a consumer protection agency was not really breaking new ground, since there were already consumer protection regulations in effect. But the concentration of consumer protection responsibility in one agency raised a number of questions, starting with "why?" Since consumer protection laws already existed and most financial regulators had a consumer protection role, why change? Why not simply ensure that the existing laws are better enforced and the existing regime better coordinated? The real question here is whether the existing regime had worked.

---

[2] Government Accountability Office, *Financial Regulation: A Framework for Crafting and Assessing Proposals to Modernize the Outdated U.S. Financial Regulatory System*, January 2009, GAO 09-216, p. 15, available at: www.gao.gov/new.items/d09314t.pdf; cited in Hillebrand testimony, *op cit.*

[3] Dennis K. Berman, "In 2010, Year of the Regulator," *Wall Street Journal*, December 22, 2009.

WERE EXISTING REGULATIONS EFFECTIVE?

The most fundamental argument in favor of changing the regulation of consumer financial products would be that the existing regulatory regime had failed. Certainly, some products and practices were inappropriate for some or all people. Mortgages that took a customer's word with regard to income, predatory lending, algorithms that rearrange checking account withdrawals to maximize overdraft fees, and similar practices drew fire once they were exposed by the regulatory reform debate. This is not surprising given the fact that the economic collapse and resulting unemployment brought rising financial distress that was exacerbated by these practices. When these dodgy practices came to light, the existing regulatory arrangements meant to protect consumers came under intense scrutiny for permitting them either through incompetence or negligence. Since the regulatory regime had failed to prevent these practices and the practices had become part of the fabric of the financial crisis, it was an easy populist target.

But how much of the blame should be laid at the feet of the regulators or the regulatory structure that divided responsibility among agencies? Would a different regime have made a difference, or did the problem really arise from an overwhelmingly casual attitude that infected consumers, lenders, and regulators alike? The answer is probably that the regulatory structure had more to do with it than many would like to admit, but less than some would accuse. On one hand, the credit card industry alone was rife with practices that were even difficult for the credit card companies to justify once they were exposed. These included, among other things,

- Sending bills close to the payment-due date, and charging high fees for late payments
- "Universal default," a practice in which the cardholder's rates can be changed based on a missed payment on another debt (or even, according to the Consumers Union, applying for a loan)
- Changing the terms of a credit card simply by providing notice, and as a result applying a higher interest rate to the existing balance

All of these practices were, strictly speaking, perfectly above-board because they had been included in the customer agreements or had otherwise been disclosed in writing to the cardholder. With no regulator specifically responsible for monitoring practices across the industry, practices that were good business and legally valid but ethically dubious flourished.

On the other hand, these iffy products did not come about just because regulators were asleep at the wheel. In the case of mortgages, the banks and regulators can justifiably point a finger at Congress and the laudable goal of increasing homeownership. The Community Reinvestment Act of 1977 set about the task of addressing discriminatory lending practices by effectively mandating the extension of credit to "low- and moderate-income" neighborhoods, regardless of the fact that low incomes and unemployment tend to suggest a deficiency in financial resources. Indeed, lending institutions were examined by regulators on the degree to which they had met their goals under the Act. And so for anyone who sees those nasty bankers as the people that lit the fuse on the financial crisis by initiating the practice of subprime lending, it is worth remembering that the banks had little choice to do so given the very clear marching orders from their regulatory masters. (It should be noted that the connection between the Act and the growth of subprime lending is not universally accepted, though supporters of this view include Fed Chairman Bernanke.)

Aside from legislative mandates, there is also the issue of individual responsibility. Consumer protection is not about protecting consumers from themselves. Blaming banks for the actions of self-indulgent over-consumers is a bit like blaming the fast-food restaurant industry for the person who eats himself to morbid obesity. Individuals are ultimately and always responsible for their financial decisions, except when representations made in their connection are fraudulent or misleading. Though serious allegations of misrepresentation have been made concerning some of the controversial practices, where this has not been proven the burden remains, at least legally, with the individual. To do otherwise would be to allow the financially irresponsible a do-over simply because they are the little guys and the lending facility is the big guy. In other words, it would be giving a bailout to the undeserving—not something the government likes to be accused of these days.

Another point made by the banks in defense of the existing regime is that if consumer protection regulations had been allowed to become overly burdensome, there would have been limited choice for consumers. Thirty-year fixed-rate mortgages may have been the best option for everyone in days past, but the flexibility of adjustable-rate and interest-only mortgages has provided additional options that have been appropriate for others. With the prevailing deregulatory mood in the markets over the past decade, the emphasis was on providing choice and letting customers make their own decisions rather than on an airbags-and-seatbelts approach to protecting customers from themselves.

While these arguments are true up to a point, any attempt to argue that the pre-crisis regulatory arrangements were adequate is doomed to fail. There is some credibility to the allegation that credit card agreements were stuffed with dodgy "traps" and there is just no way to justify accepting a mortgage application with no documentation of income or assets. More importantly, defending the existing arrangements would be political suicide—even if you were right, you would be painted as anti–consumer protection and the financial equivalent to a Holocaust denier. So if the existing regulatory approach of spreading responsibility among the financial regulators had failed, the next question was whether a single consolidated regulator was the answer.

IS A SEPARATE CONSUMER REGULATOR THE RIGHT ANSWER?

The question of regulatory structure centers on whether consumers and the industry would be well served by adding an additional source of regulation, or layer of bureaucracy, depending on which side of the political spectrum you view the issue from. Without question, adding a new entity (whether an independent agency or bureau within an existing one) would create an additional burden since the banks would still be regulated by existing regulators on a range of other topics. In the case of some non-banks the new agency would represent the first time they have been regulated. A new agency also means new rules, making for a painful and burdensome transition at a time when firms are compelled by financial circumstances to reduce costs rather than increase them. Nor can it be taken for granted that a new agency with a narrow focus on customer protection issues would be any better at regulation than were the previous regulators, since staff and management are likely to be drawn from the existing pool of talent at those regulators. Moving the same ineffective regulators into a new organization doesn't make them any better. A better alternative, said Senate Republicans, would be a council of existing state and federal regulators to coordinate consumer protection.

The American Bankers Association in particular objected to the creation of a separate consumer protection agency on the grounds that

> Creating a new consumer regulatory agency . . . would simply complicate our existing financial regulatory structure by adding another extensive layer of regulation. There is no shortage of laws designed to protect consumers. Making improvements to enhance consumer

protection under the existing legal and regulatory structures—particularly aimed at filling the gaps of regulation and supervision of non-bank financial providers—is likely to be more successful, more quickly, than a separate consumer regulator.[4]

History seemed to justify both sides of the argument. In particular, Democrats pointed to the failure of the Federal Reserve under Alan Greenspan to enforce provisions of the Home Ownership and Equity Protection Act of 1994 (HOEPA). HOEPA gave the Federal Reserve the authority to oversee mortgage loans, but the Fed did not produce any implementing rules until well after Greenspan's departure and the onset of the financial crisis (to be fair, the authority did not extend to non-bank institutions beyond the reach of the Fed, and so it would not have been a silver bullet). Proponents of the CFPA view the failure of HOEPA to halt the crisis as an indictment of the Fed and evidence that a new and more powerful regulator is needed; opponents cite it as evidence that the failure of the existing structure was attributable to poor enforcement rather than the structure itself.

Still, there are three fundamental arguments in favor a single, separate consumer protection regulator for the financial services industry, beyond the fact that the existing regime had not worked: (1) that a single regulator with a single mission could develop the expertise necessary to make good policy and to enforce the rules; (2) that a single regulator would not be as susceptible to coordination failures; and (3) that the existing structure created a conflict of interest within the regulatory agencies by making them responsible for curtailing deceptive but lucrative practices while at the same time making them responsible for the financial health of the institutions. These arguments are discussed next.

In every organization, there are departments that have a high profile and a high priority, and those that take the backseat. In arguing for a separate regulator, supporters made the point that consumer protection was too often an afterthought in agencies like the Federal Reserve or the FDIC, which had other high-profile roles to play. This implies that consumer protection is near the end of the line when passing out resources or planning examinations. It is also more difficult to attract and retain good talent when that means that working in consumer protection will be perceived as a sidelight and receive less recognition. However, if the agency has a single mission and is focused solely on consumer protection, both the available resources and staff morale will rise.

---

[4] Testimony of Edward Yingling, President, American Bankers Association, to the Senate Banking Committee, July 14, 2009.

The next point in favor of a single regulator is that the ball gets dropped less often when there are fewer handoffs. If other agencies also have some level of responsibility for consumer protection, it takes a considerable degree of coordination to make sure things are not going unexamined just because everyone thinks someone else is examining it. In addition to gaps in regulation, wasteful redundancies can also occur that can lead to conflicting regulatory rulemaking guidance, not to mention unnecessary expense for both the regulator and the bank.

While the first two points are largely true in any situation, the conflict-of-interest issue is somewhat unique to financial regulation. Regulators are used to accusing *others* of having conflicts of interest, but the pre-crisis regulatory structure built in an inherent conflict of its own. More accurately, the problem should be characterized a "conflict of missions," but it is a conflict all the same. Absent a designated agency for consumer protection, the task fell, over time, on the financial industry's existing regulators (i.e., the Federal Reserve, the Office of Thrift Supervision, and the Office of the Comptroller of the Currency). These are agencies frankly more concerned with the job of ensuring the financial soundness of institutions and the stability of the system (*ahem*). The conflict arises when a bank's revenues are substantially derived from a particular product or service, and curtailing this product or service would undermine the financial viability of the bank.

Opponents of a separate consumer regulatory agency turned this conflict of interest concern on its side, and argued that consumer protection must be housed in the same agency as "safety and soundness" regulation in order to prevent the consumer protection staff from undermining the financial soundness of the banks. This logic, it must be said, doesn't hold much weight: The only banks whose financial health would be endangered by consumer protection measures are those who can only stay in business by engaging in activities deemed abusive to the customer. Such a bank should go out of business.

As the political winds blew in the direction of a new and separate regulator, the next question was what it should and should not do—and once again, the government's views were quite different from those on the receiving end.

One existing problem that could be addressed with a new regulator was the "unlevel playing field" that existed between banks and other "non-bank" institutions that extend credit. This was one prospect that the banking industry fully supported, since the absence of any regulation on non-banks had made it more difficult for banks (especially small community banks) to compete when selling similar products. The banks had more restrictions on their activities and higher regulatory costs that needed to be carried. The extension of regulation to non-banks raised alarm bells, however, as it appeared that the scope would reach far beyond the financial services industry (later revisions narrowed the scope considerably). Indeed, the original draft as presented by the Obama Administration looked like it had been written in a rush. Its scope ranged from banks and credit card companies to real estate brokers and virtually anyone who extended credit, as well as any business that "provides a material service" to any of these financial services providers. It would also have sweeping powers to ban "unfair" terms and practices and require firms to offer standard (plain-vanilla) products conforming to standards set by the agency.

It was also important to consider who should not be covered. From the beginning, the scope of the CFPA excluded consumer protection as it relates to securities and commodities transactions, leaving these areas to their existing regulators—the SEC and the CFTC, respectively.

Many of the lending institutions within the scope of the agency were not central to causing the financial crisis, and so one of the arguments against the creation of the agency was that it punished those who had nothing to do with the crisis. This argument, of course, assumes that the goal of the legislation is to prevent another systemic crisis that looks like the last one and this is not entirely true. Many of the abuses and other concerns are issues of longstanding that have gained political momentum only as the plight of financial consumers has been highlighted in the course of the crisis. Additionally, some of the mortgage products and practices that came to life in the past decade were the genetic material from which toxic securitized assets were formed, which played such a starring role in the collapse of the financial system. To argue that they are not inherently abusive walks right into the argument that they became abusive when used by ethically casual bankers and that proper regulatory oversight could have caught and prevented the trend.

To a bank or non-bank lender that found itself within the scope of the new agency, the big question would be how that would impact its business. Clearly, an all-powerful regulator was not what the industry had in mind, but for a public already fuming at perceived abuses and for lawmakers eager to appease them, there would be no point to creating another agency if it were dentally challenged.

The idea of creating a consumer protection agency was always going to be one of the most politically sensitive, whether it had teeth or not. The debate had all the elements of a great political plot—big corporations allegedly abusing consumers, big government attempting to add another layer of bureaucracy solely to soothe the savage breast of indignant voters, entrenched agencies fighting for their turf, and the chance to take a swing at Alan Greenspan. And this would be no obscure little agency like the Federal Interagency Committee for the Management of Noxious and Exotic Weeds: It could dictate what products and services institutions could and could not provide.

In considering the arguments that were made against the creation of a CFPA, it should be noted first that no one argued against consumer protection *per se* for obvious reasons. Resistance to the proposal centered instead on the question of whether a new, single regulator was needed or even desirable, on the scope of institutions to be covered, on the specific powers to be granted to the agency, and on its impact on state regulation of banks. More to the point, the argument was that it would restrict access to credit by making some customers unprofitable for the banks.

 WHAT POWERS WOULD THE AGENCY HAVE?

From its very first draft, this agency was not meant to be toothless. Put succinctly, the agency would have the authority to determine the "manner, settings, and circumstances for the provision of any consumer financial products or services."[5] Toward this end, it would have the authority to examine firms and to request virtually whatever information it determines that it needs. While the latter powers are not vastly different from those of other regulators, the authority to dictate the manner, setting, and circumstances of providing products is. Commentators have pointed out the danger of giving a regulator the unilateral authority to designate products or services as abusive, with the result that "any such designation would create massive liability for services that were legal at the time they were offered."[6]

The first formal outline of a CFPA was floated by the Obama Administration in the summer of 2009 via a detailed draft bill published by the Treasury Department. Although significant parts of the bill were altered or removed as part of the process of getting it through committees and to floor votes, the Treasury draft served to frame the later legislation. As the Treasury Department laid it out, the CFPA was meant, among other things, to ensure that consumers received "concise and clear information that (they) can understand and use," and to protect them from "unfair or deceptive practices."[7]

---

[5] "Another Scary Czar," *Wall Street Journal*, October 8, 2009.

[6] Ibid.

[7] U.S. Department of the Treasury, "Administration's Regulatory Reform Agenda Moves Forward: Legislation for Strengthening Consumer Protection Delivered to Capitol Hill," available at www.dot.gov.

Toward these ends, the agency was to be given a broad set of powers:

- Writing rules and implementing existing statutes for consumer protection and for creating consistent rules for unregulated and lightly regulated institutions
- Supervising and examining institutions to ensure compliance and enforcing compliance through orders and penalties
- "Full authority" to create consistent standards and enforcement with respect to banks and non-banks alike
- Authority to gather information in any part of the market, from any kind of entity making the loan or providing the product or service, to respond to changes and address bad practices as they develop[8]

As noted, some of these powers are standard stuff for regulators (the authority to examine and to enforce), while others were more worrying for the industry, either because of what they said explicitly or because their ambiguous wording leaves them wide open to the interpretation of the regulator itself. Giving the agency the authority to gather information from "any part of the market" begs the question as to who is part of the market and who is not, and the very broad definition of a financial service provided elsewhere in the draft did not provide comfort, nor did the fact that the remit did not appear to place any restrictions on what kind of information could be requested (actually demanded).

Even more worrying was the full authority to create standards in the industry, since this could put the regulator in the place of designing the products and services that were acceptable, along with the parallel authority to ban practices it deems "unfair" or "deceptive."

At least in the eyes of the banks, the restrictions would also apply to non-banks extending loans or giving credit, helping to address the unlevel playing field (non-banks were less enthusiastic).

Finally, parts of the industry were unhappy that the Act would permit states to set up standards even harsher than those promulgated at the federal level. Though this would give the states more authority and would put a regulator closer to the scene for many smaller firms, the fact that the rules did not establish a regulatory ceiling meant that regulated firms could be forced to meet different standards in every state, rather than simply the federal standard in all states.

---

[8] *Ibid.*

In retrospect, the Administration's draft bill made a lot of sense if it was written looking backwards, with the intention of banning things that had happened before. But a regulation also needs to look forward, so that some thought is given to its interpretation and some level of certainty is given to the regulated firms as to how the law would be implemented.

Though the early proposals provided for an unusually powerful agency and was intended to avoid creating another toothless regulator, the negotiation process inevitably involved a considerable degree of dental work—particularly with respect to limiting its scope and its enforcement powers. In spite of all the political and populist support, the agency may well turn out to be a sheep in wolf's clothing.

A WORD ABOUT CONSUMER PROTECTION AND SYSTEMIC RISK

One of the biggest problems with risky consumer financial products was that the bank that sold the product did not assume the risk, and never had any intention of doing so. The failure to prevent the epidemic of bad loans reflects the necessity of regulating retail financial services providers in order to protect the system, but also provides a potentially powerful argument against new consumer regulations. In the old days, it could be argued, banks never created and sold such dodgy mortgages because it was bad business to give money to someone who did not have good credit and enough money. Economic self-interest dictated that they be more prudent in how they lent their money. But securitization (at least as it was practiced in the past decade) removed this market discipline because it took away a self-interest on the part of the lender from the success of the transaction. If the problem is the creation, packaging, and distribution of dodgy mortgages, the goal could be achieved much more cheaply and effectively by reforming the securitization process, for instance, through the "skin-in-the-game" provision, which would require loan origina-tors to keep some of the mortgages they create on their own books.

This argument is a good one, but it overlooks two points. The first is that too many apparently unfair practices had been identified in the course of the crisis, so merely fixing the subprime securitization problem would not address unfair overdraft charges or capricious rises in card interest rates. The second point is that it assumes that only one line of defense would be chosen, but given the gravity of the financial situation it should not have been surprising that both reforms were moved forward.

The harnessing of securitization to these products eliminated the risk from the originating institution, but then spread it around the system in a way few understood at the time. Everyone made money, and everything worked well until it didn't. One argument in favor of a powerful consumer financial protection agency is that it would help prevent systemic risk by keeping the risky instruments out of the system in the first place (note that the argument is only that it would *reduce* the risk, not eliminate it). In June 2009, Elizabeth Warren, at the time the chair of the Congressional Oversight Panel for the TARP program and the person presumed to head any new consumer protection agency, put it plainly before Congress:

> If we had had a Consumer Financial Protection Agency five years ago, Liar's Loans and no-doc loans would never have made it into the financial marketplace—and never would have brought down our banking system.[9]

CONCLUSION

In the end, consumer protection will be regulated in the financial markets. The question of whether a single agency will be created is almost a side issue now. The days of protection by means of transparency are over, especially when it turned out that consumer disclosures were transparent only in the eyes of those who wrote them. Consumer protection will be front-and-center in the regulatory oversight of the financial industry in the years to come, in whatever form the policymakers agree to give it.

---

[9] Testimony to the House Financial Services Committee, June 24, 2009.

CHAPTER EIGHT

Transparency: Letting the Sun Shine In, or Sipping Water from a Firehose?

THE CONCEPT OF TRANSPARENCY is premised on the assumption that markets, by way of individual investors and traders, need accurate, complete, and up-to-date information in order to function efficiently. With enough information, the theory goes, markets will work efficiently with minimal or no government intervention. Underlying this assumption, however, is another premise—that these investors and traders have the time, capacity, and expertise to process the information and to make sound decisions accordingly. The question is how well the theory operates in the real world. Transparency is undoubtedly good; is it good enough?

 TRANSPARENCY AS REGULATION

The answer depends in part on how you view its role. If it is a tool to make markets operate efficiently, its value is clear. But over the years it has been put forward as a means of regulating markets, or as an alternative to formal regulation.

Of course, it is not the market's job to hold the hands of investors and force them to read and digest the information that has been disclosed. After all, investors are responsible for their own decisions and if they do not make the effort to ask questions or read a prospectus they have no one to blame but themselves. To do otherwise could create a no-lose situation in which investors profit when their investments do well but hold their brokers responsible for failing to make them understand the risks if the investments do poorly. But when the typical credit card contract is 30 pages long[1] and written by lawyers, average consumers could probably be forgiven for missing a point or two.

For many years, much of market theory has taken for granted that merely disclosing information is sufficient for the market; and that the efficient market will fully digest the information and efficiently act upon it. Indeed, this Efficient Market Hypothesis held sway in academic circles for decades before the financial crisis showed just how inefficient a market can get.

Underlying the Efficient Market Hypothesis has been the fundamental assumption that markets police themselves based simply on transparency—as in Alan Greenspan's now-famous (but possibly apocryphal) assertion that laws against fraud in the marketplace are unnecessary since the market would quickly spot the fraud and act against it, for instance, by shorting a fraudulently inflated stock price. Whether he actually made this statement or not, there is little doubt that the Greenspan chairmanship was characterized by a light touch on regulation, relying on the market to police itself. In contrast, some members of Congress have faulted the Fed's failure to take action against subprime mortgage practices until after the market collapsed and triggered the financial crisis as a sign of intentional regulatory toothlessness.

As markets grow more complex and varied, there comes a point where the information is too voluminous, arcane, or ambiguous to be relied on as the principal means of market discipline. The question policymakers must ask themselves now, and in the future, is whether we have reached such a point already. If so, the notion that transparency is an effective form of regulation must be reconsidered (a polite way of saying *rejected*).

The answer will depend on the instrument and sector under consideration. Some areas, such as the buying and selling of stocks, remain straightforward enough that the publication of information such as earnings or other financials, in a standard format and schedule, is sufficient for the market to act efficiently. Yet other instruments have become so complex that even insiders do not fully understand them. Take, for example, the credit derivatives market, one of the

---

[1] Testimony of Elizabeth Warren, Chair, Congressional Oversight Panel, to the House Financial Services Committee, June 24, 2009.

easy targets for regulatory reform following the crisis. It was an easy target because the over-the-counter market, by definition not traded on any public exchange, was by its nature not transparent. But if regulators make it transparent and stop there, the instruments themselves remain complex enough to worry regulators and widespread enough to pose a systemic risk.

 ## DEGREES OF TRANSPARENCY

The term *transparency* itself is not . . . well, transparent. It is often used interchangeably with, and therefore confused with, analogous terms such as *disclosure* and *reporting*. Yet these terms have very different meanings, each being a policy option implying a level of openness different from the others. It is important to know the differences and why particular options might be chosen or rejected, and what the implications for each are on the broader world.

Reporting

The lowest level of transparency is reporting. Reporting simply means that relevant information is provided to regulators (or, in some cases, exchanges, clearing houses, or other facilities that exercise a neutral oversight function). Reports do not go to the market or the public at large, though in some cases the regulator might aggregate the information or provide it at a time sufficiently distant in the future that doing so would not commercially disadvantage the provider.

Reporting is a way for the regulators to exercise oversight of the market by allowing them to see the "big picture" (exactly how big the market is for credit derivatives, for example, and whether there are any worrying trends such as a concentration of activity and therefore risk in a small number of firms). They also allow examination of the close details of individual firms, such as their financial soundness and the extent to which they are dominant in, or exposed to, specific instruments and markets. Because more transparency is usually considered to be better than less, reporting—the lowest level of transparency— is generally reserved for that information which is sensitive or proprietary to the firm doing the reporting. Examples would be the monthly financial soundness reports provided by firms or reports that identify the specific trading activity of the firm—this information is important for regulators but could put the reporting firm at a commercial disadvantage. Reports can be required either on a periodic basis (daily, monthly, quarterly, or annually) or on request (such

72 ■ Transparency

as when suspicious activity is spotted on the market and more detailed information is required for analysis).

Disclosure

The next level of openness can be described as *disclosure.* Disclosure takes reporting a step further, by requiring reports to be made not just to the regulators and other oversight authorities, but to the market and the public at large. Disclosure therefore lies at the heart of free market theory, since the information subject to disclosure forms the core of market decision making. For example, the financial statements disclosed by publicly traded companies help investors decide whether to buy, sell, hold, or avoid shares of the company's stock. Conflicts of interest present within certain firms (such as when a firm provides research on a company that has an ownership stake in the firm) help an investor determine whether to judge the firm's actions and opinions to be unbiased.

In many cases, the information takes the form of raw, though perhaps standardized, data without context or explanation. This is done so on the implicit assumption that those reviewing the information either are market professionals themselves or are at least sophisticated enough to comprehend the meaning, importance, and nuance of the information itself. Put differently, it is assumed that the information is for the market and not for individual retail investors. Of course, many retail investors do their investing through institutions such as mutual funds and pension funds, but when they do so they delegate the role of digesting the disclosed information to the professionals at the institution. This delegation is based on the assumption that the professionals have the knowledge to understand the data even on the most complex instruments and the capacity to review the information efficiently and thoroughly.

It should be acknowledged that the financial media play an important role in making sense of raw information disclosed without context, but delegating regulatory responsibilities to the media is a rather untenable way to ensure investor protection.

Transparency

True transparency implies a greater deal of openness than either simply reporting to the regulators or the disclosure of raw information. For something to be truly transparent, it must be clear to the recipient without substantial further research or expertise. It must be self-evident, clear, and comprehensible.

It must also be easily accessible. There are many examples in the federal regulations of information that must be disclosed, and for which it is acceptable or even required that it be disclosed in the prospectus, offering circular, or on the firm's website. Yet legal documents such as the prospectus are notoriously dense and lengthy and full of terminology that is impenetrable to those who do not speak the lingo. Visiting a website may require the reader to search through several layers and false trails (is the document under "investor relations," "about us," or "regulatory filings"?) just to get to the document in which the information is contained—and this search often can begin only after the reader has registered on the website.

The lesson is that many initiatives that are touted as "increasing transparency" fall short of the implied aim of providing easily comprehended and meaningful information in a readily accessible manner. This may be because the information is really intended for market professionals, or because disclosure was deemed the most expedient compromise when the policy eked its way through the political and consultation process. More and more, though, it may be through an epidemic of complacency. When markets and instruments were simpler, transparency may have been good enough. But has the creeping complexity of instruments and markets reached the point where dumping information in the lap of the SEC staffer or the research analyst—not to mention the individual investor—merely serves to provide the illusion that the market is able to regulate itself? Is information transparent simply because it is visible somewhere, or does it require context and prominence in order to make the market work as advertised?

It would take a supremely devout free-marketeer to presume, for instance, that anyone (let alone everyone) can fully grasp the details of the risk involved in trading credit default swaps simply because trading data are reported via one of a number of central counterparties (and how can they be "central" if there are many of them?). Given the fact that even the people rating structured finance products were forced to admit they did not properly grasp their inherent risk, in spite of the fact that their black-box methodologies were fully disclosed somewhere on their websites, should serve as a warning that 21st-century reality has forced us to write a few footnotes to an 18th-century market model.

WHAT TO CONSIDER WHEN TRANSPARENCY IS THE PROPOSED REMEDY

Whenever "transparency" is proposed as a remedy to a regulatory problem, the first things to consider are who needs the information and what they need it for. If the information is meant to permit proper oversight by giving a complete and

74 ■ Transparency

detailed picture of a particular market, where the risks are concentrated, and what trends might be growing, it is appropriate to expect an approach that includes reporting to the regulatory authorities. Since reporting exclusively to regulators places all of the regulatory eggs in the least efficient basket, it should be considered preferable also to have the information made public so that market forces can also act upon the problem (for instance, to put downward pressure on the stock price of a bank that is engaging in excessively risky transactions). Absent a sound competitive reason for keeping the information hidden from the market and the public, it is reasonable to assume as a "default position" that the information should always be made public as promptly as possible. And finally, if the information is necessary in order for nonprofessionals to make informed decisions and to protect themselves, then the regulations should require not only that the information be made public but that it be done in a clear manner and by means easily and cheaply accessible by the public.

Generally speaking, we have reached the point where we acknowledge that no single individual at a financial services firm of any size can be fully knowledgeable of all the firm's activities and products. We recognize that some instruments have become so complex as to be beyond the grasp even of the professionals who work with them on a regular basis, and that this was one cause of the financial crisis. It seems contradictory, if not delusional, to then reassure ourselves that, if only the information were "transparent," the magic of market discipline would keep the markets efficient, safe, and fair.

CHAPTER NINE

Rebuilding the Regulatory Structure

OF ALL THE MODERN markets in the world, the United States has long had one of the most complex financial regulatory structures. Ask any compliance officer at a medium or large financial institution to count how many regulators have some level of jurisdiction over the firm and she will likely run out of fingers before she is through. Even before efforts to consolidate regulation began, various aspects of the industry were regulated by the Office of the Comptroller of the Currency (OCC), the Office of Thrift Supervision (OTS), the Federal Deposit Insurance Corporation (FDIC), the Federal Reserve, the Commodity Futures Trading Commission (CFTC), the Federal Trade Commission (FTC), and 50 state-level regulators for securities, for banking, and for insurance.

Such a structure clearly poses questions of efficiency and effectiveness, and the matter of regulatory structure and the division of labor was one of the more far-reaching issues in the regulatory reform debate. But the real issue is not whether there were too many agencies but whether a different structure could have prevented the financial crisis, or at least tamed it. This chapter will consider some of the issues surrounding regulatory structure and the roles of specific agencies that arose during the reform debate.

WHY SO MANY REGULATORY AGENCIES?

The first and most obvious question when looking at the regulatory landscape in the United States is why we have so many regulators. The fact that there are so many, while in many major markets there is only a single consolidated regulator or a very small number of regulators, really just reflects the fact that there are different approaches to regulatory structure. In the United States, that approach has been influenced by the economic history of the country, and in particular the occasional panics that have occurred periodically over the years.

It used to be a fairly straightforward task to divide the financial world into sectors—banking, securities, and insurance. For much of the past century, at least since the New Deal reforms of the 1930s, the law specifically forbade the mixing of commercial banking and investment banking, effectively separating the banking and securities sectors from one another. The law that created this separation, the Glass-Steagall Act, also established the Federal Deposit Insurance Corporation for the banking industry for the specific purpose of guaranteeing investors' deposits in federally chartered banks (actual regulation of the federal banking system remained with the curiously named Office of the Comptroller of the Currency, established in the 1860s). Within a year, the Securities and Exchange Commission had been established to oversee securities and derivatives. The New Deal also established new supervisory agencies for credit unions (the National Credit Union Administration), and to insure savings and loan deposits (the Federal Savings and Loan Insurance Corporation, which went bust in the 1980s as a result of the Savings and Loan crisis). In the 1970s, additional agencies were added, such as the Commodities Futures Trading Commission, the Municipal Securities Rulemaking Board, and the Office of Thrift Supervision. The insurance industry, having been comparatively blameless in the Great Crash and the even-greater Depression, managed to escape federal regulation and instead was regulated by the state insurance commissions.

The Federal Reserve had been established in 1913 and its mission remained primarily that of a central bank, but from the beginning it had certain regulatory powers as well. Partly due to the "dual banking" system in the United States, in which some banks are state-chartered and some are federally chartered, layers of regulation were added in a confusing patchwork so that different functions within the same bank—or even the same functions—could be regulated and examined by state banking regulators, the OCC, and the Fed, as well as the FDIC with respect to the safety of deposits.

As the dust settled on the recent financial crisis and officials began to assess where things went wrong, the weaknesses of the regulatory structure and the failures of particular regulators were among the first targets for criticism—from the heads of the regulatory agencies themselves, among others. As a result, the existing arrangement of responsibilities across regulatory agencies became one of the early issues for investigation within Congress. Nothing gets the ideological debate going quite like a discussion of bureaucracy and regulation, and so Congresspersons, the media, and others from all points of the spectrum took the opportunity to argue for more centralization, less centralization, the creation of new agencies, the termination of existing agencies, and moving the responsibilities around from one agency to another.

 THE SEC AND THE INVESTMENT BANKS

One of the most important shifts in regulatory responsibility occurred early in the financial crisis; the change happened quickly because it was caused by market forces rather than legislative ones. Beginning in 2004, the SEC regulated the big investment banks through the Consolidated Supervised Entity (CSE) program, established after the Gramm-Leach-Bliley Act repealed the separation of commercial and investment banking. With the liberalization of the Gramm-Leach-Bliley Act, a wave of merger activity resulted in several giant financial institutions involved in both securities and banking activities. The CSE program was meant to address the need to regulate these complex financial conglomerates and to do so within a single regulator, the SEC.

But the program was voluntary: Congress had failed to give the SEC, or anyone else, the authority to regulate the conglomerates that formed once the Glass-Steagall prohibitions were repealed.[1] That meant that the only program to regulate them, the SEC's CSE program, was unenforceable (the conglomerates could simply opt out of the program at any time). Acknowledging that the CSE program was flawed from inception, SEC Chairman Cox put it very simply: "Voluntary regulation doesn't work."[2] By the time Chairman Cox shut the program down in September 2008, there was no one left for it to regulate. Lehman Brothers was gone, Bear Stearns had been force-fed to J.P. Morgan, Merrill Lynch had been swallowed by Bank of America, and Goldman Sachs

---

[1] SEC Press Release, September 26, 2008.
[2] Testimony of SEC Chairman Christopher Cox to the Senate Banking Committee on September 23, 2008.

and Morgan Stanley had voluntarily changed their structure to become commercial banks and therefore subject to Fed regulation (with the SEC limited to regulating the banks' brokerage activities, pursuant to a Memorandum of Understanding with the Fed). Thus, the collapse of the market moved the regulation of the largest financial institutions out from under the SEC and into the Federal Reserve.

THE FEDERAL RESERVE

But the Fed was hardly viewed as a master of regulation in the aftermath of the crisis. Lawmakers questioned whether it did enough to protect customers, and observers of all stripes criticized its actions in rescuing some institutions and letting others fail.

Among the lawmakers who determine the regulatory structure of the U.S. markets, feelings have been decidedly mixed. As the two houses of Congress worked to create draft versions of the bills that would eventually have to come together to form a final law, they took differing views of what should happen with respect to the Fed's supervisory powers. The House bill, shepherded through the Financial Services Committee under Barney Frank, sought to limit its powers by taking away its consumer protection role and by limiting its unilateral authority to provide cash to failing banks, but gave it a significant role in the oversight of systemically risky institutions and activities (correcting the regulatory gap created under Gramm-Leach-Bliley). Meanwhile, the version that moved through Senator Chris Dodd's Senate Banking Committee sought at least initially to strip the Fed of most of its supervisory powers and leave it only with its role in setting interest rates and controlling the money supply. Senator Dodd voted to confirm Benjamin Bernanke to another term as chairman of the Federal Reserve in December 2009, but in doing so expressed his reservations about the powers then held by the Fed:

> I remain very concerned about the weaknesses in the overall financial regulatory system that allowed the financial collapse to occur in the first place. . . . You and I agree that the Federal Reserve should be strong, and very independent, and able to perform its core functions. . . . I worry that over the years loading up the Federal Reserve with too many piecemeal responsibilities has left important duties without proper attention and exposed the Fed to dangerous politicization that threatens the very independence of this institution.

It has been proposed that the Fed assume yet another role in controlling threats to overall financial stability. But I fear these additional responsibilities would further distract from the Fed's core mission and leave it open to dangerous politicization, undermining its critical independence.[3]

Chairman Bernanke takes a different view:

It's true, that there were weaknesses in that supervision . . . (b)ut the Federal Reserve was not the systemic regulator. It had a very narrowly described set of supervisory responsibilities—bank holding companies primarily. . . . But if you look at the firms and the markets and the instruments that caused the problems, a great number of them . . . were mostly outside of the Federal Reserve's responsibility.[4]

OTHER PROPOSED CHANGES

The proposals to shift powers into or out of the Federal Reserve were central to the reform debate, but were by no means the only method of shuffling the deck. Beginning with the Obama Administration's proposed financial regulatory framework in the summer of 2009 and continuing with the Senate and House bills, the proposals promised to make the changes to the regulatory structure the most sweeping since the New Deal. A consolidated federal banking regulator was proposed that marked two existing agencies for death (the Office of Thrift Supervision, established in the wake of the Savings and Loan crisis, and the Office of the Comptroller of the Currency, the granddaddy of bank regulators) and would absorb the bank examination powers of the others. The critical need to provide oversight with respect to systemic risk was also recognized with the creation of a systemic risk council on which the Federal Reserve would be one of many participants (with powers that varied between the proposals). Each of the proposals also sought to create a consolidated body to handle consumer protection issues, though the scope and depth of the powers granted and the form of the body (single agency or council of multiple agencies) were the subject of considerable argument. An additional new agency was proposed to establish a federal regulator for the insurance industry, replacing the state-by-state regulation that had long existed for the sector.

---

[3] Senate Banking Committee Press Release, December 3, 2009.

[4] Testimony of Benjamin Bernanke to the Senate Banking Committee, December 3, 2009.

The creation of various new regulators and councils and the demise of old ones meant that the existing agencies were facing the prospect of losing significant oversight and consumer protection powers. And so, in addition to the wranglings among lawmakers in both houses, a spitball fight broke ought among the agencies in the crosshairs, specifically the FDIC, the Fed, the SEC, and the Commodities Futures Trading Commission (CFTC), and everyone against the Treasury. On top of everything else, someone even invited new agencies to the party—for consumer protection and to monitor systemic risk.

CONSUMER PROTECTION

The idea of creating a consumer protection agency was bound to ignite some of the biggest fireworks in the reform debate, and it did not disappoint. Proposals would create a new regulatory agency, an abomination to those in favor of limited government, and that would have been bad enough in their minds. But this would be an agency with particularly intrusive powers to tell firms, large and small, involved in a broad swath of the economy, what products and services they could and could not provide. The circumstances of the financial crisis—in which consumers were among the hardest-hit victims, but whose penchant for credit helped cause the crisis—made it impossible to ignore. Chapter 7 explores the issues related to consumer protection and regulation of retail financial services.

DO WE NEED A SYSTEMIC REGULATOR?

The prospect of creating a regulator or council of regulators to monitor systemic risk is a daunting one. Not only would this add one more government agency to the pile (and one whose job description would likely include "butt heads with all other regulators"), it would create an agency with the power to declare firms as threats to the financial system and therefore worthy of special regulatory measures. Even more to the point, its task would be tremendously difficult in practice because systemic risk is about more than just size. On a day-to-day basis, the staff would need to receive mountains of data and put it into systemic perspective in order to provide warning of potential meltdowns. Does anyone even know how to do that? This task alone would require a lot of very smart people with intimate familiarity with the markets, all working together and talking with each other. When things do get to the point that someone has to break the glass and pull the alarm, the staff needs the authority to take specific actions that presumably have been thought through and walked through a dozen times before. But against this dose of reality must be balanced another: Systemic risk will not go away simply because you are not monitoring it.

Some argue that the best approach is to prevent firms from getting so big or interconnected that they threaten the system. While this is one good approach, others may argue that it would be dangerous to rely on this alone. It relies on looking at risk on a firm-by-firm basis, a practice that we have learned the hard way does not protect the system. The market is a big, complex, constantly mutating thing and it would be dangerously self-deceptive to imagine ourselves capable of spotting every threat to the system simply by keeping firms small or segregated. Even if the regulators had all the information on all the firms in the market and had the capability to continuously monitor their exposure to each other, financial whiz-kids would be busy back in the lab inventing new strains of genetically modified instruments that fall between the regulatory cracks.

TO CONCENTRATE OR NOT TO CONCENTRATE

The common thread running through all of the debate on regulatory structure is the question of how many regulators should be doing how many things. There is some logic to creating a structure that is highly specialized and dispersed, with one and only one regulator for each sector. That regulator would be highly specialized and knowledgeable. But if it fails in its role, there is no Plan B. Criticisms of the SEC for its hidebound inability to listen to warnings about a Ponzi scheme big enough to make the Fortune 500, or of the legion of banking regulators for their failure to spot fraudulent mortgage activity, are not simply criticisms of the specific agencies. They also lay the foundation for the argument that redundancy and even overlap should be built into the structure.

To many, the thought of deliberately building overlap into the system is not a matter of prudence, but one of institutionalized waste. But the question is whether the price of failure would outstrip the price of the insurance bought with the extra regulatory spending. After all, the government pays to give each paratrooper two parachutes and one of them is a total waste of money most of the time, but given the suboptimal outcome resulting from the failure of the first chute the paratroopers are grateful all the same.

This may make a reasonable argument in favor of the regulatory overlap that existed before the crisis, but it would be charitable to say that the structure was that well thought through. Too often there was little or no coordination between agencies and there were as many gaps as there were redundancies. Fixing a system in which regulatory responsibilities have infested themselves without a plan cannot be done by tinkering here and fiddling there, especially when the solution means reducing or eliminating some deeply entrenched agencies in Washington (and there are no agencies that aren't deeply entrenched). Changing the regulatory structure means changing it all at once, and only a really big upheaval like the financial crisis creates the opportunity and political cover to do so.

The debate over which agencies should do what has taken this root-and-branch approach, where nothing is off the table except leaving things the way they are. Lawmakers look to abolish or defang agencies while creating new ones in their place; agency heads have aimed for a delicate balance between accepting institutional blame for failures too obvious to deny (though carefully crafting *mea culpas* that subtly place the blame on their predecessors) and at the same time defending their turf like cornered animals.

So while the *arguments* have been about whether the Fed can be trusted with systemic responsibility or whether the states could do a better job of regulating insurance, the *debate* has been about changing the structure of regulation to one that is both efficient and effective. The goal, in other words, is to have regulators that have the necessary powers and the expertise to use those powers effectively—agencies that not only have teeth, but know how to chew. Doing so without creating unnecessary burdens on the regulated firms transforms the debate into one of political principles and attitudes toward government, and this is why the debate about regulatory reform became so heated. It is not likely to go away any time soon.

CHAPTER TEN

Rating the Raters: The Role of Credit Rating Agencies

I F CREDIT RATING AGENCIES had a fan club, it could probably hold its meetings these days in a phone booth. Having quietly performed their functions for the better part of a century, they were shoved into the spotlight early in the past decade by their sunny outlook on firms like Enron, right up until the moment the firms collapsed. When firms that are supposed to play only a supporting role in the markets are thrust into the limelight, this is usually not good news.

The rating agencies defended their actions, noting with some justification that they were misled just like everyone else, including the firms' outside auditors. But whether fairly or not, a good deal of public blame was placed on the rating agencies, and the scandals in the early 2000s started the ball rolling on a law to bring the rating agencies under regulation for the first time in their hundred-year history. As part of the Sarbanes-Oxley Act in 2002, Congress ordered the SEC to conduct a study of the role of credit rating agencies, exploring the issues raised by their role in the markets and their performance in the scandals. The following year, the SEC issued a "concept release" to provide public consultation on its thinking with respect to regulating the rating

83

industry. After the consultation and the lengthy legislative process, the Credit Rating Agency (CRA) Reform Act was passed in 2006 (the very name of the law revealed Congress's foul mood with respect to the rating agencies—and this was before the subprime crisis).

NRSRO STATUS

The law applied to those firms that had received, or aspired to receive, designation as "Nationally Recognized Statistical Rating Organizations" (NRSROs). Among its aims was to break down the perceived barrier to entry for small rating agencies, and so it provides a means by which smaller agencies could break into the magic circle of the dominant rating agencies (Standard & Poor's, Moody's, and Fitch—the Big Three). NRSRO designation had been dreamed up in 1975 and bestowed on Standard & Poor's and Moody's (and later, Fitch) by Congress in an effort to formalize what had already been the prevailing practice in the market: When the market needed an objective opinion as to the credit quality of bonds, they looked to the ratings of Moody's and Standard & Poor's (S&P). But when Congress and the SEC needed to develop a way to distinguish the quality of bonds held as capital reserves by a bank or other institution, they could not simply endorse the ratings of the two dominant agencies. So, they created the NRSRO designation and unilaterally designated the two agencies as NRSROs. The agencies had not even requested the designation, but since there were no real requirements accompanying the designation it was not really an issue to them.

Fast-forward to the late 2000s: Just when they thought everyone had forgotten about Enron, WorldCom, and Parmalat, the housing boom turned to bust, and billions of dollars' worth of AAA mortgage securities were defaulting, taking the financial system with them. Even before any deep thinking had been done on the causes of the collapse, the failures of the rating agencies with respect to these structured finance products put them on everyone's list of those responsible for the crisis. It was difficult for them to deny that their ratings had been overly optimistic given that some residential mortgage-backed securities fell all the way from AAA to junk in less than two years.

In light of the failures, it appeared that the provisions in the CRA Reform Act were too broad to be effective. They merely required NRSROs to have policies and procedures "reasonably designed" to prevent the misuse of confidential information of which its staff might come into possession as part of the rating process; to identify and manage conflicts of interest; and to make and retain specified documentation relevant to the rating process or to the agency's business operations; the provisions also prohibited certain anti-competitive practices.

What was left out was any oversight of the methodologies by which the agencies arrived at their ratings. Though the rating agencies had already accepted that regulation was coming and were fairly sanguine about the prospect, they lobbied hard to ensure that the regulations did not cover methodologies (they were so successful that the text of the law specifically prohibits the SEC from doing so). On one hand, the agencies' logic makes a good deal of sense. If the SEC starts to pass judgment on what is and what is not a valid approach to rate a given type of security, the methodologies of the agencies will soon converge on the approach that has met with the SEC's approval. Not only are the regulators less qualified to make such a decision, but there would be little interest in the agencies to think of better ways to determine the ratings. Moreover, there is little point in passing a law to open the industry to competition if the result will simply be more agencies doing the same calculations.

On the other hand, in leaving the methodologies to the complete discretion of the rating agencies, the regulators entrusted market competition to determine whose ratings were more accurate. In theory, the financial industry would recognize the agency with the most accurate methodologies, and the agency with the most accurate methodology would be rewarded with the most business. The problem was that the people choosing which agency would rate a security are the issuers of those securities, whose inherent interest is in the *highest* rating, not the most accurate one. This *issuer-pays* model has been condemned in the aftermath of the financial crisis and will be discussed later in this chapter. It is sufficient here to say that there are arguments on both sides of the issue, but the upshot is that the assumption that there is a market mechanism that provides discipline over rating methodologies is misplaced under the dominant issuer-pays model.

To be fair, even if the regulators had looked at the rating agency methodologies as soon as the CRA Reform Act went into effect, it is unlikely they would have recognized the weaknesses that eventually surfaced with respect to residential mortgage-backed securities (RMBSs) and other toxic assets. The regulations implementing the Act did not go into effect until September 2007, well after the poisonous securities had been given their cheery ratings.

This raises the question of why the rating agencies themselves did not recognize the weaknesses, either (or why those within the agencies who did raise concerns were ignored). Clearly, the agencies got these ratings wrong. No matter how you look at it, when a rating agency slashes the ratings of billions of dollars' worth of securities from AAA to junk levels in one fell swoop, the initial rating was just plain wrong. How, then, could the agencies get it so wrong?

One theory goes that it was simply a matter of pleasing the issuers who were paying them to rate the RMBS securities. While this may be true up to a point, part of the problem lay also in the way the ratings were done—those methodologies and models that the regulators are not supposed to look at. The problem is that a rating is an opinion of the likelihood that the bond will stop paying interest or will go into default, and that means it is all about probabilities. When assessing probabilities with any precision, as we all learned in high school, you take historical data and arrange the outcomes into a bell curve. The fat, middle part of the bell curve represents the most common outcomes and the tails are the rarest outcomes. At the risk of oversimplifying the problem, rating agency models were based on the fat part of the bell curve. Worse, they were based on historical data and so they were backward-looking and did not very well represent those economic situations that had not occurred recently.

Think of it this way: In meteorology, there are some big storms that are characterized as *hundred-year* events because they happen only about once a century; even if you do not prepare for the storm, you will be fine most of the time. If you base your forecasts only on weather data from the past 50 years, you might completely overlook the possibility of a hundred-year storm. But when it hits, the Gulf of Mexico takes up residence in New Orleans. The housing crash, combined with the flood of subprime mortgages and with rising interest rates, created a hundred-year storm. The SEC said as much in the findings it published in July 2008 after an investigation of the structured ratings process at Fitch, Moody's, and S&P:

> According to the ratings agencies, credit raters relied upon historical data in order to predict future behavior. . . . (T)he performance history of the types of subprime mortgages that dominated many of the RMBS portfolios . . . has been very short. Further, the performance history that did exist occurred under very benign economic conditions. . . . (I)t appears that the parameters of the models were re-estimated by executing the model with new data infrequently.[1]

---

[1] Securities and Exchange Commission, "Summary Report of Issues Identified in the Commission Staff's Review of Select Credit Rating Agencies," July 2008.

Is it fair to blame the rating agencies for ignoring the hundred-year storm? Perhaps not, if ratings were strictly a mathematical exercise. But the reason ratings are done by analysts and not by robots is so that the process can include judgment and nonempirical "qualitative" factors. To do otherwise reinforces a false sense of security, a false precision, in the validity of the process.

External input (i.e., external to the rating model) was available to anyone reading the papers—and in some cases the warnings came from within the agencies. As far back as 2005, the chief economist at one major agency was predicting that the housing market had peaked and a downturn was inevitable.[2] Similar warnings were made from outside the agencies months or years before the housing market fell off a cliff. In November 2005, for example, the Associated Press wrote of the consensus forming that the housing bubble would burst, quoting from reports by Merrill Lynch, Goldman Sachs, Lehman Brothers, and the Center for Economic and Policy Research (CEPR).[3] The CEPR's published reports, going back as far as the summer of that year, had been particularly specific in their predictions—that the housing bubble would burst and throw the economy into a recession, and likely a deep one; and that the housing bubble would "put major strains on the financial system and require a federal bailout of the mortgage market":

> Of course, if the economy is in a recession, then many homeowners will have no choice but to default on their mortgages. Rising house prices have led many homebuyers to stretch themselves as far as possible to be able to afford monthly mortgage payments. Losing a job or being forced to take a new job at lower pay will leave many recent homebuyers unable to make their payments. Similarly, if interest rates rise, as virtually all economists expect, homebuyers with adjustable rate mortgages will find themselves paying much more on their monthly mortgages. Many homeowners will be unable to make these higher payments.
>
> If there is a large increase in the rate of mortgage defaults, then the mortgage holders will experience big losses. While many banks and financial institutions still hold large amounts of mortgage debt, most mortgages become the basis for mortgage-backed securities, a market that now exceeds $6 trillion. This market will be put in danger by a large wave of defaults following the collapse of the housing

---

[2] Mark Zandi, Chief Economist at Moody's Economy.com, interviewed on National Public Radio's *Weekend Edition*, November 27, 2005.

[3] Ellen Simpson, "Housing Bubble's Burst Could Cost 1 Million Jobs and Cause a Recession, Experts Say," Associated Press, November 13, 2005.

bubble. It is likely that the federal government will have to bail out the market in mortgage-backed securities to prevent a cascading series of defaults.[4]

The CEPR's forecast couldn't have been more accurate. The point is that there had been an increasing consensus among economists, the firms originating and holding RMBSs, and even within the rating agencies that the housing market was headed for a fall and that it would take the mortgage market with it. No matter what the financial models within the rating agencies were saying, the rating agencies were responsible for giving rating opinions that conformed to reality, not to the models. Yet the first downgrades of subprime mortgage ratings did not occur until June 2007, nearly two years after the first warnings and only after the housing market collapse was well underway and undeniably a reality.[5]

The issuer-pays model is a clear conflict of interest that could distort ratings, but it is not the only one. Each of the three major rating agencies is publicly traded or the subsidiary of a publicly traded company. In the case of Moody's, it is the principal subsidiary of Moody's Corp.; Fitch is one of three subsidiaries, and probably the largest, of the French company, Fimalac. Standard & Poor's Ratings is less directly a contributor to its parent's earnings, as it is one of several subsidiaries of publisher McGraw-Hill. When you work at a senior level for a publicly traded company, you are responsible for reporting figures on a quarterly basis, and from the top down, managers' revenues goals reflect the short-term time horizon inherent in publicly traded companies. This phenomenon is not unique to rating agencies (and is arguably less of a factor at S&P and Fitch than at Moody's, given their respective corporate structures), but at least one former rating agency official testified that this environment led to a perverse revenue-related culture at the agency, as stock options and other related incentives turned "management's focus increasingly to maximizing revenues," and an atmosphere in which rating shopping by issuers flourished.[6]

At Moody's, revenues skyrocketed. Observers point out that the company's own public filings document a shift from rating relatively straightforward bonds to rating structured finance products for which they could charge up to five

---

[4] Dean Baker, *The Housing Bubble Fact Sheet*, Center for Economic and Policy Research, July 2005.

[5] Testimony of Jerome Fons to the House Committee on Oversight and Government Reform, October 22, 2008.

[6] Testimony of Jerome Fons, former Managing Director of Credit Policy at Moody's Investors Service, to the House Committee on Oversight and Government Reform, October 22, 2008. Available at www.fonsrisksolutions.com.

times more for a deal.[7] This shift led to an expansion of profit margins to over 50 percent, a nearly unheard-of figure in the market.[8] As the drive to rate more and more structured deals accelerated, Moody's revenue structure changed as well. Far from the stodgy old rater of corporate bonds with steady but respectable income that it had been in the 20th century, by 2007, the majority of the firm's revenues came from structured finance deals.[9]

Additionally, the rating agencies can and do find themselves rating the debt of firms that hold a large portion of their stock. Happily, the evidence does not indicate that this particular conflict has distorted ratings. Berkshire Hathaway, the well-known and respected investment vehicle of Warren Buffett, is the largest shareholder in Moody's Corp., having invested in the Moody's IPO in 2000. In spite of this financial relationship, Moody's downgraded Berkshire Hathaway's AAA debt rating in 2009, a move that will over time cost Berkshire Hathaway a considerable amount of money and limit the activities in which the company can engage.

HOW RATINGS ARE MADE

It is not possible to judge the extent to which ratings are distorted by conflicts of interest or outright greed without at least a basic knowledge of the rating process, though some have tried. NRSROs are required by the CRA Reform Act to make public a description of their rating processes, and so those who wish to delve deep into the details can visit the relevant rating agency websites. But a simplified version goes something like the following.

Corporate and Municipal Bond Ratings

Bonds issued by companies, as well as municipal and government bodies, are assigned to an experienced analyst (sometimes assisted by a recently hired analyst), who analyzes the bond in accordance with the methodology developed for the industry in which the issuer operates (e.g., U.S. airlines or European pharmaceuticals). The methodology is the description of what information to gather and how to process the information to arrive at a rating (what conditions would lead to an AAA rating, to an AA rating, etc.). The

---

[7] Gretchen Morgenson, "Debt Watchdogs: Tamed or Caught Napping?" *New York Times*, December 6, 2008.
[8] Ibid.
[9] Ibid.

statistical models are the algorithms that predict the outcomes of various scenarios, such as what would happen to an airline if the price of oil rose to $100 per barrel. The analyst does his or her homework and comes up with the rating he or she believes is correct, but this is only the beginning of the process. The analyst next presents his or her views to a rating committee that may be as few as a handful of staff or a gaggle of 20 or more, depending on the size and sensitivity of the rating. After the analyst presents his or her analysis and proposed rating, a vote is held among the committee to decide the actual rating. The fact that ratings are decided by a committee rather than one individual is an important means for ensuring that the rating is not unduly influenced by one individual and, according to the rating agencies, is an important antidote to the issuer-pays conflict of interest because most of the committee has no revenue goal that might be affected by an angry issuer.

Rating committee procedures are formalized in written documents and are designed to ensure open and free discussion, even to the point that voting is done in reverse order of seniority in order to prevent junior analysts from being overly deferential to their managers rather than voting their own views. Written memos are prepared for each rating committee that include a description of the discussion. The SEC requires all documents that helped form the basis of the rating opinion to be retained so that they may later be inspected by SEC investigators in the course of a routine examination or an investigation.

The rating process does not guarantee pristine ratings that are always untainted by conflict, much less ratings that are always accurate. It is true that the analysts themselves do not have specific revenue or market-share goals as part of their bonus scheme and performance evaluations, but if their first- or second-level supervisor does, the effect is little diminished.

The process does, however, go a long way toward preventing the kind of capricious and sycophantic ratings that much of the public may have come to assume as events have transpired.

Ratings are given both to issuers and to specific series of bonds, and the two may sometimes differ. An issuer may have, for instance, an overall rating of AA—and that rating will be an important input into the specific rating for any of its rated debt. But some of that issuer's debt will be senior and some will be subordinated, meaning that in case of bankruptcy the holders of senior debt get paid first and the subordinated debt holders get paid afterwards, in the order of their subordination. Other factors that bear on the likelihood of a particular bond's payment of interest and principal will also be analyzed. The same even holds true with respect to country ratings, so that the "sovereign" rating of a country may impact the rating of all companies located in that country, depicting the nation's economic environment.

Structured Finance Ratings

The description provided earlier applies to the most straightforward securities. The process is somewhat more problematic when it comes to structured products. The role of the rating agencies with respect to structured finance products is also described in Chapter 4, which discusses structured finance products more specifically. Some of that discussion bears repeating here.

When a rating analyst is rating a corporation issuing a bond, or a particular series of bonds issued by the issuer, it is generally a matter of looking at the company's present finances and prospects or the bond's structure as it is. In contrast, structured finance products are still on the drawing board when they are presented to the rating agencies. Even grasping whom to consider as the "issuer" of a structured product is problematic; usually it is a *special-purpose vehicle* (SPV), set up by a bank or other financial institution as an off-balance-sheet entity to buy a pool of assets and create the structured investment. The SPV is created as an off-balance-sheet entity so that the (often dodgy) investments in the pool do not affect the bank's financial balance sheet and credit rating, and so that it is "bankruptcy remote," limiting the bank's liability for its handiwork if the SPV goes belly up. So, the SPV is an entity set up for the sole purpose of issuing the structured security and not to engage in any other business, making it fundamentally different from corporations or municipal entities that issue more pedestrian debt obligations.

When the "arranger" (SPV), or more likely its banker, approaches the rating agencies, it has not yet bought the assets (e.g., mortgages or credit card debt) that will inhabit the pool and provide the income stream of interest and principal payments that become the structured securities payments to its holders. Instead, it presents the characteristics of the assets it will buy and represents to the rating agency that the assets it eventually does purchase will in fact meet those characteristics. For instance, an arranger putting together a residential mortgage-backed security (RMBS) would describe the mortgages it would purchase in terms of some three- or four-dozen characteristics, such as the credit scores of the mortgagees, the loan-to-value ratios, the percentage of jumbo versus conforming mortgages, the geographic dispersion of the homes, and so on.

Because the assets have not yet been purchased, there is always time to change the pool's characteristics if the pool's tranches do not receive the rating desired by the arranger. And that's where things can go astray. The arranger customarily approaches two or even three agencies for a rating, but does not need all three ratings. It is in the arranger's interest to take the highest rating, and to the victor goes the rating fee, and so there is at least an implicit incentive for the analyst to help the arranger get to the rating it wants for the security (invariably, AAA for the senior tranche). This generally means adding "credit enhancement," such as overcollateralizing the loans in the pool, or it could mean a change to the characteristics of the underlying assets. But the rating agencies aren't supposed to advise these potential clients; otherwise, they could be construed as part of the group creating the investment and their legal departments would have a fit (liability and all that). But in this "iterative process," as the rating agencies describe it, there is a thin line between being helpful and being part of the team. Regulatory proposals in the European Union have taken a particularly aggressive view with respect to the advisory nature of rating agencies in the structured finance process, and a federal court opinion in 2009 made the point outright that the rating agencies were in fact part of the syndicate creating the securities that were the focus of a lawsuit.[10]

WHAT REALLY KEEPS THE RATING AGENCIES UP AT NIGHT (AND IT IS NOT YOUR MORTGAGE)

Which brings us to the issue that is arguably the biggest concern for rating agencies, if their lobbying activities are any indication: *civil liability.* Although the agencies are packed with PhDs devising mathematical models and they spend millions on complex computer resources, all designed to delve through mountains of data to find the fine distinction between an AA rating and a single A, they insist that their ratings are just opinions. And they have stuck to that story even though government regulations and market practice give the ratings themselves the authority to determine how a security is treated for capital purposes or other uses. For instance, if a company loses its AAA rating, its commercial paper is no longer eligible to be held by money market funds and it loses a very important means of overnight funding. Indeed, the lowering of Bear Stearns' credit rating has been widely cited as one of the tipping points in its demise, precisely because these "opinions" are treated by the market as empirical and (theoretically) objective analysis and implicit recommendations.

---

[10] *Abu Dhabi Commercial Bank v. Morgan Stanley & Co. Inc., et al.,* 08-7508 (S.D.N.Y. September 2, 2009).

Of course, in our litigious society, the consequences of viewing a rating as a recommendation could be dire for the rating agencies. If investors were able to sue the agencies even just for the really big blunders (Enron, RMBSs, Icelandic banks, etc.), their liability could put them out of business in one punch. And so the rating agencies deploy considerable sums to defend the proposition that a rating is just an opinion.

And they don't stop there. They also claim that ratings, being published opinions, are protected by the freedom-of-the-press provisions of the First Amendment. This notion has been attacked as ludicrous by various lawmakers (not to mention real journalists), but it has had a surprising measure of success in the courts. Yet the tide is turning. Perhaps as a result of years of bad publicity, important people are starting to question whether protecting the rating agencies is what the founding fathers had in mind when they wrote the First Amendment. These people include federal judges and chairmen of congressional committees writing new laws to regulate the agencies. They cite important distinctions between the rating agencies and the more traditional press, such as the fact that newspapers are paid by the people reading the newspaper (or advertisers), not by the subjects of their stories, or that ratings sometimes are "private" and not publicly disseminated. Worse still for the rating agencies, some observers believe that they are more vulnerable with respect to subprime mortgage-backed securities due to their limited scope and distribution.[11]

This battle will likely be slugged out for years. Even if Congress limits the First Amendment defense for rating agencies by statute (which, as of the time of this writing, has been proposed but not enacted), the agencies are likely to fight the issue up to the Supreme Court. More important than the legal technicalities will be the practical argument. If rating agencies can be sued any time they get a rating wrong, there will soon be no more rating agencies. Moreover, when, exactly, is a rating wrong? Clearly, if a security rated AAA defaults, the rating was wrong. But rating agencies typically have a dozen levels, each with gradations, so is a rating somewhere in the middle a prediction that the bond will default or that it will not? If the weatherman tells you there is a 45 percent chance of rain and it rains, was he wrong? He didn't say it would *not* rain, after all.

---

[11] Nathan Koppel, "Credit Raters Plead the First: Will It Fly?" *Wall Street Journal*, April 21, 2009.

THE END OF THE NRSRO?

Another initiative well underway at the time of this writing is the removal of NRSRO status. Whereas the thought of losing their press pass truly keeps rating agency lawyers awake at night, the agencies have greeted the prospect of losing NRSRO status with a collective yawn. The Big Three do not need it (and the little seven just don't want the NRSRO designation limited to the Big Three). As the head of S&P put it, "Standard & Poor's traces its origins back 150 years, long before any rating mandate, and would certainly be able to compete in an open market."[12] NRSRO status was not created to benefit them; it was created to give the regulators a means by which to label some debt securities as better than others, and it was a lot more palatable to embed references to NRSRO ratings than to say "ratings from S&P or Moody's." Long before there was an NRSRO status, there was a rating industry and the rest of the financial services industry was dependent on it. The establishment of NRSRO status was in fact a reflection of the dominance of Moody's and S&P, not its creator. Financial institutions went to the rating agencies because they needed them long before they were told to do so by the government, and so if all references to NRSRO ratings are removed from federal regulations, there will likely be little or no impact on the revenues of the rating agencies. All that Congress and the SEC would accomplish is to give themselves two new, and potentially bigger, problems. First is the problem that the creation of NRSRO status solved: How do you provide an objective standard for distinguishing the levels of safety of securities held as capital by financial institutions? Capital adequacy rules rely on the ability to identify the weaker assets and require more cash or similarly hard assets to be set aside as a cushion for their potential default. Absent references to NRSROs, could any firm call itself a rating agency and start handing out AAA ratings to the highest bidder? Dodgy or desperate or outright fraudulent ones might. The counterargument is that the market would push legitimate banks away from such fly-by-night agencies and push them toward agencies widely recognized to have a better reputation. Of course, that would mean the existing NRSROs and the Big Three in particular. Congress's attempt to "end the oligopoly" would not succeed simply because NRSRO status did not create the oligopoly.

The second problem is that NRSRO status is effectively the only means by which the rating agencies are regulated in the United States. If references to

---

[12] Devon Sharma, "Why Rating Requirements Don't Make Sense," *Wall Street Journal*, January 18 2009.

NRSRO status are removed from the regulations, there is really no reason for a rating agency to be an NRSRO any more—just the disadvantages, cost, and exposure of being regulated. If they were to withdraw from NRSRO status, the SEC would lose those powers it has only recently gained over the rating agencies—including the power to examine them, to require certain documents to be kept, and to discipline them. Removing reference to NRSRO ratings, then, would make regulation of the rating agencies a completely voluntary regime. And one lesson the SEC says it has learned from its failed experience with investment banks is that *voluntary regulation does not work.*[13] Even if the revised laws prohibit voluntary withdrawal from NRSRO status, this would create a strange and uncomfortable situation in which the government first required agencies to register, then slammed the door shut behind them after taking away the only benefit of registering.

So, however viscerally satisfying and electorally rewarding it may be to take a swing at the rating agencies, the removal of reference to NRSRO status amounts to cutting off your nose without even spiting your face. The better option is to enforce the regulations and to be prepared to remove NRSRO status from one or more of the agencies where appropriate.

The prospects for real enforcement are increasing. SEC examiners conducted their first NRSRO examinations in late 2007 and early 2008, and have since been camped out in at least one other NRSRO for a deeper look at specific issues. The SEC has already amended frequently the rules it issued in 2007 to implement the CRA Reform Act, each time making the rules more stringent. It has also taken steps to create a separate office responsible for oversight of the rating agencies, reporting directly to the chairman of the SEC. Still, no sanctions have yet been imposed on any rating agency.

This is not because the examiners have failed to find any deficiencies. The SEC published a summary of its findings after the 2007–2008 examination, and serious shortcomings were identified.[14] The report dealt only with the three largest firms and focused on the rating processes for RMBSs and collateralized debt obligations (CDOs), but even this narrow look found disturbing deficiencies. It was this report that disclosed the infamous e-mail in which an analyst said that a deal could be structured by cows and they would still rate it.

---

[13] "Chairman Cox Announces End of Consolidated Supervised Entities Program," SEC Press Release, September 26, 2008.

[14] Securities and Exchange Commission, "Summary Report of Issues Identified in the Commission Staff's Review of Select Credit Rating Agencies," July 2008.

One of the deficiencies noted in the report returns us to the nature of the rating process itself. The report noted, at least with respect to the RMBS and CDO ratings, that monitoring of ratings to ensure they are still accurate was often either not documented, poorly performed due to inadequate staffing, or even not performed at all.[15]

When you see a rating on a bond or other debt security, it is reasonable to assume that that rating is current and valid—and that it would be changed if circumstances warranted. By and large, that is the case and that is why rating agencies conduct monitoring of ratings they have issued. Indeed, they generally have indicated to the public that securities are monitored unless they are clearly identified as *point-in-time* ratings. The thoroughness and vigor of those efforts are likely to vary in an organization with over a million outstanding ratings to keep an eye on. Monitoring then becomes a matter of setting up alerts to tell the analysts when a rating may require a review, and the process then becomes dependent on (1) knowing what information is relevant, (2) having accurate and complete data from the issuer, and (3) setting the alert parameters correctly (and not repeating the mistake of looking solely at the middle of the bell curve of historical data). If any one of these three steps is not done correctly, the surveillance team may never look at a security that is on the verge of failure. The problem is particularly acute for municipal and other government obligations, which make up a significant proportion of the ratings of the Big Three. In addition to the sheer volume of public finance issuers, many do not issue bonds frequently and so are not subject to new alerts that would trigger a review. As such, a bond issued by a relatively small municipal authority could be outstanding with a rating given to it years before, and it would be reviewed only if the rating agency's monitoring system flagged it for review. The question then becomes how robust the monitoring system is and how complete its dataset is: Would it know whether the municipality had a pension obligation that had become vastly underfunded, or whether a county treasurer had bought highly risky and complex derivative products to hedge against interest rates but that had turned toxic? If a financial crisis and the resulting falloff in tax revenues caused a sharp increase in municipalities suffering from their own financial crises, would the system and the staff be able to keep up with all of the alerts, or would the staff simply reset the parameters to yield a more manageable workload?

So, the new SEC office responsible for rating agencies will have a full plate for the foreseeable future. One thing seems clear, though, and that is that the

---

[15] *Ibid.*

industry that once did its job in comparative anonymity and without the burden of regulation will become one of the most closely watched, by the regulators, by the press, and by the courts. For those agencies with international operations, the scrutiny will be no lighter; the European Union and Australia, among others, have already brought the rating agencies under regulatory supervision.

 ## CONFLICTS IN THE RATING AGENCY BUSINESS MODEL

Mention has already been made of the issuer-pays model and the conflict that inevitably ensues. Even the rating agencies acknowledge the conflict, but point out that the conflict can be managed (a position that the SEC expressly supports through its regulations, which place the conflict on the "must-be-managed" list and not on the "prohibited" list). There are in fact policies and procedures that can diminish the impact of the conflict, assuming that the compliance or risk management departments have the authority and independence necessary to enforce the procedures. An alternative model, already adopted by at least one smaller agency, is for the "user" to pay for the rating (i.e., an institution considering purchasing the bond). This is essentially the model used by the big agencies for most of the first hundred years, but it became untenable as a way to support the agencies given the number of free riders who would see the rating after someone else had paid for it. Beyond the question of its economic viability, the user-pays model also carries its own potential conflict of interest. If an institution pays a rating agency to rate the bonds it buys, it will not be pleased if the agency subsequently downgrades a large number of those ratings, reducing the value of the bonds that had already been bought. After a while, it will go to a more reliably agreeable agency.

Other models have been floated that are less rife with conflict though they would not be easy to put into effect. These range from plans for investors to pay money into a pool from which the raters would be paid, after having been chosen at random to rate any particular deal, to proposals to nationalize the raters and put them on the government payroll.

 ## ARE RATING AGENCIES UTILITIES?

The notion of nationalizing rating agencies leads to a separate issue, and that is the very nature of the rating agencies. On one hand, they are a kind of utility for the market. Ignoring the economists' definitions of a utility, the point is that the agencies perform a service for the rest of the market, the market really cannot function without it, and there are only a small number of firms that are capable of providing the service. At the same time, they are businesses—either publicly traded, or the subsidiaries of publicly traded companies. And many blame the shift in culture from "utility" to "business" as one of the primary reasons behind their voracious appetites for revenue growth, 50+ percent profit margins, and mortgage-backed securities deals.

The fact is that they are both, or rather that they are utilities that act like businesses because that is where the incentives of their decision makers lie (as discussed in Chapter 6 on compensation). As Moody's former president said in an interview with the *Wall Street Journal* a month before his departure, regarding his efforts to make the agency "friendlier" to issuers: "We're in a service business. . . . I don't apologize for that."

Of course, there are many publicly traded utilities in the United States, but their business activities are closely regulated to ensure that their revenue imperative does not lead to abuse. The last time we had a publicly traded but lightly regulated utility, its name was Enron.

CONCLUSION

It used to be that market forces were all that were required to ensure the rating agencies did their business with probity, transparency, and vigor. There are many theories about what went wrong: the issuer-pays model, failure to keep pace with the growth of the industry, and complacency, among others. But one thing that surely failed was the discipline of reputational risk. Every company will say that its reputation is important, but for rating agencies the threat of losing their reputation for objectivity and accuracy was everything. But reputational risk works only when *one* firm loses its reputation and the customers take their business elsewhere. When the whole industry loses its reputation, there is no other place to go. And that is the conclusion policymakers have come to regarding rating agencies. While policymakers agonize over whether there is such a thing as a firm that is too big to fail, key congressional leaders have already owned up to the fact that the ultimate sanction cannot be applied to the handful of rating agencies, regardless of whether they have NRSRO status. Representative Paul Kanjorski, chairman of the House subcommittee redrafting rating agency regulations, told the *New York Times* in late 2009, "We want to do as much correction as we can . . . but we don't want to kill the institutions because we have nothing to replace them with."[16] Observers agree that the prospects of strong regulation of the industry are growing more remote. As far back as June 2009, the *Wall Street Journal* paid a backhanded compliment to the industry by congratulating the agencies' lobbyists:

> If world-class lobbying could win a Stanley Cup, the credit-ratings caucus would be skating a victory lap this week. The Obama plan for financial re-regulation leaves unscathed this favored class of businesses whose fingerprints are all over the credit meltdown. . . . The Obama plan does make plenty of vague suggestions, similar to those proposed by the rating agencies themselves, to improve oversight of the ratings process and better manage conflicts of interest. The Obama Treasury has even adopted the favorite public relations strategy of the ratings agency lobby: Blame the victim.[17]

This is a good point for a reality check on the rating agency bashing. Whatever their failures, and they are many and real, they have also gotten a lot of things right. They have gotten most things right, in fact, for a hundred years. Whatever the failings of a handful of senior managers, some of whom have since been defenestrated by the firms themselves, the bulk of the staff and managers at the rating agencies do not succumb to the conflicts inherent in their business model. Good regulation from the SEC and good governance from within will be the key to rehabilitating the agencies and their reputations. Whatever the outcome of that rehabilitation, it is clear that the rating agencies will continue to play a central role in the marketplace. Love them or hate them, we've got to have them.

---

[16] David Segal, "Debt Raters Avoid Overhaul After Crisis," *New York Times*, December 7, 2009.

[17] "Triple-A Punt," Review and Outlook, *Wall Street Journal*, June 23, 2009.

CHAPTER ELEVEN

The Politics of Regulation

Congress does two things well—nothing, and overreacting.

Rep. Mike Oxley, co-author of the Sarbanes-Oxley Act

REGULATION IS A THOROUGHLY political process; this is perhaps the key point to remember in understanding why regulations turn out the way they do. By and large, all important financial regulations start with a law that has been drafted, negotiated, debated, compromised, amended, and voted through at least a House committee, a Senate committee, floor votes in both chambers, and finally presidential approval. And of course there's the formal public consultation and the less-visible lobbying at every stage of the process.

This certainly makes for democratic regulation, but not always for good regulation. What is best for the markets or for investors is not always the thing that is politically achievable given the wide range of interests that must be accommodated. In addition to the back-and-forth of partisan politics, politicians must take into account the positions of the industry (which rarely speaks with one voice) and other interest groups as well as the public. Nor is the best regulation the most popular with the voters, and overreaction to slake the thirst of a braying electorate can easily be as harmful as a failure to act. The Sarbanes-Oxley Act is frequently cited as an example of this phenomenon, and some have also argued that Congress's enthusiasm for extending homeownership was as disastrous in the long run as it was politically pleasing in the short run.

So what may start out as a coherent and effective regulatory proposal must run a gauntlet of compromises as it winds its way through House and Senate committees, does a couple of laps up and down K Street, on to the floor votes in Congress, and across the President's desk before it lands in a regulator's in-box. Along the way, the goal is often to water down the regulation, to limit its scope, or to carve out exemptions for particular interested parties. That's not to say that the process is wholly destructive; good debate among lawmakers and insightful commentary from the industry and from academia can prevent the passage of proposals that have more unintended consequences than intended ones.

The value of the political process lies not so much in the negotiation and the compromise but in the transparency it brings, and in putting on the record the legislative intent and the arguments considered in the course of the deliberation. The fact that regulatory reform is made in public keeps it honest, if not necessarily effective.

THE POLITICAL PROCESS

The regulatory process is no simpler than anything else that has been in the hands of civil servants for two centuries, but for explanatory purposes a common route can be laid out that is fairly straightforward and reflects the path taken by big-issue regulations like the ones that have composed the reform of financial regulation. Like other legislation, it all begins with discussions in the appropriate committees of Congress. In the case of large programs like financial reform or health care, the congressional hearings may be preceded or accompanied by a document from the Administration laying out the President's desired approach (as did President Obama in June 2009). The committees most frequently and directly involved in financial regulation are the House Financial Services Committee and the Senate Banking Committee, although significant hearings on financial reform were also held by the House Committee on Oversight and Government Reform and the Joint (House and Senate) Economic Committee.

It is in committee that most of the give-and-take occurs in drafting the legislation. The committee is comprised of Congressmen and Congresswomen who either had some level of prior expertise in the subjects brought before that committee or (it is hoped) have developed some level of expertise since. They are at any rate assisted by a professional staff who do in fact have significant expertise, and this helps ensure that the right issues are discussed and that the best witnesses are called when the issue comes up for a hearing. Though the Administration may present a proposal that serves as a starting point for discussion, it is in the committees that the ideas of what will go into the draft bill are first floated, discussed, and horse-traded. Some of this process occurs in publicized hearings, with witnesses called from government agencies, the industry, consumer groups, and academia. Other decisions are made in the hallways and offices by congressional staff and by the Congressmen and Congresswomen themselves. A proposed bill is eventually floated and given to committee members for "markup," which is the process of adding, deleting, and otherwise mutating the text until a compromise text is achieved. A vote is then taken on whether to send the bill to the floor of the House or Senate (as the case may be) for vote.

The entire committee process can take a very long time, even under the best of circumstances. In the case of financial regulatory reform, the process took nearly a year from the time debate started in earnest (after the fall of Lehman Brothers) until draft bills had even made it out of the House Financial Services Committee and the Senate Banking Committee. There are several reasons for this. First, a big and important bill often has many different issues to address. In this case, separate hearings needed to be held on everything from hedge funds to credit derivatives, from rating agencies to executive compensation. Moreover, even the big issues have to share the stage with other big issues. Congressional committees have such broad remits and cover so many issues that it is often months between hearings on a particular subject. Moreover, Congresspersons sit on multiple committees and perform constituent services, and have to manage their time and staff resources accordingly (Senator Dodd, chairman of the Senate Banking Committee, played a key role in health-care reform legislation as well as financial regulatory reform). So, bills are unlikely to get the committee's undivided attention for very long regardless of how politically important they may be.

The delay in getting a bill drafted and out of committee can have a real impact on the nature and scope of the ultimate regulation. It is important to realize that the lawmakers are never more than two years away from the next election (each Representative in the House; one-third of the Senators). A two-year gap between elections, in practice, means a year-and-a-half or less before the campaign season kicks off in earnest. In close elections in hotly contested districts, it is important for a candidate to be able to demonstrate that he or she had taken a "tough" (i.e., extreme) stance on an issue, even if that position was later quietly given up in a compromise. This is a concern even when a single party controls the White House and both houses of Congress, and it is a common misperception that the party in power can simply push its own agenda through. Some of those in the majority may have especially close elections coming up, and although towing the party line may help ensure one's popularity with the party Whip, it may sit less well with those who will decide whether the Representative or Senator will be back at all. Particularly when Congresspersons must also answer for potentially unpopular votes on eye-popping deficit spending or on health care, the incumbents are well served to have a bit of work they can point to in order to show that they can be aggressive in standing up for the "little guy" in the election booth.

Another way in which the long gestation period of a bill can affect its outcome is that it enables opponents to engage in tactics to delay the bill's enactment. This may be as a service to those whom they believe would be hurt by the legislation (the industry groups paying into their reelection funds, to give a cynical example), to wait until public interest in the issue has waned, or even to ensure that the bill does not come about until after the next election, when there may be a more benign president or a different majority in one of the houses in Congress.

As a result, there can be two diametrically opposed forces working on a bill—one that tends toward more forceful measures to please the pitchfork-bearing electorate and the other seeking to ossify the bill until it can be safely neutered or defeated. Which force prevails will depend on a number of factors and may not always be easily predictable. Indeed, the answer may vary from measure to measure within the same bill.

The bills related to financial reform provided a clear spectacle of the impact of politics on regulation. At the very foundation of the debate was an ideological struggle between those who wish to limit government's role in the markets and those who wish to expand it, at least in the financial markets. But there were a substantial number of areas in which there was agreement, and others where compromise was achieved without gutting the provision in question. There were also positions taken that were likely done for the folks back in the district and quietly jettisoned later as part of a compromise; the Congressperson could later claim the decision to back off was a tough but necessary compromise. There was even outright rebellion based on concerns only marginally related to the task at hand, as when the Black Caucus threatened to withhold support from its own party's bill in the House unless the Administration gave special economic relief (unrelated to regulatory reform) to minority-owned businesses

104 ■ The Politics of Regulation

in general and radio stations in particular, and very particularly to one business that was being pestered by Goldman Sachs and GE Capital to repay some $300 million in commercial loans.[1]

Which leads us to the *L* word. It's safe to say that lobbying has a bad reputation, which is only partly deserved. The contribution of large sums of money to a particular candidate may look to all the world like an attempt to buy a vote (in the future), but to the interest group making the contribution it is more a matter of trying to ensure that the candidate who wins is the one who has (in the past) demonstrated a keen understanding of the issues. More to the point, lobbying isn't just about campaign contributions; it's also about getting information to the lawmakers that will help them make an informed decision. And while the lobbyist's information may not be a shining illustration of empirical objectivity, as long as the source of the information is out in the open the recipient can weigh whether the information is reliable.

The notion of *regulatory capture*—that regulatory agencies tend to favor those they regulate, either because they are dependent on the industry for information or in order to curry favor for future job prospects—can be extended to the legislative world in a kind of *political capture*. Apart from the obvious influence of campaign contributions or under-the-table sweetheart mortgages, political capture can manifest itself through the industry's domination of the information flow to legislators. The outcome of legislation is of immediate importance to the financial services industry and so they expend considerable resources to influence legislation, whereas consumers' concerns are diluted across a range of issues.

Given the importance of potential changes to financial regulation to the financially regulated, it should come as no surprise that the industry outdid itself in pressing home its points.

The figures for the first three quarters of 2009 from the Center for Responsive Politics show that the pace did not slacken as the legislation matured. The Securities and Investments industry group spent nearly $65 million in lobbying (not counting campaign contributions), with the Insurance industry spending nearly double that figure (the Insurance industry group took the silver medal to the Healthcare and Pharmaceuticals group, which had challenges of its own to worry about). Within the Securities and Investments group, the biggest spenders were the likes of Goldman Sachs, Morgan Stanley, the CME Group (which recently established a clearing facility for derivatives trades that would benefit nicely from proposals to force derivatives dealers to

---

[1] Eric Lipton, "Black Caucus Seeks to Ease Radio's Woes," *New York Times*, December 2, 2009.

The Political Process ■ **105**

clear their trades through a central clearing facility), and trade associations for mutual funds and hedge funds (which are likely to be brought into new regulatory regimes) and for private equity funds (which are spending a lot of money to make sure regulators do not confuse them with hedge funds). And the great-granddaddy of them all was the U.S. Chamber of Commerce, which managed to find over $65 million in the middle of a recession for its lobbyists to spread around in the first nine months of 2009.[2]

Some might take from this the lesson that a lot of money is being spent to distort the legislative process, by firms that claim not to have a lot of money any more (arguably, taxpayer money from the TARP program went in one door and then out the other to influence legislation). But it is important to recognize that these industry groups are the primary source of information as to how complex markets and instruments work and for avoiding unintended consequences. Also, big business isn't the only group that has had its checkbook out; the American Association of Retired Persons (AARP) spent over $5 million, more than anyone in the Securities and Investments industry group.[3]

So, although many blame the regulatory structure for the failures of oversight that led to the financial crisis, it should be recognized that the regulators are playing cards dealt to them by Congress. The structure, the laws, and even the resources available to the regulators are the result of what the politicians agreed to based on ideology, compromise, and their own electoral self-interest. Whether this is good or bad, it is important to recognize that regulations are as much a creature of politics as they are of economics.

---

[2] Figures are available at www.opensecrets.org.

[3] www.opensecrets.org.

CHAPTER TWELVE

Nice Law, Now Go Do It: Regulators and Compliance Officers

ONCE THE DUST SETTLES and the lawmakers have moved on to other tasks, the work of regulation has just begun. Laws commonly need to be supplemented by regulations written within the appropriate regulatory agencies, and these sometimes even need to be supplemented by rules from the various industry organizations. These rules are put out for discussion with the industry and the public, both through the publication of draft rules and, in some cases, public roundtable discussions with industry, consumer, and academic representatives. Ultimately, the firms themselves review their internal policies and procedures to determine whether any changes are necessary, and what level of notification and training for the firm's staff is required.

The process and players will vary from sector to sector and according to the type of issue involved. This chapter will seek to give a sense of how the process works and the level of effort involved in ensuring that the aims of the original legislation are carried out in the field. To keep the illustration simple, it will focus on a single sector, the securities industry, with a discussion of the work of the relevant sections of the Securities and Exchange Commission (SEC) and the Financial Industry Regulatory Authority (FINRA), and the compliance functions within regulated firms.

THE SEC

If you stop and think about what we expect regulators to do, it becomes clear how wide their remit is and how thinly spread their resources are. Taking the SEC as an example, it writes the rules that put financial laws into effect; it approves prospectuses for new securities offerings; it supervises the exchanges, investment management companies, and investment advisers; it investigates insider trading and market abuse; it oversees corporate finance issues; it coordinates policy with its counterparts in other countries; it examines nearly 5,000 brokerage firms; and it responds to customer complaints and tips. It does all this with a staff of about 3,500—smaller than some law firms—spread out among 11 regional offices plus headquarters in Washington, D.C. Insofar as the SEC is traditionally heavy on attorneys, an SEC staff member below the government Senior Executive Service level might eventually make as much as a first-year associate at a large law firm. (The SEC's reliance on attorneys and its difficulty in retaining experienced talent have had profoundly negative consequences for the public. These problems and their resolution are discussed in Chapter 15.)

HOW THE SEC RULEMAKING PROCESS WORKS

Rulemaking is the process by which federal agencies implement legislation passed by Congress and signed into law by the President. Major pieces of legislation, such as the Securities Act of 1933, the Securities Exchange Act of 1934, the Investment Company Act of 1940, and the Sarbanes-Oxley Act, provide the framework for the SEC's oversight of the securities markets. These statutes are broadly drafted, establishing basic principles and objectives. To ensure that the intent of Congress is carried out in specific circumstances—and as the securities markets evolve technologically, expand in size, and offer new products and services—the SEC engages in rulemaking.

Rulemaking can involve several steps: concept release, rule proposal, and rule adoption.

Concept Release: The rulemaking process usually begins with a rule proposal, but sometimes an issue is so unique and/or complicated that the Commission seeks out public input on which, if any, regulatory approach is appropriate. A concept release is issued describing the area of interest and the Commission's concerns and usually identifying different approaches to addressing the problem, followed by a series of questions that seek the

(continued)

> (*continued*)
> views of the public on the issue. The public's feedback is taken into consideration as the Commission decides which approach, if any, is appropriate.
> **Rule Proposal:** The Commission publishes a detailed formal *rule proposal* for public comment. Unlike a concept release, a rule proposal advances specific objectives and methods for achieving them. Typically The Commission provides between 30 and 60 days for review and comment. Just as with a concept release, the public comment is considered vital to the formulation of a final rule.
> **Rule Adoption:** Finally, the Commissioners consider what they have learned from the public exposure of the proposed rule, and seek to agree on the specifics of a *final rule*. If a final measure is then adopted by vote of the full Commission, it becomes part of the official rules that govern the securities industry.
> (*Source:* SEC website, *www.sec.gov*, accessed November 28, 2009.)

This chapter is not meant to be a comprehensive overview of the SEC as an organization, but rather an illustration of how the work of the SEC and other regulatory agencies is done. Specifically, it will look at the day-to-day activities of a department whose work has been central to the unfolding and resolution of the financial crisis, the Office of Compliance Inspections and Examinations.

EXAMINATIONS AND INSPECTIONS

The Office of Compliance Inspections and Examinations (OCIE) is responsible for the conduct of the SEC's examination program, including determining who will be inspected in any given year, what areas of focus will be highlighted in the inspections, and what general issues will be the subject of special inspections.

Although OCIE staff are located in the regional offices as well as in Washington, D.C., it cannot examine everyone every year. Instead, the OCIE uses a *risk identification* and *risk assessment* methodology to determine who and what will be inspected.[1] Put simply, the bigger the organization and the greater the risk its business poses to individual investors and to the market, the more often and more vigorously it will be inspected. Firms subject to OCIE examination run the full range of market participants—broker-dealers,

---

[1] "OCIE Overview," http://sec.gov/about/offices/ocie/ocieoverview.pdf, accessed November 30, 2009.

investment advisers, Self-Regulatory Organizations (discussed in greater detail in the following chapter), clearing agents, and credit rating agencies, among others. Depending on the type of examination and the issues likely to arise, the examination team may be augmented by SEC staff from other departments such as Trading and Markets or Corporate Finance.

The SEC conducts four types of exam. The most common and least ominous for the targeted firm is the *cyclical* examination, so named to reflect the fact that the examination is routine in nature and conducted on a (risk-based) periodic basis, usually every two to three years. Firms with a high number of customer complaints, those that fared poorly in previous examinations, and those whose business puts them in frequent contact with retail and unsophisticated investors are likely to find themselves inspected more often than others. As such, a firm like Madoff Investment Securities, which did not have a high number of customer complaints (Ponzi schemes rarely do, since everyone is happy until the music stops), dealt primarily with wealthy investors, and had not had particularly bad previous inspection results, may fly under OCIE's radar for years at a time.

The second type of examination is the *cause* examination. These occur when the OCIE staff have reason to believe that specific violations of federal securities laws are occurring or have already occurred. Cause examinations are frequently initiated as the result of whistleblower complaints, customer complaints, stories in the press, or tips from other agencies. Again, the Madoff scandal could have been averted earlier had a cause examination been conducted based on tips received from third parties or internally generated red flags. But it wasn't conducted, and that is why a great deal of hell had to be paid when the scheme came to light.

A third type of examination is the *risk-focused* examination, known more colloquially in the industry as a *sweep.* Sweeps are meant to identify emerging risks, to assess how widespread and serious the risks are, and to determine how firms are addressing the risks. Examples of recent sweep examinations include those regarding the sale of mortgage-backed securities, sales of inappropriate investments to senior citizens, and the quality of the ratings process for structured securities such as the now-infamous mortgage-backed securities.

Finally, the SEC has responsibility for the oversight of those *Self-Regulatory Organizations* (SROs) to which it has delegated close supervision of the markets (most prominently, the Financial Industry Regulatory Authority—FINRA). On the principle that an organization can delegate tasks but not responsibility, the SEC examines the work of the SROs to ensure that the SROs' examinations were rigorous and comprehensive.

CONDUCT OF EXAMINATIONS

So how are exams conducted? In most cases the examiners do not show up unannounced and unexpected. While unannounced examinations are conducted for cause examinations in which it is feared that evidence may be destroyed or documentation falsified if the target firm is forewarned, it is generally more efficient for the firm and for the SEC to give notice a few weeks before the examination is on site. And so the first step in most examinations is for the SEC staff to send the firm a letter notifying it of the examination and containing a list that requests certain information or documents that SEC examiners will review as part of the examination. Some of the information is to be sent to the SEC for review prior to the exam, partly in order to help the staff prepare and partly to do everyone a favor by keeping the actual visit to the firm as short as possible. In the past, it was not unusual for a firm's Compliance Department or General Counsel's Office to attempt to restrict the document production, but the Bernie Madoff scandal has since made the SEC staff far less agreeable to restrictions or even requests for an extension to provide the information.

When the examiners arrive for the on-site portion of the examination,[2] they commonly conduct initial interviews with the Chief Compliance Officer and other members of senior management. This interview gives a bit more detail about the firm and its operations, and often helps to determine the scope of the examination. The examiners also do a walkthrough of the firm's offices to gain an overall understanding of the firm's organization, flow of work, and control environment (are conflicted groups, such as Research and Trading, sitting in a common area?). For the duration of the examination (which may take days or weeks), the examiners conduct interviews, spot-check documentation, and make supplemental requests. An important axiom for Compliance Officers with respect to regulatory exams is that if a task wasn't documented, it didn't happen in the eyes of the examiners. If an examiner pulls a customer complaint file at random and it does not show that the complaint was resolved or is actively under review, the SEC will not accept the compliance department's word that everything was taken care of but just not documented. At the end of the examination, the examination team will conduct an exit interview with the Chief Compliance Officer and other key staff members, to

---

[2] In some cases, the entire examination is conducted by reviewing documents at the SEC office and so there is no on-site portion of the examination.

Conduct of Examinations ■ **111**

discuss the preliminary findings and to provide the firm with an opportunity to provide additional information regarding points about which concern has been expressed.

The examiners then go back to the SEC offices and over the coming weeks finalize their examination report (SEC policy is to complete the process within 120 days of leaving the firm). They may ask follow-up questions or request additional documentation, and will confer with other parts of the SEC if special expertise is required. When everything is wrapped up, they will send the firm a written notification that the exam has been concluded. They will send the firm either a "Deficiency Letter" outlining specific areas in which the firm did not meet regulatory standards in the judgment of the SEC, or a "No Further Action Letter" if the examiners found no deficiencies. If the staff found particularly serious deficiencies, they will refer the matter to the Commission (the five actual commissioners) and this may lead to a formal investigation. Whenever a firm has received a Deficiency Letter, it has 30 days to respond in writing, including any steps that it has taken or will take to address the problems and to ensure that they do not recur. Except in sweep examinations and a handful of other circumstances, the results of the exam are not made public.

This description of a typical exam might imply that the life of a member of the SEC staff is pretty straightforward, moving from one examination to the next. But, like most of us, they work on several things at a time and at any given time may have five or more projects underway, including examinations and actual investigations. Investigations are longer-term in nature and are aimed at determining whether serious violations have occurred. They may be initiated based on the findings of examinations, from customer complaints, from referrals from self-regulatory organizations such as FINRA, from the Enforcement Division and other parts of the SEC, or (occasionally) from reading the newspaper.

Supervising the efforts of the staff are Branch Chiefs, the SEC's first-level supervisors. Their role has been likened to that of a project manager for the staff attorneys assigned to them. With respect to the conduct of investigations, the lead attorney leads the investigation and determines the tactics, but the Branch Chief manages the broader strategy (i.e., what violations are to be investigated and when the investigation is complete).

Understanding the workload of the SEC staff and the administrative processes involved in examinations and investigations provides important insight into how the SEC managed to miss a multibillion-dollar Ponzi scheme in spite of the fact that outsiders, and some of its own staff, had raised concerns. If you've ever watched a TV crime show, you've likely seen a cop (along with his partner or dog) working on one case at a time, which he or she or they solve within one hour minus time for commercials. It doesn't happen that way, and it doesn't work that way for SEC staff, either. At any given time, they have a good half-dozen projects in various states of completion or inactivity in their in-boxes, and they receive a good number of tips from outside sources each week. Many of the tips are off the mark. More to the point, when a complaint does appear to merit further review, that's one more project to be worked on. That does not mean that good tips are ignored or that the staff are not eager to find and catch violations, but rather that there is an incentive to close a complaint without further action if the complaint is not black-and-white.

Does this excuse or even explain the failure to spot the Bernie Madoff scam? Not at all—the tips raised regarding his activities were clear and merited far more attention than they received. The SEC itself has said so, in a series of Inspector General reports that describe in shocking detail all the things that did not happen. It does, however, highlight the many moving parts that have to come together on a daily basis to make the process work. It also highlights the danger that a similar scheme will be missed in the future.

FINRA

In the securities industry, the work of the SEC is supplemented by self-regulatory organizations (SROs), which were established along with the SEC in the wake of the Great Crash of 1929. The most important of the SROs is the Financial Industry Regulatory Authority (FINRA). It is not a government organization, but many of the regulatory oversight functions established by law are delegated to it. FINRA establishes rules for the operations of broker-dealers, most stock markets and other trading facilities, and certain other parts of the industry. FINRA rules are detailed and often technical in nature, and are intended to ensure that regulation keeps pace with the changing market.

Any firm that wishes to do business as a securities broker or dealer in the United States must register with FINRA and is subject to examination by FINRA staff in much the same way as the SEC examines firms, although FINRA is the first line of defense and inspects all firms rather than a sample of them. Within registered firms, anyone who deals with the public (brokers, or registered representatives, in industry parlance), as well as their managers and other key staff, must also register with FINRA. To do so, they must pass an examination and a routine background check, and each year they must meet standard continuing education requirements.

In addition to writing rules, examining firms, and licensing firms and individuals, FINRA performs the frontline surveillance of trading on the NASDAQ stock market, the NYSE, and other trading venues. It does this by using highly advanced computer systems to detect unusual activity in share prices or volumes and other factors that may indicate the presence of insider trading, the manipulation of prices, or other forms of market abuse. Analysts who are familiar with the markets and who specialize in detecting market abuse routinely review the alerts generated by the system and conduct an initial assessment of whether further investigation is required. These investigations are similar to those conducted by the SEC, although FINRA investigations tend to focus on violations committed by FINRA-registered firms or individuals. Large cases and cases involving nonregistered individuals may be referred to the SEC or law-enforcement authorities. Although FINRA does not have the authority to bring criminal or civil charges, it may levy fines and suspend or revoke the registration of a firm or individual. This effectively kicks them out of the industry and takes away their livelihood, and even lower-level sanctions are made public. The prospect of FINRA sanctions is not viewed lightly in the industry.

FINRA conducts a number of other functions critical to the fair and orderly operations of the markets, including monitoring the financial health of member firms and running the industry's dispute-resolution service.

COMPLIANCE DEPARTMENTS

It should be evident at this point that regulators cannot be everywhere all the time, even if the rules they write and enforce are. To be effective, rules need to work their way through the system and embed themselves in the firms where business is done. For this to happen, there needs to be someone or some group of people who know the rules, know how they are applied and how they are expected to be fulfilled, and can interpret them for the dozens or hundreds of situations that might fall within their reach. For this job, firms hire compliance officers.

It could easily and mistakenly be assumed that compliance officers are the representatives of the regulator within the firm. It is not uncommon for business line managers who have been told 'no' once too often to take this view. But it is more accurate to think of compliance officers more like other control functions such as Internal Audit or Legal, whose job is to protect the firm by ensuring that it follows the rules and does not expose itself to regulatory enforcement action, civil or criminal liability, or reputational damage. More than other risk functions, though, their activities directly impact the extent to which the regulations conceived by lawmakers are effective, the extent to which markets operate in a fair and efficient manner, and the extent to which investors are protected.

The idea of a separate compliance department staffed with professional compliance officers did not spring fully formed into existence by regulatory fiat but rather evolved as the requirements became more detailed and the businesses to which they applied became more complex. In the later decades of the 20th century, the role was commonly viewed as part of the work of the Legal Department, a not-unreasonable view since following rules and regulations is closely akin to following laws. Although more recent years have seen the development of professional compliance officers with specialized training and education, the legal ancestry of the field can still be seen in the preference among some firms for compliance officers with law degrees and for compliance departments that report to the General Counsel. This pattern, though shrinking, was likely supported by the SEC's own hiring practices, in which investigators for years would be lucky to even get in the door without a law degree (a rather odd obsession, it must be observed, since the FBI and other federal agencies have no such policy or preference).

Compliance departments are headed by a *Chief Compliance Officer* (CCO), though the title sometimes varies. In most cases, most notably for broker-dealers and credit rating agencies, the firm is required by law or regulation to officially designate by name the person filling this role so there is no ambiguity either within the organization or among the regulators and the public at large. Depending on the size of the organization, the extent of its overseas operations, and the diversity of products and services it provides, the CCO will be supported by a staff to carry out the range of compliance responsibilities. A few of the typical supporting roles are described next.

Business Unit Compliance Officers

Perhaps the most fundamental role of a compliance officer is to provide guidance to the business lines on a day-to-day basis, answering the question, "Can I do this?" Because the business lines themselves can be so diverse, it is often necessary to assign a specific compliance officer or group of compliance officers to each business line as a dedicated resource. In this way, they not only can focus on a more limited range of laws and regulations (e.g., equities trading, bonds, derivatives) but also can become conversant in the business line itself.

This helps the compliance officer come up with alternative approaches should the one envisioned by the business line be unacceptable for some reason. More to the point, it helps the compliance officer know when someone from the business line is trying to pull the wool over his or her eyes.

One type of business line compliance officer particularly worth mentioning is the trading floor compliance officer. This is perhaps the most stressful compliance role, since it requires the compliance officer to make decisions very quickly and very correctly. These officers are located on the trading floor specifically so that traders can ask them questions and get approval to do trades in real time, sometimes while the other party is on hold and nearly always while the market is moving. Add to this the fact that they are dealing with highly strung Type-A personalities whose livelihood is partly dependent on the trade in question, and it is clear that this is no job for the weak stomached, weak minded, or weak willed.

Another compliance role that is particularly important, and that may be considered a business line compliance role, is that of "retail" compliance. In some firms, this may not exist as a separate function, but the role is performed one way or another in any firm that does business with individual clients. Regulations generally distinguish between institutional investors, who are deemed to require less protection, and retail ones (at least with respect to broker-dealers).

The need for business line compliance officers has fueled a trend over the past decade or two in which the compliance profession has become more and more specialized. Whereas in the early or mid-1990s compliance officers were generalized (indeed, compliance was often considered a specialty within the legal field), a glance today at compliance job postings shows few positions for generalists other than those at the highest level. Most of the postings will be for "fixed income compliance," "compliance reporting," "investment adviser compliance," and so on. As regulation is reformed, this trend will only continue and perhaps accelerate, as requirements increase in scope and complexity and as additional sectors are brought under the regulatory umbrella.

Monitoring

Many of the functions performed by a compliance department are dependent on automated systems that initiate alerts when suspicious activity occurs. The most sophisticated of these are those located in firms with securities trading activities, in which computerized programs conduct surveillance of all trading activity to detect potential violations of securities laws (such as manipulating the price of a stock or trading on inside information) or of internal risk management procedures (such as exceeding individual limits on the size of the bets a trader can take in the market). Monitoring staff review the alerts and may quickly determine that there is no cause for alarm (e.g., a quick runup in the price of a stock is explained by news that came out that day), or they may follow up by investigation of the circumstances through interviews with the traders involved. Compliance monitoring also includes communications monitoring (in particular, e-mail monitoring through sophisticated programs that use artificial intelligence to detect insider trading or other unauthorized communications).

An important monitoring function is located in the so-called "control room," which keeps highly confidential lists of deals the firm is working on and the individuals who are aware of the deals. It is standard practice in most financial firms to require employees to disclose their personal trading activities and those of their immediate families, and to ensure that copies of their trading records are sent directly from the employee's brokerage firm to the compliance department so that they can be reviewed against the control room deal lists. Even in those cases where employees are required to get permission from the control room before executing a personal trade, this post-trade review serves as an important backup and is generally a focus of examinations by regulators and SROs.

Customer Complaints

Customer complaints are a part of doing business in any sector of the economy. But in financial services, they also constitute an important element of the compliance function by alerting the staff to potential wrongdoing. While it is as true here as it is elsewhere that many complaints are unfounded, each must be investigated since it not only could be true, but could be the tip of a much larger iceberg. Complaints made in writing to customers are therefore logged, investigated, and tracked so that managers and regulators can identify in each case how the complaint was handled, what the outcome of the investigation was, and how it was finally resolved. In this sense it must be said that the regulated firms were by necessity performing the tasks that the SEC's Inspector General found were not performed during the period in which Bernard Madoff was operating his Ponzi scheme.[3]

---

[3] "Review and Analysis of Examinations of Bernard L. Madoff Investment Securities, LLC," U.S. Securities and Exchange Commission Office of the Inspector General, pp. 3–4.

Examinations and Reporting

Some firms, particularly those that engage in many different sectors of the financial industry, are subject to regulation and examination by so many different regulatory agencies that being examined is a full-time job. For this reason, they establish dedicated sections within the compliance department to take responsibility for the full examination process. They receive the initial notification and provide the documentation requested, notify relevant departments and individuals of the pending examination so that they are appropriately prepared, ensure that workspace and resources are provided for the examiners, act as the liaison between the examiners and the firm once the on-site examination has begun, and coordinate post-exam follow-up.

In some cases, the same section will also be responsible for information requests from regulators that are not related specifically to examinations. Particularly in the case of larger firms, it is common to receive requests for information or documentation on specific transactions or specific clients. These may be entirely routine, as when a market surveillance department asks for information about an unusual trading pattern, or they may be related to a more serious matter such as the identity of an individual who made a large purchase of a stock prior to a big news announcement. In most cases, the inquiry does not imply any wrongdoing by the firm itself, but the firm is the party with the knowledge or the documentation necessary to assist the regulators in determining whether and how to proceed with an investigation.

Advertising and Marketing Review

The way in which financial services are marketed is closely scrutinized and highly regulated. There are two main areas of concern. The first is ensuring that the way in which services and products are marketed and sold is not deceptive. In particular, advertising (in any form) that implies a guarantee of returns, implies that an investment that has done well in the past will therefore do well in the future, or that provides false information is banned and firms must demonstrate that they have specific measures to prevent such advertisements from seeing the light of day. The other issue is disclosure. Given the emphasis on transparency as a tool of investor protection, it is necessary that regulations actually require the disclosure of information concerning the risks and other factors that should be considered before investing in a particular product. Marketing compliance officers review all literature, advertisements, and web pages to ensure that they conform to the relevant regulations, and that risk and other information is disclosed when and to whom required.

As is the case with many other aspects of compliance, the global nature of business and the growth of the Internet have complicated the marketing review process. Regulations vary from country to country to country, and even from state to state, yet the Internet is of course accessible from all over the world. This is the reason why you sometimes need to select the country in which you reside before going further on a website, and are directed to the site conforming to the relevant regulations (there are other legal and marketing reasons for separate websites as well). Mass e-mailings can also cause regulatory difficulties, since they often make no distinction as to the country of the recipient and could result in marketing that does not include the appropriate language or that constitutes an offer to sell products in a country in which the firm is not registered to do so.

Compliance Systems

Whether conducting surveillance of trading activity, monitoring communications, tracking complaints, or delivering training, the world of the compliance officer is increasingly all about gathering and organizing information so that it can be analyzed in the most efficient fashion and presented in the most usable manner. The larger or more complex the firm, the more difficult and more essential this challenge becomes. As this trend developed, compliance departments began to recognize the importance of close contact with their firms' IT staff to help develop tools that would assist in their work. More and more, though, compliance technology has become a specialized discipline in its own right, and many firms have their own internal IT staff to develop, implement, and update systems unique to their requirements.

There are three principal advantages to maximizing the use of technology in the conduct of compliance activities. The first, not surprisingly, is efficiency. Especially in large firms, those dealing in a wide range of products, or those that are geographically dispersed, there is simply too much data to be analyzed manually. Who can watch every e-mail or every trade, or check that every file has all the necessary information? Even those tasks that can be done manually, such as collecting information for routine reports to regulators, may be done more efficiently by an automated or semi-automated system. Being able to do more with fewer people is critical to the success of the CCO, and if a process can be automated, the CCO can deploy that member of the staff to other tasks that require human judgment.

Typical issues for these units include identifying what databases in the firm contain the information necessary for analysis (e.g., the current list of all employees so that the list can be checked against a list of all employees who have taken mandatory annual training), determining the best way to consolidate information, constructing firewalls so that confidential information is not accessible by those who do not have a need to know the information, and ensuring compatibility of systems with the platforms used in the department and other parts of the firm. These units are also able to keep track of development in compliance technology and to evaluate the effectiveness of specific products being pitched to the firm by outside vendors who are in the business of developing compliance technologies.

IT projects in the compliance department, as elsewhere, are expensive and complex, and so their implementation often requires close supervision. The best compliance systems professionals also have project management skills and experience, so the person most familiar with the system is also the person managing its implementation.

Other Functions

The business of ensuring compliance is neither simple nor straightforward. For all of the work involved in the tasks already mentioned, there are still others that are often performed by the compliance department, such as:

- Detecting and reporting potential money-laundering activity or the use of the firm's facilities for corruption and other forms of financial crime
- Training
- Assisting in the Due-Diligence process for potential corporate actions
- Drafting, circulating, and updating internal policies and procedures
- Developing the firm's positions on proposed regulations in order to provide formal comments during the draft regulation's consultation process

And what is more, firms with branch offices around the country must themselves conduct compliance examinations of the branches to ensure they are complying with the rules, and overseas offices have different or additional rules to follow in accordance with local national law.

 CONCLUSION

As important as the political process is to regulating the financial industry, laws that just sit on the books would do no good for anyone. The way these laws are implemented through more detailed rules and regulations, and the way in which the regulators, industry organizations, and financial firms ensure that they are carried through, is what makes a regulatory initiative a success instead of a failure. The quality of the organizations and the people who lead and staff them, and the attitude toward compliance within regulated firms, will be critical in the success of regulatory reform, whatever the outcome of the political wrangling that starts the ball rolling.

CHAPTER THIRTEEN

Cost-Benefit Analysis

ANY TIME A NEW regulation is proposed, or significant changes to an existing one are contemplated, it is certain that the question will be raised as to whether the benefits derived from the new measures will outweigh the costs of implementing them. It is logical to do so. It would not make sense to implement a proposal that will in the end do more economic harm than good. Second, it forces the debate into a rational, empirical, and presumably objective analysis isolated from political motivations, special interests, or emotion (at least in theory). Finally, performing such an analysis is a good way to focus on the direct and indirect effects of the proposal, thus assisting in the discovery of any unintended consequences that may be worth avoiding.

On this basis it would be difficult to argue against a rational and objective cost-benefit analysis. Indeed, it is an accepted part of the regulatory process, and some regulators require a formal cost-benefit analysis to be performed for any significant regulatory proposals, including the Financial Service Authority in the United Kingdom.

In practice, however, performing a cost-benefit analysis is extremely difficult. The reasons for this are described in what follows, but they come down to this fundamental truth: It is usually relatively easy to quantify (or exaggerate) the costs of a proposal, but nearly always impossible to quantify accurately and fully the benefits. This is particularly true in the case of public-good objectives such as those related to customer protection: How, exactly, do you calculate the monetary value of an incremental increase in customer protection? Moreover, the insistence on a cost-benefit analysis assumes that regulation must never cost more than the measured value of the benefit. It assumes that there is nothing so important that we would be willing to assume a net loss to the market, resulting in lower profits.

As simple as it sounds on the surface, cost-benefit analysis has become a highly technical economic process, and as a result there are volumes of academic literature concerning the intricacies of how it might be performed and the factors that may or may not be appropriate to consider, as well as debate as to whether cost-benefit analyses are useful (including, inevitably, cost-benefit analyses of cost-benefit analysis). This chapter seeks to avoid stepping into the academic quicksand from which the reader might never emerge, though if you wish to explore the issue on a more academic plane you are welcome to do so.

BASICS OF COST-BENEFIT ANALYSIS

There is no single methodology or even general framework for conducting a regulatory cost-benefit analysis. Most methods, however, share common characteristics to ensure that the process is as precise as possible, but as flexible as is practical.

Before making any measurement of costs or benefits, the analysis must identify as many of the costs and benefits as possible. These might be direct or indirect, and the important thing is to make the analysis as inclusive as possible. When identifying these costs and benefits, it is also important to determine as well as possible whether they are quantitative or qualitative in nature—whether they can in fact be measured. Cost-benefit analysis recognizes that not all factors will be quantitative, and indeed that the mere fact that something is more qualitative does not necessarily mean that it is less important (think, for instance, of Homeland Security regulations whose ultimate goal is the prevention of deaths from terrorist incidents). When assessing costs, most cost-benefit analysis considers both cost to the industry of implementation, and cost to the government (or the industry) of monitoring compliance.

Once the costs and benefits have been laid out, it is next necessary to measure them. This is normally a two-step process: *quantification* and *monetization.* The first is a direct measurement (or estimation, to be more accurate) of the impact of the proposed regulation on a particular cost or benefit source. For example, it may be estimated that the regulation will reduce paperwork requirements across the industry by 50,000 pages or will require an additional 5,000 hours of training. This is not very useful in and of itself, since it says nothing about the actual financial cost or benefit arising from the proposal. Monetizing the costs and benefits, to the extent possible, serves to provide a common unit of measurement for the whole range of costs and benefits, which might otherwise be expressed in such incompatible terms as pages, hours, and dollars. Only then can a meaningful assessment in terms of the financial viability of the proposed regulation be proposed. Not all factors are quantifiable, some are quantifiable but not monetizable (time is often difficult to monetize unless it is in the context of an hourly fee), and some are both quantifiable and monetizable. Because regulations are meant to be in effect into the future rather than simply at a point in time, a calculation is normally performed to express the costs and benefits in current dollars, in order to recognize the *time value* of money.

Once costs and benefits are estimated, they may be expressed as a specific number (which is nonetheless understood to be an estimate) or as a range. If the estimate is expressed in both a quantified range and a monetized range, the monetized range may not be a straightforward multiplication of the quantified range by a fixed cost, but will generally reflect the fact that the per-unit cost is also subject to variation. For example, an estimated cost of an additional 50,000 to 100,000 pages of paperwork and financial range of $5,000 to $20,000 reflects the fact that the price per page could be as little as 10 cents and as much as 20 cents (the price range reflecting the lowest estimated quantity at the lowest per-unit price and the highest estimated quantity at the highest unit price).

In most settings, the cost-benefit analysis is not simply an examination of one particular proposal. In the U.S. federal system, described in more detail below, the process is intended to include the costs and benefits of alternative regulatory approaches as well, and of course the costs and benefits of not regulating. Thus, a full cost-benefit analysis is likely to include not simply a number on the cost side and a number on the benefit side, but a series of analyses for comparison.

It should be stressed that a cost-benefit analysis is not always about finding the most *effective* approach but rather the most *efficient* one that meets or exceeds the desired level of effectiveness. The most effective way to prevent embezzlement from client accounts may be to conduct independent audits of

124 ■ Cost-Benefit Analysis

each and every account at the end of every business day, but it is considered sufficient and more efficient to conduct periodic risk-based audits, at a far lower cost, instead.

Once the analysis is completed, what happens? It is not as simple as merely determining whether the number in the "costs" column exceeds the number in the "benefits" column, and proceeding if the benefits number is larger. Among the reasons for this, three stand out: First, if the numbers are expressed in a range, there could be overlap, which makes it unclear as to the actual outcome, as when the costs are expected to be in the range of $1 million to $2 million and the benefits to be in the range of $1.5 million to $2.5 million. The exact numbers in practice could turn out to be a cost of $1 million and a benefit of $2 million (regulation was a good idea) or a cost of $2 million and a benefit of $1.5 million (regulation was a bad idea). Second, the qualitative factors need to be considered, even if they do not fit within the mathematical calculation. Third, given the political environment in which the process occurs, it is common for interested parties to contest the validity of the analysis.

Arising partly from the recognition that the result of a cost-benefit analysis is merely an imprecise estimate and partly from the recognition that qualitative factors may outweigh those factors that are easily measurable, few would argue that regulatory policy should be strictly determined on the basis of such an analysis. Many of those who are aware that the analysis occurs but are not well-versed in the process miss this point. In what follows, we will examine why cost-benefit analysis is conducted even given its limitations. But first, we will delve deeper into how the analysis can go awry.

Problems in Measurement

The first problem that arises is the first step of the process—ensuring all direct and indirect costs and benefits have been identified. This is a highly subjective undertaking that requires a thorough familiarity with the industry and with the issue under consideration. The costs need to include the costs to the government of administering the regulation as well as the costs to the industry, which may include the hiring of new staff or engaging outside firms to perform a task, training, recordkeeping and information technology requirements, as well as similar costs to firms providing relevant services to the regulated firm (e.g., additional recordkeeping and training requirements). Most of these costs are quantifiable and monetizable, though the estimates are likely to be highly variable based on a wide range of assumptions. Some benefits are also quantifiable and monetizable, though many are not and are therefore regarded as qualitative, such as investor protection or promotion of confidence in the markets.

From this arises the second problem in measuring costs and benefits—what do you do with the unmeasurable factors? The answer is that policymakers end up with an equation that you know to be incomplete, because you can compare only the quantified (and indeed monetized) factors, which may in fact be more important.

Monetization is itself a process fraught with imprecision. Even when factors are quantifiable, their characteristics may lead to different ways of calculating a price, with different levels of precision and ranges of assumptions. On one hand, it may be easy to assess the cost of 100 extra hours of work by a government employee at the GS-12 pay grade, since the salary for such a resource is precisely known and can be estimated with a fair degree of confidence into the future. On the other hand, the price associated with other factors may depend on assumptions as to market conditions, the number of affected transactions or customers (which may impact the marginal or per-unit cost of the change), exchange rates, interest rates, and the emergence of technologies or other alternatives as a result of the regulatory change. As a result, monetization treats all inputs as if they were equally easy to monetize.

Though the cost-benefit analysis process is meant to bring a rational and scientific approach to policymaking, it is in some respects trying to treat an art like a science. Simply putting a number on something may give merely the illusion of accuracy, precision, and quantifiability. Even when the assessment is done, it is based on a series of assumptions and estimates, and so any precise figure provided for either costs or benefits should be taken with a shaker full of salt.

Other Problems

Other limitations arise that are not directly related to the measurement of factors, but rather to how the process is carried out. First, costs and benefits are generally expressed in terms of an entire industry or market, rather than at the firm level. This facilitates interpretation by virtue of simplicity (one cost figure and one benefit figure), and indeed many benefits accrue to investors as a whole. However, costs tend to be borne by individual firms. Though some costs will fall less heavily on smaller firms, the danger arises that the additional cost cripples individual firms even though the overall cost is less than the overall benefit. Although federal agencies are normally expected to weigh the impact of regulatory costs on small and medium-size businesses, the costs are not always perfectly scalable and as a result some businesses can and do become unviable or find themselves forced to change the way they do business. A classic example is raising the minimum wage, which may benefit the workforce as a whole but may lead to the loss of jobs as small businesses operating on thin margins find that they cannot afford the increased cost. A related point is that the costs and benefits often do not even accrue to the same parties. When one party pays the cost and another receives the benefit, society may have a net gain but the business bearing the costs may see only the increased burden.

Second, the time horizons of costs and benefits may not be the same. Costs are commonly borne immediately, while the benefits may take years to appear (or, as discussed in the following, may never actually appear). For example, when Congress mandated the creation of the National Market System in 1975, which served to integrate trading in all U.S. stock markets and create a single virtual exchange decades before other markets attempted to do the same, the costs of creating the necessary infrastructure were immediate and considerable. The benefits of a single market, over time, surely have paid back this investment in spades. Yet in an environment of quarterly earnings and annual bonuses, it may be difficult to justify equal weighting to a dollar of immediate, certain cost and a dollar of deferred, uncertain benefit.

Third, policymakers conducting the cost-benefit analysis are often—in fact, usually—at the mercy of those who will be regulated to provide the data on which the estimates will be based. This presents a clear conflict of interest for the parties furnishing the information and could lead to some estimates being no more accurate than a man who measures his height standing on his toes and measuring to the tips of his fingers with his arms stretched over his head. As the section on cost-benefit analysis as a lobbying tool points out, this reliance can lead to strikingly different estimated costs for proposed regulations.

Whoever is measuring the costs and benefits is faced with defining the parameters of what is likely to happen or unlikely to happen in the future—in essence, how much of the bell-curve to assume when estimating costs and benefits. The tendency is to assume that things will occur somewhere in the middle of the bell curve—a curve that is often a backward-looking set of data based on past scenarios. Consider, for instance, the cost of deposit insurance for FDIC-insured banks. This cost is borne by the banks themselves, since the pot from which deposit insurance is paid is funded through assessments on each individual bank. The size of the pot is therefore a direct factor in determining the cost of the regulations requiring deposit insurance, and it is determined according to historically based scenarios. In the event of a financial crisis that leads to the closure of an unusually high number of banks (the "tail" of the bell curve), the pot may need to be enlarged or replenished. This means an inaccurate estimate of costs and a second dip into the pockets of the banks. (This analytic fallacy of focusing on the middle of the bell curve has had wider implications, as when the credit rating agencies assumed mortgage repayments would remain reliable and the real-estate boom would not go bust.)

The unpredictability of markets leads also to a broader limitation to assessing costs versus benefits. Regardless of whether the cost estimates are accurate, it is certain that they will be paid. Sometimes, however, the benefit may never be visible since the aim is to prevent an undesirable outcome. The benefits arise only when you need them, in an unusual or catastrophic situation. If you measure costs and benefits at any time before the catastrophe, the assessment will show that costs greatly outweigh benefits. The analysis will show that regulation makes no sense right up until the day you wish you had it. This is the argument with respect to the need for regulation to break up institutions that are too big to fail, or at least to lay out a plan of how such an institution would be dissolved in an orderly fashion in case of collapse. It is also the argument in favor of the more pedestrian and less controversial issue of bank deposit insurance. In fact, all regulations of this nature can be likened to insurance. The premiums paid by an individual for health insurance may be substantial and will on the surface feel like money wasted, but the utility of the insurance takes on a whole different character when it is needed. And what if the catastrophe never occurs? Was it worth it to pay all those costs in the first place? Was the money spent on gas masks during the London Blitz wasted?

The final limitation to be discussed is misunderstanding or misrepresenting the aim of a cost-benefit analysis. Cost-benefit analysis is meant to be a tool that aids in making the ultimate decision, rather than for determining the outcome in a strictly rational and uncontestable way. Policymakers understand that the estimate is just an estimate, and in this respect policy analysis differs from financial analysis. More to the point, even if the figures were absolutely reliable and correct and pointed to an increased net cost, there are some things that policymakers judge to be worth paying for (hence the $12 trillion budget deficit in the United States). This is simply another way of looking at the importance of the "qualitative" factors. In the intensely political environment in which regulations are incubated, political factors may impel legislators to press for or against regulation in a given area because it is in their best political interests to do so, and if the cost-benefit analysis backs their position, so much the better.

THE BENEFITS OF COST-BENEFIT ANALYSIS

Given all these limitations, then, why even bother performing a cost-benefit analysis? Do the benefits of performing this time-consuming and resource-draining exercise outweigh the costs?

Generally speaking, the answer is *yes*, with some qualifications. The three principle reasons for conducting the analysis are: (1) In practical terms, it is difficult to justify *not* doing a cost-benefit analysis, (2) it focuses attention on the goals of the proposal and the relevant factors to be considered, and provides discipline to the process, and (3) it provides a useful comparison between various alternatives.

First, as a practical matter it is difficult to justify *not* doing some manner of cost-benefit analysis on a proposed piece of legislation. Indeed, the question of whether a proposal is worth doing—whether the benefits will outweigh the costs—is implicit in most of the debate that occurs with respect to regulation, anyway. Conducting a systematic analysis, even with the limitations inherent in the process, at least gets the considerations out in the open where their merits can be debated. And if the regulatory agencies do not do a cost-benefit analysis, one or both sides of the debate will surely offer their own and these analyses are likely to be even less reliable than one performed by a more-or-less neutral government agency.

With respect to the second rationale, the cost-benefit analysis provides a framework for considering both the regulatory issue and the proposed solution from a critical angle. By giving consideration to the range of direct and indirect costs and benefits, the process may point to unintended consequences that had not been considered before. When the process includes a requirement to send the proposal to other relevant agencies for review (as is the case with U.S. federal regulations), additional costs or regulatory redundancies may also be identified. Attempts to quantify and monetize these factors, however empirically weak the process may be, can nonetheless be helpful in describing the magnitude of the cost or benefit, sometimes contrary to expectation. And even with a fairly cursory analysis, the process can serve as a filter against bad regulation that is put forward for political or other reasons but that would clearly make bad policy. Also, identifying the cost factors and estimating benefits allows for post-implementation reviews that can watch the identified costs to give early warning of problems, and that can assess benefits against their expected benchmarks to determine whether expectations were valid. Indeed, a sunset provision based on such reviews would serve as a safeguard against ineffective regulations that turn into The Thing That Wouldn't Die.

Of course, some of these benefits would be achieved with any kind of formal regulatory review or through the public consultation process, but given the prominence of the cost-benefit analysis as a tool and the presence of other reasons for using it, it does make sense to see these factors as direct benefits of the cost-benefit analysis process.

The third rationale arises from the common requirement in cost-benefit analyses (explicit in U.S. federal regulations) to analyze and compare all reasonable regulatory alternatives, not simply "enact this regulation" or "do not regulate." This activity may itself bring to the surface alternatives that had not been considered or had been written off as unworthy without serious consideration. More importantly, however, it allows a focused and systematic weighing of alternatives to determine which is likely to be more cost effective and what factors might change the assessment. It slows down the rush to regulate, or the rush to a particular regulatory solution that may be more politically palatable but nonetheless unwise. And while the fact remains that the analysis of each alternative will be imprecise and based on assumptions, the relative merits of the various alternatives (including no regulation) can still be made clear.

So the answer isn't really that cost-benefit analyses are worth doing because of the *product*, but rather because of the *process*. The outcome of the analysis is likely to be less reliable and precise than we would like, but the very process of performing the analysis focuses study on the aims and goals and helps to ensure that all viable alternatives are considered, stripped of their political encumbrances.

GOVERNMENT USE OF COST-BENEFIT ANALYSIS

Here is the good news: Federal agencies are required to perform a cost-benefit analysis on most proposed federal regulations as part of the process of developing and issuing them. Though the requirement has its roots back in the Nixon Administration, its present form was instituted via an Executive Order of the Clinton Administration in 2003 (Executive Order 12866), which is still in effect with only minor modifications. The bad news: EO 12866 does not apply to the so-called independent regulatory authorities, including the SEC, the CFTC, the Fed, or the FDIC (though, as we shall see, this does not mean that the agencies do not perform these analyses of their own accord). The reason for this rather strange exclusion is lost to history.

Because it lays out official and longstanding government policy with respect to regulation, it is nonetheless useful to explore EO 12866 as it is applied across the rest of the federal government. Among other things, Executive Order 12886 lays out the government's official Statement of Regulatory Policies and Principles, including a requirement to assess "all costs and benefits of available regulatory alternatives, including the alternative of not regulating."[1]

Though excluded from most of the procedural requirements of the Executive Order, the independent agencies are required to submit their annual regulatory plans to the White House office responsible for conducting cost-benefit analyses, the Office of Information and Regulatory Affairs (OIRA) within the Office of Management and Budget, and they do on occasion submit proposed regulations to OIRA for review.

Jurisdictional and procedural issues aside, the point is that the federal government has had a policy of assessing costs and benefits of proposed regulations and that the policy has changed little regardless of the party in power. As a result, independent regulatory authorities such as the SEC generally perform their own cost-benefit analyses. In these analyses, the Commission staff attempt to identify which costs and benefits can be quantified (can be measured) and monetized (a price can be associated with the result). They then use various financial models to estimate the costs, which generally may be given in ranges rather than a precise estimate. For example, it may be determined that a regulatory change will reduce the paperwork burden on the total industry by 500,000 to 1,250,000 pages (quantified), for an estimated total saving of $75,000 to $200,000 (monetized).

 ## COST-BENEFIT ANALYSIS AS A NEGOTIATING TACTIC

You don't have to be a federal agency to perform a cost-benefit analysis. Lobbyists often perform, commission, or call upon the government to perform an analysis. As a negotiating point it makes sense to do so. First, when they perform the analysis themselves, they make the call on all the subjective judgments with respect to how costs and benefits are measured. The result can be dramatically different from the "official" cost-benefit analysis and this alone can cast a doubt on the government's analysis if it does not favor your position. An example comes from a letter to the SEC from the Center for Capital Markets Competitiveness of the U.S. Chamber of Commerce in July 2009 about a proposed regulation concerning the custody of client assets at investment

---

[1] Executive Order 12886, Sec. 1, in *Federal Register*, No. 58, Vol. 190, October 4, 1993, p. 51735.

advisory firms. Addressing the cost of auditing all client accounts rather than a risk-based sample, the letter states:

> . . . the SEC's estimate of an additional annual cost to advisers of $8,100, on average, for surprise exams appears woefully understated. It is our understanding that surprise audits are likely to cost between $20,000 and $300,000 for small and medium-sized advisers to over $1 million for the largest investment advisers.[2]

Of course, it can very well be that the Chamber of Commerce's figures are accurate or at least more accurate than those of the government. But when an industry group provides a cost estimate at such wide variance with the official and presumably more objective figure and does not accompany the estimate with the supporting data or methodology, the estimate must approached with caution.

Sometimes a lobbying organization will commission a study from a third party rather than performing the analysis itself. This makes sense when the organization lacks the resources or expertise to perform the analysis itself. Yet the fact that the analysis was performed by a third party does not necessarily mean that it was performed by an *independent* party (after all, the one who pays the piper gets to call the tune).

Calling for the government to perform a cost-benefit analysis (in those cases where it is not already required to do so) also has the advantage of slowing down the process. It is often viewed as important to break the momentum of a proposed reform, and calling for a time-consuming cost-benefit analysis serves this purpose well, whether intentionally or coincidentally. The hope is that the delay may mean that the political sentiment in favor of the proposal has cooled as the public's short attention span is diverted elsewhere. Less cynically, such a delay could be a deliberate goal because the political momentum behind a proposal may be a product of the heat of the moment and breaking the momentum would allow for more dispassionate consideration of the proposal.

So, it makes sense for a group opposed to a regulatory proposal to perform, commission, or call for a cost-benefit analysis—in this way they can challenge the official analysis or delay its implementation for months. And there is not much to lose in doing so; who is going to argue against checking whether benefits exceed costs?

---

[2] Letter from the Center for Capital Markets Competitiveness to the Securities and Exchange Commission, July 28, 2009, available at www.sec.gov/comments/s7-09-09/s70909-830.pdf.

CONCLUSION

Knowing whether a regulation is worth doing before committing to it is the essence of sound regulatory policy, and so cost-benefit analyses are in general useful tools to ensure that regulations are efficient and effective. Though they slow down the decision-making process and can appear misleadingly precise, they serve to focus analysis on the outcomes, indirect consequences, and alternatives to proposed regulation. Regardless of how accurate or useful the analysis itself may be, the process of conducting the analysis makes it a useful part of the regulatory process, and about as close to an objective assessment of its merits as there will be.

CHAPTER FOURTEEN

It's a Small World, After All

THROUGHOUT THIS BOOK, THE point has been made that regulations are highly influenced by political considerations, and a focus has been placed on how the political and policy processes play out in the United States. But a description of the regulatory process and the factors that influence it would be incomplete without a discussion of foreign and international regulation. For a number of reasons, the requirements of foreign regulators and the guidelines and recommendations of international organizations can have a significant impact on U.S. regulations and market practices. This chapter gives a brief overview of the overseas bodies that can influence U.S. regulation, how they work, and how their influence can work its way into the U.S. markets and ultimately your wallet.

 SUNDAY IS THE NEW MONDAY

If you have ever listened to the morning business report before the stock markets open, you probably heard something about how the markets in Asia did and how those in Europe were doing. You probably also heard something along the lines of the market in one region carrying through the trend of the region that had opened before it. This is partly due to that great driver of short-term market movements—the herd instinct—but it is more directly a reflection of the interconnectedness of markets. There are few very big banks or securities firms that are not also global, or at least regional, and both money and securities whip around the globe nearly as easily as they do within a single country. Financial markets are as globalized as the rest of the global economy, and perhaps more so, since prices, trends, panics, and failures are transmitted much more quickly across computer networks than along the sea lanes. When government officials and market chieftains worked through the weekend to save Bear Stearns, and later to not save Lehman Brothers, they knew they needed to have a plan in place before the end of the weekend and the opening of the next week's markets. But they knew that the deadline wasn't 9:30 Monday morning, when the markets opened in New York, but instead Sunday evening—Monday morning Tokyo time—when the Asian markets opened. If no plan had been announced until the New York market opening time, the Asia markets would already have traded an entire session and Europe would be halfway through its trading day, giving panic a good long time to sink in. Sunday, as the saying on Wall Street goes, is the new Monday.

So the markets themselves are linked through the flow of money and instruments across them. Doubts on the ability of Greece to meet its bond obligations sent markets in Asia and the United States into an immediate swoon in early 2010 for precisely this reason. And so poor oversight overseas may ignite a crisis which spreads quickly across the ocean, and that should concern us. But the interconnectedness—the mutual dependency—of global markets is also produced by the regulations that govern the markets.

When regulators take different approaches to the oversight of global firms, it is often the case that the entire firm complies with the most restrictive local regulation. For example, if the regulations in France require that certain documents be retained for six years but the equivalent requirement in the United States is only for four years, it may not be worth the effort and expense to distinguish what needs to be kept for each different time period, and so everything may get kept for six years. Or if U.S. law requires that any company whose stock trades on a U.S. exchange publicly release its financial results on a quarterly basis while other regulators require only semiannual results, large foreign companies have little choice but to abide by the more stringent requirement if they wish to tap the deeper U.S. capital market.

Privacy laws are notoriously fickle from one jurisdiction to the next and this can be the bane of the both regulated firms and those who regulate them. Regulated firms may face conflicted requirements and thus have separate procedures for different regional subsidiaries: In the United States, a securities firm is required to monitor the personal securities trades of its employees and so is expected to receive copies of each employee's personal brokerage account statement; requiring employees in the European Union to provide the same documents would likely be illegal. For regulators, privacy laws may not only make it difficult to peer into the bank accounts of potential perpetrators, but may also make it difficult to establish information-sharing agreements with jurisdictions whose laws prohibit the sharing of personal information with a country that does not have equally stringent privacy regulations.

But differing overseas regulations do not merely affect the poor benighted compliance officer at a global bank or the equally benighted civil servant; they also affect consumers and investors. When the Greek government took a rather casual attitude toward collecting taxes while spending generously on government programs until its credit rating begged for mercy, U.S. and other markets plummeted and people's investments ran for cover as the pros pondered whether the multinational euro would come flying apart. Meeting multiple and often conflicting requirements simply because a firm operates in other countries, or even simply because it has customers in other countries, eats up resources and costs money. It is not in the nature of these firms to absorb that cost if they can instead pass the cost on to you. This is to say nothing of the potential cost of multimillion-dollar fines for failing to meet the regulations of another country. Consumer choice may also be limited by overseas regulation, and not just because a large foreign market regards a particular practice to be misleading. If you call your broker and tell him or her that you would like to buy shares in a Russian company, the response may well be a dial tone. It's not that Russia doesn't have a stock market (it has several) or that its stock market is tiny, but rather that the country is judged by many to be somewhat unfussy about its regulatory regime and legal framework. So your broker may not deal at all in Russian securities and you may have to postpone your plans to own shares of the latest Siberian startup and settle for something more pedestrian (and more vigorously supervised).

OVERSEAS REGULATORS

It seems that every nation wants to have three things to be a country: a flag, and airline, and a stock market. Although a handful of countries have merged stock exchanges (notably the French/Belgian/Dutch/Portuguese Euronext, which also includes bits from the UK and the United States), not one has given up the privilege of having its own regulator. But that does not mean that

136 ■ It's a Small World, After All

all regulators are equally influential. Generally speaking, and not surprisingly, the most important regulators tend to be those for the countries with the largest markets. Though regulatory initiatives in Asia (especially Australia) and other regions can have a significant impact on regulation in the United States, Europe is the most influential overseas region in the U.S. markets.

The European Union

The European Union is often misunderstood by Americans—and with good reason since it is often misunderstood by Europeans themselves. The EU now consists of 27 countries, ranging from Germany, France, and the UK at one end of the scale to Cyprus, Estonia, and Malta at the other. Though the number of Member States has increased dramatically as the EU's boundaries march east, several west European nations, including Switzerland and Norway, remain outside of the fold (though not entirely outside the EU's orbit). Not all Member States use the euro as their currency, either because their economies have been judged too woozy to qualify for the single currency, such as Bulgaria, or because they smelled a rat and wanted nothing to do with it (the notoriously contrary Brits). An explanation of the history, organization, and legislative processes of the EU is well beyond the scope or aim of this book, but suffice it to say that its regulatory processes and tortuous negotiation rituals are not built for speed.

Along each stage of the process, negotiations occur along several dimensions at once: Member States versus other Member States, regulators versus market participants, sector versus sector (i.e., banks and securities firms each trying to feed the other to the wolves), individual firms versus other firms (e.g., a big stock exchange versus a little one), and even among the major EU organs responsible for the process—the powerful Commission, the largely consultative Parliament, and the Council, which is the final stop for a prospective directive, plus the specialist agencies responsible for each sector. The complexity of this circular firing squad makes the political process in the United States seem a bit minor league, but, surprisingly, much of EU regulation is actually pretty good.

A handful of EU directives and regulations are particularly important and illustrate the influence of European legislation on the U.S. markets. The Markets in Financial Instruments Directive (MiFID) is the general law covering everything from dealing with customers to establishing a stock exchange. MiFID sets the ground rules for "best execution," the concept that a broker must get the best deal for its customer when executing a trade (a surprisingly weak requirement before MiFID), and whether, how, and how quickly market prices must be made public to the market. The idea behind MiFID—which took well over half a decade to negotiate, draft, review, negotiate again, adopt, and implement—is to make the requirements uniform across the EU in order to avoid trench warfare among Member States attempting to promote or protect their local securities firms, stock exchanges, and other market participants. The Prospectus Directive governs the filing requirements for securities offered in the EU (including the securities of U.S. companies that are to be offered in the EU) or admitted to trading on an EU-regulated market (including U.S. securities that will be listed and traded on an EU stock exchange, even if no new shares will be issued in order to do so). The Regulation on Credit Rating Agencies, while in principle providing regulatory requirements for rating agencies located in the EU, takes aim right between the eyes of the major U.S. rating agencies by requiring among other things that they be "subject to requirements at least as stringent as those of the [EU] Regulation"[1] and that EU regulators are able to monitor the U.S. rating agencies' compliance with the EU Regulation. In effect, "systemically important" U.S. rating agencies are required to meet the stringent EU regulations or cease rating European companies. These requirements reach deep into the operations and governance of the rating agencies, ranging from the rotation of analyst assignments to the composition of their boards.

EU privacy laws are notoriously fickle, at least if you are sitting in an office in the United States. Perhaps reacting to historical totalitarian excesses, European privacy laws are fiercely protective of personal information and communications. The result is, frankly, to hinder the ability of most companies to enforce laws and internal policies: It is generally illegal for firms to monitor employee communications and Internet usage, the backbone of preventing insider trading among financial firms in the United States, or to pass personal information (home address, etc.) across borders without the consent of the person involved. This can be somewhat damaging to an investigation if, for example, the individual must be asked permission for the regulatory authority in one country to pass along information on that dodgy wire transfer to police officers in the United States. Financial firms that operate in multiple jurisdictions sometimes find themselves writing different procedures for their European subsidiaries, and as a result suffer from weaker controls in that region.

The impact of European regulation occurs not only in the cross-border reach of specific rules, but even in the very approach of the regulators to

---

[1] "Consultation Paper: Guidance on Registration Process, Functioning of Colleges, Mediation Protocol, Information Set Out in Annex II, Information Set for the Application for Certification and for the Assessment of CRAs of Systemic Performance," Committee of European Securities Regulators, October 21, 2009, at paragraph 64.

oversight of the market. For years, the battle lines were drawn across the English Channel, pitting the approach of the UK, which emphasized self-regulation by the market and the use of broad principles rather than detailed rules, versus the more stringent approach of the "Club Med" countries of France, Italy, and other southern European markets. The debate between "principles-based" and "rules-based" approaches began to seep into U.S. regulatory discussions in the middle of the last decade.

The idea behind a principles-based regime seems sound: Rather than try to write detailed rules to cover each aspect of every market, which may then be circumvented by sly market participants, the regulators would write principles that set forth the aims they are trying to achieve. This does not mean that regulations wouldn't be written, but rather that they would cut to the chase and say "Treat your customers fairly." Nor, in practice, did it mean that the FSA's principles-based Handbook of regulations was short and to the point: At 8,000 pages, the full Handbook would actually require *two* hands plus a wheelbarrow to carry (the book you are now reading would fit within the Glossary at the beginning of the FSA Handbook, with about 150 pages to spare).

For years, the United States and the UK took differing views of how to regulate. The U.S. system was based on detailed rules, supplemented by formal guidance from the regulators meant to interpret the rules as markets evolved. The advantage of this approach is enforceability: If the rule says that you must provide customers with a certain document with specific information within a certain timeframe, you either did so or did not. If you did not (or more precisely, if you cannot document that you did so), you have violated the rule. There is no room for debate as to whether you violated the rule. The UK, as noted earlier, took the principles-based approach and as such did not need to reassess and interpret rules as the market evolved at an ever-more-rapid pace.

Shortly before the onset of the financial crisis, the SEC began a shift toward principles-based regulation. Chairman Christopher Cox, among other officials, made it clear throughout 2007 and clear up until the end of his tenure in 2009 that he favored a move toward a principles-based regime along the lines of that used in the UK, particularly in such areas as accounting. The appointment of Mary Schapiro from the market's self-regulatory organization, the Financial Industry Regulatory Authority (FINRA), did not augur well for those seeking an about-face given her track record supporting regulation by principle and market discipline.[2] In the end, regulators on both sides of the Atlantic quickly drew back from singing the praises of principles-based approaches in the wake

---

[2] "Starting the Regulatory Work," *New York Times*, January 7, 2009.

of the financial crisis. Given the failures in oversight that featured so prominently in the collapse of the markets, indignant politicians and shame-faced regulators have been far more inclined to talk about nailing down rules than to extol principles. Still, the swing of the pendulum from rules to (almost) principles and back demonstrates that regulators in both the United States and Europe each pay attention to how the other approaches regulatory problems, and are likely to continue to do so.

INTERNATIONAL ORGANIZATIONS

International regulatory organizations do not cut a very impressive figure in the media since they are international (and therefore somewhat remote), regulatory (*yawn*), and organizations (i.e., bureaucracies). Still, they are worth keeping an eye on, since in some cases they set the mold for later legislation at the national level, and in others they are the place where national regulators get together to coordinate or negotiate global regulatory approaches to urgent problems.

The Group of 20 (G-20) is a forum for the finance ministers (Treasury Secretaries) and central bankers of 19 countries plus the European Union, ranging in size from the United States to Indonesia, which together represent 85 percent of the world's gross national product. The output of G-20 summits is high-level stuff, generally joint communiqués the bulk of which have already been scripted by functionaries before the summit began. But the summits are not all cocktail parties and press conferences; since they are attended by top financial leaders, the meetings and communiqués are significant in that the attending nations stake out their positions on economic and regulatory issues at these summits. The financial crisis has raised the urgency of coordinating financial regulations so that firms do not fly off to the jurisdiction with the weakest regulations, and to avoid foisting conflicting requirements on firms that operate in more than one country. The profile of the G-20 was raised substantially in the immediate aftermath of the crisis since it was the first place where the top leaders of the major (and a few minor) markets set forth their agreed reform priorities, such as reforming compensation, regulation of rating agencies, and accounting standards. Detail and implementation were left to the national regulators, and to other international organizations such as the Financial Stability Board (FSB).

The FSB is the forum where high-level principles and themes are fleshed out, and as such the FSB has a more direct impact on U.S. regulation than does the G-20 (its membership is slightly larger than the G-20, and includes other international organizations as well as finance and central bank representatives from member nations). In addition to proposing means by which the G-20 goals could be achieved and monitoring member nations' progress toward achieving G-20 goals, the FSB sets its own agenda with respect to problems to be addressed, studies and surveys to be conducted, and guidance to provide to member nations. Compliance with the FSB's guidelines is not mandatory, but most countries do not want to be seen to be against most of the commonsense measures, and failing to implement guidelines that they have endorsed via the FSB is fodder for the press. As such, the FSB's guidance frequently makes its way into U.S. markets, either directly through U.S. laws and regulations or indirectly through enactment in Europe or other important regions.

A sampling of recent publications from the FSB demonstrates its function in providing cross-border surveys of existing practices and practical guidelines for addressing the big issues:

- A peer review on compensation practices in the financial industry among member nations
- Guidance to assess the systemic importance of financial institutions, markets, and instruments
- Implementing guidance for achieving G-20 goals, including strengthened regulation of credit derivatives and of the structured finance market

Additionally, there are specific regulators for each of the major sectors of the financial industry: securities, banking, and insurance. The Basel Committee for Banking Supervision (BCBS) is probably the best known of these organizations, since it has given its name to the Basel and Basel 2 capital standards by which banks' financial soundness is judged (though in the United States, implementation of the Basel standards has been a bit à la carte). The International Organization of Securities Commissioners (IOSCO) has established a set of Objectives and Core Principles of Regulation for the securities commissions (including the SEC) that are members of the organization, as well as a number of voluntary codes that can serve as the framework for regulation at the national level (e.g., the U.S. Credit Rating Agency Reform Act of 2006, which was the first legislation in any major market to regulate the rating agencies, largely repeated the Code of Conduct Fundamentals for Credit Rating Agencies issued by IOSCO a year and a half earlier). Similarly, the International Association of Insurance Supervisors (IAIS) has issued a set of Insurance Core Principles as well as standards on such matters as licensing, on-site inspections, and disclosure of risks). Unlike the securities sector, however, there is no single regulator in the United States for the insurance sector (which is primarily regulated by the states), and so the implementation of IAIS standards in the United States is uneven. Of the three sectoral organizations, then, IOSCO has the most direct impact on financial consumers in the United States.

CONCLUSION

It would be easy both to understate and to overstate the degree to which overseas regulators and international organizations affect the regulatory arrangements of the U.S. financial system. In some cases, the impact is real and direct, for instance, EU privacy or rating agency regulations, while in other cases, it is indirect or incompletely felt (global insurance standards). In the end, knowing how regulation is being done overseas is not as immediately important as knowing what is going on in Congress or at the Fed, but it is a good way to understand other ways of approaching regulatory problems and of seeing new trends that may wash ashore in the months or years ahead.

CHAPTER FIFTEEN

Where Do We Go from Here? Conclusions, Observations, and Recommendations

THE REFORM OF THE financial markets has been underway for some time now. The shape of the new regulatory world is probably less radical than many had seen as inevitable or necessary back in 2008, when the desperate times seemed to be calling for desperate measures.

That doesn't mean that the show is over and we should all go home now. The work of reforming the markets is far from complete, and many issues remain. Moreover, the complex and rapidly changing nature of the market dictates that regulatory measures will need to be reviewed periodically by lawmakers and policymakers to make sure that we don't try to regulate new markets with old techniques.

Toward that end, this chapter sets forth regulatory approaches that build on the points made in the previous chapters. Some have already been raised in the course of the policy debate; some have not. Though they are, hopefully, founded on sound logic and valid conclusions about the state of the market, the reader should take his or own critical view to them—after all, doing so is the point of this book.

142

MODERN MARKETS ARE TOO COMPLEX TO REGULATE THEMSELVES

Markets in 2008 were too complex for anyone to see all the positions, exposures, and balances inside a single firm at any given time, let alone the entire system. It has gotten no better since then. The lack of transparency and the increasing interdependence resulting from this complexity mean that we can no longer rely on markets to regulate themselves—they're too complex for anyone to see and absorb all the relevant information. Recognizing this limitation is critical to effective financial reform.

A greater role for regulation is therefore necessary to bolster oversight of the markets and to help avoid future crises. We should no longer accept a situation in which entire markets are opaque or important sectors are un-regulated. And we should not assume that the next crisis will look like the last. To say that we should not regulate a particular sector or product simply because it wasn't a cause of the previous crisis misses the point and attempts to fight the last war instead of the next.

Complexity also means that regulation must include looking at risk to the system, not just to one or two firms—hence the need for a systemic risk regulator. Setting up an interagency council to monitor risk across the system gets two cheers. It won't be as strong a separate agency, since interagency councils run the risk of degenerating into routine meetings among officials who have other priorities. But half a loaf is better than nothing, and it would be foolhardy to have no coordinated systemic oversight simply on the grounds that the negotiated solution might not be perfect.

However we plan to address systemic risk, the point is that the growing complexity of the market has increased its inefficiencies and the market's ability to recognize them. Since regulation is meant to address these inefficiencies and protect the market, it is vital to recognize the need for regulation as a way to protect the market when it can't protect itself.

Of course, if the markets are so complex that they can't spontaneously regulate themselves, they're probably too complex for the regulators to be relied upon as well. But the increased protection afforded by active oversight provides a second line of defense. Recent history clearly demonstrates the need to increase regulatory oversight rather than rely on theoretically self-regulating market mechanisms.

Even with two lines of defense, we can never hope to have complete transparency of everything in the market, nor can we hope to efficiently analyze and process what information we do have. It would be reckless to base policy on the assumption that we can absolutely prevent any future crises either through transparency or by limiting the size and activities of financial institutions. That means we need to prepare for how we would handle the next crisis *now*, not the weekend that it happens.

PLANNING FOR THE NEXT CRISIS

Without a doubt, preventing a future crisis should be the top priority of policymakers. A great deal of discussion has taken place as to how this should be done. The Volcker Rule—keeping firms from getting too big or too risky—has some merit, though the practical difficulties in implementing such limits may severely weaken its effectiveness. But plans that discourage firms from becoming too big or too entrenched, such as those which impose a higher capital requirement for firms above a designated level or which engage in particularly risky activities should be given serious consideration. Policymakers would be derelict in their duty if they do not even attempt to prevent another crisis.

But it would be dangerously foolhardy to assume that there will be no future crisis, and policymakers would be equally derelict in their duty if they do not prepare a Plan B to react to a brewing crisis. The absence of a plan to address a pending meltdown will serve only to create the confusion and uncertainty that turns a crisis systemic. That is the key to Plan B—swift action to avoid the panic and uncertainty that naturally occurs when an important firm fails.

One of the main points of this book has been that the system was not brought to the brink by liquidity problems at any individual firm—it was laid low by fear and the rumors bred by the uncertainty of who was exposed to whom and by how much. It was the fear of the unknown that turned failing firms into pariahs overnight, and turned the system to financial rubble. Firms instinctively acting to protect themselves will rush to the exits unless they have some assurance that the failing firm will have the necessary capital to pay its debts and continue operations at least in the immediate future.

The question is how to prepare. Our instincts, ideology, and sense of justice may tell us that failing firms should be left to their own fate (and the worse that fate, the better). But the reality is that positive action by the government to provide interim support to the failing firm is the best, and perhaps the only, way to stem a lethal crisis of confidence and to keep the panic from going systemic. When cooler heads prevail, it can be decided whether to send the firm to the gallows, and how to do so in an orderly fashion.

As discussed at the beginning of this book, the support should not be a guarantee that those dealing with the failing firm will get every penny back. Firms holding securities of the failing bank should be forced to take a haircut, unlike the 100-cents-on-the-dollar deal that AIG's creditors got. Otherwise, failing firms' debt would have the implicit government backing of a no-lose bet, skewing the market for those and other securities. It might make sense for short-term securities such as repos to be exempted, if this were done strictly to avoid drying up the overnight funding for the firm.

Finally, and obviously, the firm that received government support would be required to pay back every penny, plus interest.

Among the proposals to provide interim support have been variations on the theme of establishing a resolution authority, funded with money by the banks most likely to put the system at risk. This has been opposed in some quarters because it presupposes that it would be used to bail out irresponsible banks permanently, offending our sense of justice and demonstrating that risky behavior carries no negative consequence. Such concerns are misguided. The establishment of a resolution authority need not presume that the bailout will be permanent—the money could be used to prevent systemic collapse in the near term and to keep the firm going while it is put through bankruptcy in the long term. Moreover, it takes money to keep a firm going while it is being wound down, and it is far better for that money to come from industry contributions than from the taxpayer.

Even if it is decided to save the institution instead of putting it in bankruptcy, we should not swallow whole the notion that doing so will encourage other institutions to act recklessly. As pointed out earlier in this book, killing off institutions aims at the wrong target: It is far better to impose sanctions on the individuals making the decisions than the corporate entity which served as the vehicle of their recklessness. People, not organizations, make decisions. If the senior managers are tempted to assume that their firm would be bailed out in case their risk taking goes south, let them be assured that if that happens they would be (1) fired, (2) barred from any senior executive role or board directorship in any publicly traded company or any firm, public or private, in the regulated financial industry, and (3) subject to federal civil sanctions (which could bankrupt them). The regulators should have some discretion in determining to whom the sanctions should apply (lest the threat of sanction keep qualified directors from coming in to help rescue a failing company), but the threat of sanction should be real.

Another source of debate has been how and when to fund the resolution authority. The argument against "pre-funding" the pool is that it penalizes all firms now for a crisis that may never happen. But the alternative (leaving the pool empty until it is needed) would mean passing the hat in the middle of a crisis, when other firms may be just as distressed (either because of their proximity to the failing bank, or because they are affected by the same external factors that are causing the other bank to fail). While it's true that pre-funding the pool will tie up millions of dollars of capital that the firms could use more properly, this cost would be a factor in deterring firms from becoming systemically important in the first place.

Thus, a resolution authority should be established with a range of options which include saving the firm permanently, breaking it up into smaller firms or putting it into bankruptcy in an orderly fashion. Two critical measures must be included in the resolution authorities arsenal: the power to dismiss senior managers and board directors of the company, and the authority and resources to provide immediate interim support to the failing firm in order to keep short-term financing of the firm from disappearing.

The thorny question remains as to which institutions should be eligible for this kind of emergency assistance. The simple, but not particularly helpful, answer is that a list cannot be drawn up in advance. If it really were all about too big to fail, perhaps it would be easy to draw some arbitrary line above which firms are too big to fail (a bad idea). But as this book has argued, it is really about interconnectedness, exposure to particular instruments or markets, and other factors that make the firm systemically important. One of the primary roles of the systemic risk regulator therefore must be identifying which firms are reaching the stage where their failure could threaten the rest of the industry. If and when the firm begins to fail, policymakers will already have an idea whether the firm in question is systemically important and why. The regulators could then move swiftly to assure the market that the government support program is a possibility if the situation further deteriorates.

THE NEED FOR A PROFESSIONALIZED REGULATORY SERVICE

No matter how regulation is improved and markets are reformed, everything depends on the quality of the monitoring, of the enforcement, and of the decision making of the regulators. The entire regulatory structure is built on the assumption that the regulators will do their jobs and do them well, once provided with the information and authority to do so. When you consider the nature of the reforms that have been proposed or enacted, they all assume the

The Need for a Professionalized Regulatory Service ■ **147**

presence of competent regulatory authorities. If the staff at a regulatory agency is inexperienced, poorly trained, or fails to communicate well, all the reform will go for nothing. Increased transparency will merely lead to piles of information rather than a clear picture of the market, and tougher rules will go unenforced or will be enforced in an incoherent manner. The regulation of the market rests on an effective, experienced, professional regulatory service.

Yet in reality the agencies suffer from high turnover and poorly trained staff, at least by financial industry standards. Prior to the Madoff scandal and the subsequent internal investigations by the SEC's Office of the Inspector General (OIG), there was little training done and even now the training is rudimentary.

One weakness is the lack of diversity in the backgrounds of those conducting the agency's work. While legal training is useful in some respects to investigative and examiner roles, a more diverse range of skills, especially those related to the financial markets, would provide the SEC with a more capable staff (no federal law enforcement agency requires a law degree for its agents, and indeed the FBI actively seeks a diversity of educational backgrounds and experience). Moreover, once an attorney has worked at the SEC, and perhaps received an advanced Master of Laws degree at government expense, she is able to leverage even a few years of experience into a princely salary at a Wall Street law firm. This makes the issue of training a bit moot, since training staff with such a high turnover is like pouring water into a bucket riddled with holes.

Certainly a legal background is useful in regulatory work. Legal training implies an ability to think analytically, to view problems from multiple points of view, and to argue those points in a cogent fashion. But a legal background, especially when it is limited to academic training, is not the only background that engenders these qualities. To place a slavish emphasis on a particular background is not a mere exercise in academic elitism; when the safety of the nation's markets is at stake, it is reckless. Other agencies learned long ago the value of recruiting from a more diversified pool of experience, and have not suffered the high turnover or embarrassing failures that led the SEC to its recent changes.

The result has been a workforce that is narrowly based and narrowly trained, in which many do not know the market and therefore are not in a position to dispute misrepresentations, and with a low average level of experience. It's no surprise that Bernie Madoff was able to intimidate so many examiners with bluster and jargon, and a Ponzi scheme big enough to be in the Fortune 500 went undetected for years.

There are, of course, those who do stay in the organization, gain valuable experience, and seek training to make themselves more effective. But in the end the existing arrangements have not worked and have placed our financial system at risk. It is difficult to argue against massive change in the face of massive failure.

The staffing reforms being implemented by the SEC are a good idea, but they are short-term fixes. Conducting additional training and hiring a few non-lawyers are clearly steps in the right direction, but they are not enough. If the staffing issues merely required fine-tuning, then tinkering around the edges would be sufficient.

Similarly, changes to the structure of the SEC may be useful but they do not address the fundamental problem of building a stable and effective professional staff. Changes to the organization chart may create or move around positions, but if those positions are frequently vacated, the organizational changes are largely meaningless.

Perhaps the greatest problem is retention. Unless the regulators can stop the rush to the exits among their staff, more training will just mean better trained ex-staffers representing defendants, and creating new divisions will only move vacancies around on the organization chart.

The situation demands a more fundamental change, and not just within the SEC. A stable, experienced, well-trained regulatory service is necessary across all financial regulatory agencies in order to make the new regulatory structure more than a fig leaf.

CREATING A FEDERAL REGULATORY SERVICE

Put simply, the federal financial regulatory system should be professionalized. As in other critical agencies and functions at the federal level, specialized and organized training, defined career progression paths, and special compensation and pension arrangements should be adopted to attract and retain a professional core of regulatory professionals. The best parallel is the Foreign Service. Though Foreign Service Officers (FSOs) may serve in a number of different agencies, all are required to meet common professional requirements. The Foreign Service Institute provides residential training throughout the FSO's career, as well as distance-learning courses, and FSOs are paid on a different scale from other government workers.

To be more specific, a program should be considered that includes the following:

1. A separate career designation be provided for financial regulatory staff in relevant agencies, modeled on the Foreign Service (i.e., a Financial Regulation Service). Like the Foreign Service, the designation would apply

across regulatory agencies and so would involve professional staff in such agencies as the SEC, the CFTC, the consolidated banking regulator (which replaces the Office of Thrift Supervision and the Office of the Comptroller of the Currency), the FDIC, and possibly parts of the Federal Reserve.

2. Application for selection as an officer in this service should be competitive, with specified entry routes similar to those used by the FBI, for instance: 25 percent of each year's intake to be lawyers, 25 percent of intake to be accountants and risk management professionals, and 50 percent to be "diversified," which would require a bachelor's degree plus three or more years of relevant industry experience. A special emphasis within the latter category should be placed on recruiting former professionals from regulated industries and seasoned investigators from law enforcement agencies.

3. A Financial Regulation Service Institute should be established to provide initial training to new officers. The curriculum should be developed and taught with the assistance of industry professionals. The training should be thorough enough to provide a good grounding, but should recognize that it provides only a foundation for experience in the field. Routine rotations back to the Institute should be made for advanced training, management assessment and training, updates on new products and services, and other continuing education.

   The Institute should also offer a program for a small group of state-level regulators in the same way that the FBI Academy has offered the National Academy program for state and local law enforcement officials. In doing so, the Institute would help foster coordination among agencies through common training and through the establishment of professional relationships among attendees.

4. Financial Regulation Service officers should be on a separate pay scale similar to the Foreign Service pay schedule in order to be competitive with outside employment.

5. Full or partial retirement should be available after 20 years of service. While this benefit is normally reserved for law enforcement and military personnel, it would be an important factor in retaining experienced staff. Midcareer professionals are particularly vulnerable to recruitment away from regulatory agencies. The knowledge that leaving would mean forfeiting a pension to which they would be entitled in a few years' time would be a strong motivation to stay, at least until they were eligible for the pension.

This proposal is not as radical as it sounds. In addition to military and law enforcement personnel and foreign service officers, professionalized corps within the National Health Service and the National Oceanographic and

150 ■ Where Do We Go from Here?

Atmospheric Administration also have the benefit of early retirement. If we believe the staff of these agencies are important enough to receive this benefit, certainly it is also worth doing for the guardians of our financial health in order to keep them in government service.

Creation of a federal regulatory service along the lines just described would increase the stability of the organization and the average experience of those conducting oversight, examination, and investigative functions. It would increase communication within and among organizations by establishing professional relationships among regulators, as occurs among graduates of the FBI Academy and the Foreign Service Institute. It would ensure adequate training based on current market trends and products, both for entry-level regulators and for mid- and senior-level ones. And it would mean that training stays with the regulators and does not merely benefit the firms that will hire staff away after a few years.

By managing the career progression and development of this stable pool of rising professionals, regulatory agencies would also be able to identify future needs and plan for them through focused recruitment and career development rather than plug gaps as they occur.

It would not come cheaply. But the net increase in cost would address critical problems in the very organizations on which all reform depends. The change simply needs to be done, and it needs to be done now so that the benefits of professionalizing financial regulation have the opportunity to take effect. The government has written some pretty large checks over the past three years as a result of the crisis, and by comparison this money would be far better spent on a professionalized regulatory service.

The arrangement should also be supported by the industry. First, it would improve the quality and consistency of regulation in all agencies with responsibility for financial regulation. Second, although the program aims to reduce turnover, those professionals who do leave, or who leave after 20 years of service, will be better trained and more professional. This would create a much better pool of talent from which to recruit than the current pool.

Virtually every legislator, policymaker, pundit, and journalist who has commented on the causes of the crisis has pointed to failures of the regulators as major contributors to the financial crisis. If we don't improve the quality of these agencies, we will suffer the same consequences again: multibillion-dollar Ponzi schemes operating unfettered for decades, disastrous risk-taking within firms, and systemic risk sitting like a time bomb in the midst of the financial system. Moreover, the reforms that have been proposed or enacted place even more emphasis on the regulators by making information transparent on the assumption that regulators will have the knowledge and experience necessary to understand and assess the information. Without a cadre of well-trained core regulatory professionals, the regulatory agencies on which so much depends will continue to be sheep in wolves' clothing.

 ELEVATING THE COMPLIANCE PROFESSION

What of the other side of the coin—the compliance officers (including risk management professionals) inside the regulated firms? Starting largely as a function of firms' legal departments, compliance has been growing as a separate profession since at least the 1990s. Although in some firms the compliance department remains subsumed within the legal department, more and more firms are making the chief compliance officer a direct report to the CEO. Specialized qualifications have been developed such as FINRA's Certified Regulatory and Compliance Professional and the Society of Corporate Compliance and Ethics' Certified Compliance and Ethics Professional (though the latter is not specific to the financial services industry), and some universities either offer a graduate degree in financial compliance or incorporate compliance and regulatory courses into their business and law curricula. Specialties have developed within the compliance field, so that professionals concentrate in areas such as anti–money laundering, compliance policy and procedures development, and compliance IT systems, in addition to specializing in particular sectors such as equities, options and derivatives, fixed income, and investment advisory and fund management. An entire industry has developed to support the technological and information needs of compliance departments.

Though all of these developments imply that compliance is maturing as a separate profession, its place within a firm is a trickier proposition. Compliance is not a profit center within a firm, and in the financial industry the profit center has been king (at least before the financial crisis). Compliance is, in effect, a control function similar to the internal audit or ombudsman/inspector general function. For this reason, it must have the same level of independence and authority that other control functions enjoy. The compliance function should report directly to the chief executive officer, if not to the Board of Directors itself. There are two reasons for this: First, the compliance officer will occasionally need to put the brakes on initiatives that could be lucrative to the firm but that may, for instance, create unacceptable conflicts of interest. When the chief compliance officer walks into the meeting to say *no* to the initiative, he or she needs to have equal standing and authority with the business line managers.

Otherwise, the CCO walks into a gunfight armed with a knife. The second reason is that the chief compliance officer should have regular, direct access to the chief executive officer to provide unfiltered and candid assessments of the state of compliance in the organization. Even reporting through the legal department can prove problematic if the General Counsel places more focus on avoiding litigation (avoid documentation) than on regulatory compliance (document everything).

Regulators and legislators have shown signs of recognizing the importance of ensuring that compliance departments have sufficient independence and authority. Proposed legislation has included requirements for chief compliance officers to report directly to the Board of Directors in firms such as credit rating agencies and derivatives clearing organizations; the self-regulatory organization FINRA has developed the certification program for compliance officers mentioned earlier, and FINRA regulations for securities broker dealer firms require both the designation of a chief compliance officer and that the chief executive officer certify each year, after consulting with the chief compliance officer, that the firm has effective internal controls in place.

As discussed in Chapter 12, the compliance function is effectively the first line of defense in regulation, acting along with other risk and control functions to avoid the kinds of excesses that contributed to the financial crisis. Given its role in carrying regulation through the "last ten yards" into the firm, its position should be elevated in order to ensure its independence and its authority. Toward that end, regulations should be amended to specifically require that the chief compliance officer report directly to the chief executive officer or to the Board of Directors. Initiatives already underway to develop a licensing procedure for chief compliance officers should be finalized and be made mandatory as well, along with continuing education requirements similar to those in other professions.

DECISIONS ARE MADE BY INDIVIDUALS, NOT ORGANIZATIONS

Too much of the debate on regulatory reform has focused on the actions taken by organizations. If they wish to prevent reckless behavior, policymakers should focus on the incentives placed on the individuals who actually make the decisions that lead to increased risk. People make decisions based on what they see as their own interest, rarely that of the organization. Even when it appears that they are acting to benefit the organization, they do so because it is in their interest, for example, because they own shares or because increased revenues mean a bigger bonus pool. For this reason, there should be a regulatory focus on incentives.

When people are making seven-, eight-, and nine-figure salaries in the midst of an economic meltdown, it offends our sense of justice. But capping salaries is not going to prevent another crisis, and is really appropriate only in TARP-funded firms. Time and effort are better spent addressing the way in which pay is structured in firms, at least among those who have it in their power to put the firm (and the economy) at risk. This will not be easy, but the goal should be to align as well as possible the risk horizon with the payout horizon. Clawbacks and other "malus" provisions are also likely to be helpful.

But if the goal of reforming compensation is to remove incentives to take risk, then the regulatory approach ought to go straight to the heart of the problem and address the performance goals on which a person's incentive compensation is based. Control functions within firms should have the authority to review the performance goals for analysts, traders, managers, and others, and to identify those goals that create an incentive to take excessive risk. As a practical matter, it is neither possible nor desirable to prohibit goals that encourage risk taking, but identifying those employees whose goals encourage risk enables management and control functions to monitor their activities more closely. In reviewing performance goals, the control functions should also seek and prohibit any goals that create a conflict of interest.

Review of the controls placed on performance goals should also be a standard part of regulatory examinations.

As mentioned in Chapter 6 on compensation, there will always be an incentive to take risk because people are ambitious. But taking reasonable precautions regarding how people are paid, and what they have to do to earn their pay, will be a good step in the right direction. Crises start with excessive risk and excessive risk starts with someone deciding it is in his or her interest to roll the dice. Maintaining some level of vigilance over incentives is thus the first line of defense in preventing crises.

KEEP THE RATING AGENCIES—BUT ON A SHORT LEASH

Bashing the ratings industry is all good sport, but most of the work they do in the markets is accurate and praiseworthy. Even the rating agencies admit now that they got it wrong on structured finance ratings, and the reemergence of structured finance instruments is a profoundly worrying development. But not all rating agencies were equally culpable in the structured finance sector, and their work on more pedestrian products like boring old corporate bonds has been reasonably accurate.

More to the point, we really don't have much of an alternative to them. Fixing the issuer-pays model may prove useful, particularly with respect to the publicly traded agencies. Removing the First Amendment fig leaf that protects them from investor lawsuits is also a good idea and would allow the Founding Fathers to stop spinning in their graves like lathes.

Removing reference to NRSRO status is not a good idea unless there is some other regulatory hook by which to keep the agencies on a short leash. Otherwise they will de-register and no longer be subject to regulation, and at any rate the big agencies would not lose much market share. If we're going to cut off our nose, we might as well at least spite our face.

PUT DOWN THE PITCHFORKS

There's no way around it: Some people got very rich taking bigger and bigger risks in order to make more and more money, and when it all went south they were able to walk away. The price was paid by others who had no connection to the markets but have lost jobs and homes, and have had their personal finances ruined and their families put under enormous strain. It offends our sense of justice, and rightly so.

But our wounded sense of justice should not drive our policy decisions. Fixing the markets and preventing future meltdowns requires a more dispassionate view of what went wrong. Yes, there are specific individuals whose greed and arrogance drove them to make decisions the rest of us have to pay for. Financial regulation should look at what incentives drove them to take these risks and what controls can prevent people like them from causing future catastrophes. Should they be punished? You bet. But that's what the courts are for.

Moreover, changes to the regulations should not be driven by political calculation. Of course, telling politicians not to court votes is a bit like telling them not to scratch an itch, but good regulation should be based on what works, not on a collective case of populist road rage.

CONCLUSION

As financial reform proposals have worked their way through the political process and a very public debate, they have been subjected to a number of forces which have nothing to do with their effectiveness—political bargaining and populist anger chief among these. It's important to view the reforms from a practical point of view—what will work, not what fits our particular view of the world as it should be. That means that we should plan to avoid crises, but be prepared for when crises occur in spite of our best efforts. It means there should be a regulatory profession staffing the agencies we assume will put reform into effect. And it means we may sometimes need to hold our nose and come to the rescue of those we would rather watch implode or put up with sectors we need more than admire. Doing these things doesn't mean we have abandoned our ideals. It means we are regulating markets as they are, not as we wish they were.

CHAPTER SIXTEEN

Judging for Yourself

THIS BOOK'S GOAL IS to explore the concepts and problems surrounding financial regulation, particularly in the context of ongoing efforts to correct problems that caused or contributed to the financial crisis. It is meant to provide a guide to those who understand the impact of financial regulation on their own economic wellbeing and wish to come to their own conclusions regarding regulatory reform. Its discussions aim to assist in understanding most of the issues that surround regulation, but it would also be helpful to provide a general view of how people might judge proposals for themselves.

Evaluating a regulation is not a straightforward calculation, as Chapter 13 on cost-benefit analysis contends. There must be some room for judgment, and two people may look at the same factors and come up with completely different views. But it is still worthwhile to have a framework for attacking the question of whether a given regulation is worth your support. Here are seven questions that should help frame such an analysis.

Is the goal of the regulation worthwhile?

The first question is the most important, the most obvious, and probably the most difficult to answer. But if you do not believe that the goal is worthwhile in

156

the first place, there isn't much point in going further. For example, if you do not believe that insider trading should be illegal because you believe it is simply part of an efficient market, you will not support regulations to prevent the practice no matter how effective they are in doing so. However, you may view excessive risk as having been a key factor in the collapse of the markets in the past decade, and so you would support measures that discourage excessive risk taking so long as you believe them to be effective.

Is the regulation likely to attain that goal?

The next question is where much of the debate lies: Will the proposal actually work? Depending on the nature of the issue being addressed, the answer may be complicated and based on best guesses. For this reason, it is useful to see the arguments presented in support of, or opposition to, the measure—from journalists, from the industry, from consumer groups, from academics, and from politicians. That does not mean the arguments should be swallowed whole, since these arguments will by their nature be biased. But choosing a few relevant industry and consumer groups and following their positions on the issue and reading (or viewing) testimony in relevant congressional hearings will help to obtain a balanced view.

Whatever else is said regarding the effectiveness of the proposal, remember also to factor in human behavior and self-interest. Ask whether the incentives provided by the measure are the right ones and whether there are any incentives already in place (including greed) that might influence a decision maker to ignore the proposed regulation. Market theory goes only so far in predicting behavior in the markets.

Are there any unintended consequences?

Once you have considered the intended consequences, it's time to think about the unintended ones. As is the case with judging whether a proposal will do what it set out to do, the public comments of market participants are likely to prove helpful in finding unintended consequences since it is they who are closest to the market. If their analysis is misleading, someone else is likely to say so. Be particularly wary of arguments that assert that a proposal will drive a particular segment of the industry offshore (such as regulating hedge funds or capping pay). Although this has happened on very rare occasions, it is not likely that an entire industry would fold up its tents and head en masse to Macau simply to be in the most permissive regulatory environment.

158 ■ Judging for Yourself

Are there other ways to achieve the same aim?

As mentioned elsewhere in this book, the cost-benefit analysis process is probably more valuable as a means of identifying alternative approaches than as a balance sheet to determine the financial wisdom of a regulatory proposal. This leads to a point that should be obvious but is often overlooked, and that is the importance of considering whether there are other approaches that might be more effective, or simpler, or cheaper. Some alternatives will be raised in the course of congressional hearings, public consultations, and the government's cost-benefit analysis, but it is also worth taking a step back and asking some general questions for yourself. If the regulation is based on formal requirements—such as breaking up banks that get "too big"—would the same aim be better achieved using market incentives instead (requiring higher capital reserves for big banks, thus making it cheaper to stay small)? Would transparency be sufficient, since market forces would then come to bear? Is no regulation at all a viable alternative, as was decided with respect to proposed transparency requirements for credit derivatives in the 1990s?

What exemptions exist? Do they make sense?

In the next step, it's time to get cynical. The final version of the legislation or its implementing regulations is likely to have exemptions that identify certain types of firm or activity to which the requirements will not apply. These exemptions may apply to firms based on size (e.g., hedge funds with assets under management of $100 million are exempt from certain federal registration requirements), the type of customer (firms that deal only with institutions are generally exempted from customer protection rules designed to protect retail customers), or activity (securities firms are exempted from the rules of the Consumer Financial Protection Agency). These exemptions are often wise or even necessary from a practical point of view, but they could also be the result of successful arm-twisting by the firm or industry in question. The question to ask yourself is whether the exemption makes sense (there is no need to apply retail investor protection rules to firms with no retail customers) and whether it will create a gap in supervision (exempting securities firms from the rules of the Consumer Financial Protection Agency does not, since they are already covered by similar rules from the SEC). Rule proposals circulated by the relevant regulator are a good source for identifying all of the exemptions and the reasons for them, since they are discussed in detail as part of the proposal process.

If the rule contains transparency provisions, does it have the right level?

As discussed in Chapter 8, the term *transparency* is frustratingly ambiguous in its use among policymakers. Where a rule aims to provide transparency, it is worth considering the level of transparency that is actually achieved. If the goal is to enable the public to see and understand a particular piece of information, true transparency requires that the information be in more-or-less plain language and that it be easily accessible if not actually prominent (not on page 218 of a prospectus or four levels down in a website for which you must register to gain access). If the information is necessary in order for market discipline to function but is not necessary for the general public (e.g., certain financial information required in the annual statements of publicly traded companies), the information should be disclosed but need not be put in the language of the nonprofessional. If the information is necessary for the market but cannot be identified with specific firms without putting them at a disadvantage in the market (for example, short interest information or credit derivatives trading volume), it is sufficient for the information to be published in aggregate. Finally, if the information is necessary in order for regulators to perform their oversight function but is commercially sensitive and not needed for market purposes (such as information on amount of leverage at a firm), the information need only be disclosed to them.

The level of transparency provided in a regulation may be the result of compromise rather than effectiveness; it would be inadvisable to assume the level of transparency is the one in the best interest of the market and public (in retrospect, few would argue now that it was a good idea to provide no transparency at all to the credit default swap market, even though it was considered and proposed by the Commodities Futures Trading Commission).

It is also worth saying that transparency may not be the best solution for a conflict of interest. In theory, disclosing a conflict allows the market and investors to judge whether they wish to do business with the conflicted firm, but it does not make that conflict go away. Any time you see "disclosure" as the principal remedy to a conflict of interest, it is worth wondering whether that was the best solution or the one that was politically achievable.

Is the right agency responsible?

If you have made it through the first six questions and are still in favor of the regulation, you should still think about how it will be implemented. One of the factors that may impact implementation is which agency is responsible for it. The issue of who should do what in the regulatory world was one of the more contentious in the course of the reform debate, with senior officials defending their turf like mother grizzlies. It does in fact require some explanation why, for instance, the Federal Reserve would have customer protection responsibilities, or why the NASD could both own and regulate the NASDAQ stock market until it was forced to divest.

Addressing this question can be done from at least three angles. The first is one of resource and expertise. Some firms are best positioned and their staff best trained to look at "prudential" issues, meaning questions of the financial soundness of firms. Others are better placed to handle customer protection issues, with a higher proportion of investigators and attorneys and fewer accountants and financial examiners than the prudential regulators. When it comes to systemic oversight, the regulator's span of control is important, so that it can see as many of the moving parts in the system as possible.

The second angle is state-versus-federal supervision. In many cases, it makes sense for regulation to be done at the most local level because the firms involved are small and focused on the needs of their particular communities—this is the fundamental rationale for the "dual banking system" in the United States, with some banks chartered at the state level and some at the federal level (consequently, the regulation of banks occurs at the state and federal levels). There is also little need for the federal government to be involved in the regulation of a firm that does all of its business within one state, and these intrastate firms are commonly exempted from federal regulation. This also frees up resources of the perpetually strapped regulatory agencies. While the SEC is not likely to have the time to pay much attention to the goings-on at a two-person investment adviser in Truth or Consequences, New Mexico between trips to Goldman Sachs and Morgan Stanley, the state regulator in New Mexico likely will.

The third angle is government regulation versus self-regulation. The delegation of authority and work from federal regulators to the industry, especially in the securities industry, is well established and has generally been successful. Self-regulatory organizations are reasonably well funded and able to pay something close to the market rate and benefit from the expertise that derives from their proximity to their member firms. In other cases, though, effective oversight and enforcement requires the government's authority and clear independence from the regulated firms.

CONCLUSION

The reform of the financial system will affect everyone in a very direct way. Credit cards, mortgages, bank accounts, insurance, the safety of our pensions and investments are all potential targets of regulation that will change things for good or for bad. Each person should come to his or her own conclusions rather than swallow whole the arguments made by those involved in the process—including my own. By asking the right questions, readers can set about coming to their own conclusions regarding the proposals.

Appendix 1: Summaries of Regulatory Concepts and Issues

BELIEVE IT OR NOT, people have for decades been devoting good chunks of their careers to thinking about financial regulation. I am not making that up (I'm one of them). As a result, the discipline has developed its own lexicon, and debate has settled around specific conceptual issues—conceptual, that is, until the financial crisis made them very real and pressing.

It has been said that academic fights are more vicious than those in the real world because the stakes are so low. By the time the financial crisis reached its peak, the debate on these academic issues had moved into the real world and the stakes were no longer so low. This book has aimed to discuss many of the critical issues in practical terms and some detail, but for an informed view of the debate it is also appropriate to have at least a nodding acquaintance with some of the conceptual issues around which reform has at least implicitly revolved. This appendix will give a brief description of some of the terms and concepts. In some cases, as with *systemic risk*, there is an extensive and hopefully practical discussion elsewhere in this book. In other cases, the basics are laid out here and readers who wish to delve deeper are encouraged to pursue that interest through the wealth of material available elsewhere.

 MORAL HAZARD, TOO BIG TO FAIL, SYSTEMIC RISK

The financial markets have never been level playing fields, and there have always been some giants that dominate their sectors. At the same time, markets are intended to be ruthlessly Darwinian places, where the strong

164 ■ Appendix 1

feed on the weak and where the slow and sickly in the herd meet a quick and inglorious demise. So it was not long before the question arose as to what to do if a failing firm is so big and so central to the rest of the system that its collapse could take the rest of the system with it. This was a question of two parts: first, whether it is possible for a firm to become so big that its failure would cause irreversible destruction to the system, and second, what to do when such a firm teeters on the brink of collapse.

This has not always been an entirely academic parlor game, since large firms have felt the icy hand of death on their shoulders before—Barings and Long Term Capital Management, among others. But the crisis thrust the question into the real world, and questions of ideology and principle gave way to expediency and practicality. That is not necessarily a bad thing; it simply reflected the fact that big decisions needed to be made immediately if not sooner.

As discussed in greater detail in Chapter 2, the notion of a firm being too big to fail is really shorthand for a firm being too *interconnected* to fail. In a complex system like the modern financial market, failure spreads like a virus rather than a series of dominoes precisely because the failing institution is connected to a vast array of other institutions, each of which is itself equally embedded in the system. And this is the link to the concept of *systemic risk*, the idea that some events can trigger a collapse of the entire system (usually, but not always, the collapse of one or two large institutions). The question for policymakers when a big firm is in danger is whether its collapse would trigger a systemic collapse, and if so, what to do about it.

The simple answer might well be to intervene on behalf of the failing firm just in case. There are, of course, strong arguments against this approach, and in their purest form they argue against saving any institution in any circumstance. One argument, of course, is that it is not fair to bail out a big firm when the other firms have acted more prudently—especially if it is those firms, or the taxpayer, that must foot the bill for the rescue. But, as is argued elsewhere in this book, justice and revenge are not the most pressing concerns of regulators facing a systemic crisis and these tasks are better taken up by others. The other argument against a bailout, though, holds that such a rescue is bad policy in the long run because it guts the very notion of market discipline. If firms know that the government will bail them out if their bets all go wrong, there will be no restraint in the market. Better to let the failing firm go down; this is the core of the theory of *moral hazard*.

Moral hazard theory holds that when the government steps in to bail out a firm, and particularly a financial services institution, that firm and all other firms absorb a lesson that firms that are deemed too big to fail will always be bailed out. Knowing that they are now working with a safety net, the theory goes, they will take more risks than they normally would, and even inordinate risks.

Whereas systemic risk has moved from theory to painful reality, moral hazard is still largely a theory. No firm is likely ever to acknowledge that it is taking on additional risk because of its assumption that the government will bail it out. As Chapter 3 on moral hazard discusses, it is debatable whether the individuals who make strategic risk decisions would ever do so anyway—in which case the whole concept of moral hazard is undermined. A more likely manifestation of moral hazard is the assumption by *others* that a firm would be bailed out, which would imply that the market would accept a lower interest rate from its debt and the rating agencies might award the firm a higher credit rating. The upshot is that the government safety net would give an unfair advantage in the marketplace to firms that are formally designated or implicitly assumed to be too big to fail.

The distortion of the market implied by moral hazard is part of a broader issue that appears frequently in regulatory debates, and that is the matter of keeping a "level playing field."

UNLEVEL PLAYING FIELDS

Just as it is not fair to play football on a field where one team goes downhill and one uphill, the notion that the structure of the market created by market regulation would place some at an inherent advantage over others is a constant concern. The idea is that financial services firms engaging in the same or similar activities should be subject to the same regulations.

This argument has been used both in support of new regulation and to oppose it. It supports new regulation when the market itself has distorted the fairness of competition. For example, the creation of a new Consumer Financial Protection Agency, described in Chapter 7 on consumer protection, aimed among other things to extend regulation to non-bank lenders that previously had not been subject to regulation. In the absence of regulation, they had fewer restrictions on their activities and lower overall costs, putting them at an unfair advantage over banks (at least according to the banks).

The unlevel-playing-field argument may also be used to support revising existing regulations when they appear to be applied capriciously or to favor one set of firms over another. An example would be the revision of the "best execution" rule in the UK. Best execution is the rule that aims to ensure that brokers who execute a trade for their clients do so at the best terms (usually, the best available price); well into the early years of this century the official regulatory definition of *best execution* was to execute on the London Stock Exchange, regardless of whether better prices were available on other venues. This regulation made it virtually impossible for competing startup exchanges to gain momentum, and the reform of best execution regulation—the leveling of the playing field—is one of the factors that led to the explosion in the number of alternative execution venues in the past ten years.

Finally, the unlevel-playing-field argument is sometimes used to oppose new regulations, and you are likely to see it in one form or another in discussions concerning regulatory reform over the course of the next few years. Proposed regulations that distinguish between large and small firms or between types of traded instruments will inherently create a greater burden on some firms and thus potentially put them at a disadvantage in the market (e.g., the proposals to cap salaries at certain large investment firms put them at a disadvantage in recruiting and retaining experienced staff).

One point worth making is that some argue that markets are not naturally level in the first place, so regulatory efforts to change the contours are not necessarily as bad as one thinks. This argument is based on the assumption that markets in the real world have their own inherent distortions and so regulation that favors one group of firms over another may be aiming to "undistort" the market.

The idea that regulations might distort the markets is itself a manifestation of the concern that regulations could impact the market in ways no one had anticipated. This notion is more commonly known as the *unintended consequences*.

UNINTENDED CONSEQUENCES

The fact that things sometimes go differently than planned is hardly a fresh new idea, and it is of course not unique to the financial markets. The formal expression of the phenomenon is attributed to the field of sociology and specifically to Robert Merton, the man who also gave us such catchy terms as *self-fulfilling prophecy* and *role model* (a term with less application to the financial services industry in recent years).

A formal exposition of sociological theory is best left for sociologists, but suffice it to say that systems as complex as regulated financial markets are more prone to unintended consequences than less complex environments. This is largely because it is simply too difficult to anticipate the cause-and-effect relationships in a system with so many interactions. So, it would have taken keen insight or a time machine to anticipate that efforts to increase home-ownership by creating alternative standards for mortgages would result down the line in a near-collapse of the world economy (though some did predict something similar). Additionally, the market tends to adjust as individuals take their business elsewhere or create new products to get around recent restrictions. For example, restrictions on short sales (a way to bet on the downward movement of a stock's price) would result in higher volumes of derivatives trades rather than less speculation in the market.

Unintended consequences can arise from a number of different sources, but the two most important are ignorance and error. The distinction is important in developing financial regulation because it implies two different ways of attempting to prevent unintended consequences, though it is likely that both ways are used. Those arising from ignorance, on one hand, are fundamentally caused by a lack of visibility into the sector of the market addressed by the regulation. If you do not know the size or distribution of the credit default swap market, you fail to see that AIG is dangerously exposed to bond defaults and that AIG's collapse would itself cause widespread harm across the industry. Error, on the other hand, derives primarily from a misunderstanding of how the market is likely to react to a given proposal. This sounds rather condescending toward policymakers, but the markets are complex things and prone to human behavior as much as to textbook cause-and-effect relationships. The fear of error in this regard is one of the primary reasons why regulators propose rules before they implement them, reviewing comments from all interested parties but in particular those from the industry itself. Of course, the trick then is to distinguish the valid concerns and arguments from the spin (a distinction that sometimes is lost even by those presenting the argument).

One final point should be made about unintended consequences, and that is that they sometimes are not all that unintended. Simply because a regulation has additional, or derivative, effects on the market beyond those clearly stated does not mean that they were unanticipated. Particularly in the highly political environment in which reform has taken place, crowd-pleasing effects such as lowering profits for particular firms may be more of an *unspoken* consequence than an unintended one.

In seeking comments from the industry in order to avoid unintended consequences to proposed regulations, policymakers tacitly acknowledge that some people are better placed than others because they have a closer seat to the action. This idea carries forward into the very structure of regulation, through the establishment of self-regulatory organizations.

 SELF-REGULATION

Self-regulation in the financial services industry is largely embodied in the Financial Industry Regulatory Authority (FINRA), formed in 2007 by the merger of two earlier self-regulatory organizations (SROs), the National Association of Securities Dealers (NASD) and the regulatory arm of the New York Stock Exchange (NYSE). FINRA is not a government organization, but many of the regulatory oversight functions established by law are delegated to it. FINRA establishes most of the rules for the day-to-day activities of broker-dealer firms and certain other parts of the industry. It performs sophisticated surveillance of trading on the NASDAQ stock market, the NYSE, the American Stock Exchange, and the International Stock Exchange (under contract to those markets) as well as over-the-counter trading in equities (trading in shares not listed on an exchange). Importantly, virtually any firm that wishes to do business as a securities broker or dealer in the United States must register with FINRA and consequently must abide by its rules and submit information on its financial soundness on a periodic basis. These firms are also subject to examination by FINRA examiners in much the same way as the SEC examines firms, except that FINRA is the first line of defense and inspects all firms. Additionally, the brokers, managers, and other key staff at a FINRA-registered firm must be licensed by FINRA, which means passing the relevant exams, having a clean criminal record, and meeting continuing education requirements. Like their firms, individuals are subject to disciplinary actions by FINRA and these disciplinary actions are available on the FINRA website for all, and particularly for potential clients, to see.

FINRA itself is subject to SEC oversight, both through routine examination and through the rulemaking process, whereby FINRA rules and significant rule changes must be proposed publicly first through the SEC. This oversight is neither pro forma nor toothless; in 1996, an SEC investigation into the activities of firms on the NASDAQ market, which at time was both owned and regulated by FINRA's predecessor the NASD, found that the NASD had not been sufficiently vigorous in its oversight of the market. As a result, the SEC ordered the NASD to make a number of major changes, including selling its cash cow, the NASDAQ market.

There are several advantages to self-regulation. Because it is governed by a board consisting of industry senior managers, its focus and strategy are informed by the view from the trenches. In fact, FINRA often provides formal and informal input to the SEC and to congressional committees on market matters. Perhaps inevitably, this arrangement leads to occasional charges that it is too cozy with the industry it is meant to regulate, but (the 1996 investigation side) the arrangement works well and is regarded as a better approach than simply leaving everything to the SEC. Another advantage of self-regulation is that its investigative and disciplinary process is generally more nimble than that of a government regulator. The reason is simple: Membership and licensing with FINRA is a contractual matter that is entered into voluntarily. If a firm or member breaches FINRA rules, it has also breached that contract and is subject to disciplinary actions up to and including expulsion (as well as fines and referral to the SEC or to prosecutors). This has the very important effect of making it mandatory for registered firms and individuals to provide whatever information is asked by FINRA staff—there is no taking the Fifth.

Finally, since SROs are not part of the government they are not subject to the government pay scale. Though most FINRA staff could make more money "on the outside," and this has historically translated into relatively high turnover, the pay has been generally higher than in the SEC and the turnover lower.

As noted earlier, the fact that FINRA is as much a creature of the market as it is a creature of policymakers raises concerns that it might put more emphasis on *self* than *regulation*, and not be vigorous in its oversight (not "robust," in the overused jargon of regulators and compliance officers). As with so many other issues in financial regulation, this one has been blessed with its own catch-phrase: *regulatory capture*.

REGULATORY CAPTURE

There is a phenomenon called the *Stockholm syndrome*, whereby victims of a kidnapping or hostage-taking come to identify with their captors and even to side with them against their rescuers. It would not be too far of a stretch to say that regulatory capture is a variation on that theme, though it would bring howls of protest from both the regulators and the industry.

Though FINRA is the organization most closely linked to the financial industry, the concept of regulatory capture applies to all regulators: FINRA,

170 ■ Appendix 1

the SEC, the Fed, state regulators, and so on. The basic idea is that regulators take it easy on the regulated, for a variety of reasons that could be overt or subconscious.

The basis for regulatory capture derives from the same things that cause high turnover at regulatory agencies. Regulatory staff are paid less than those they regulate. Whereas it may be cynical (not to mention untrue) to argue that regulatory agencies are staffed with mercenaries who are merely serving time to burnish their resumes, people do have mortgages, educations, and retirements to pay for. The natural path is to seek employment with a firm that has a need for your experience, and so that path leads to firms regulated by the agency. That is hardly a bad thing for the public interest, since the presence of former regulators within the industry provides insight and a broad view of the industry and its issues, and helps to promote a culture of compliance that might otherwise be lacking. The hazard, of course, is that regulatory staff might seek to curry favor with the firms they regulate while they are employed as regulators.

To be fair, this is not a phenomenon unique to regulators. Law firms are fairly stuffed with former-prosecutors-turned-defense-attorneys, as are corporate legal departments. And the public view is even more jaundiced when it comes to politicians and political employees, who are barred by law from working for a firm for which they were responsible for a set number of years.

So, yes, it is possible that individual regulators will consciously or subconsciously make decisions that ingratiate them with their wards, but this is a general concern in public service and does in fact have its benefits to the industry and to the public interest.

Another variety of regulatory capture is all about information rather than people. As has already been mentioned, regulators and policymakers (including politicians) are somewhat removed from the day-to-day operation of the markets. Self-regulation is one remedy for this problem, and another is the well-established process of seeking comment on regulatory proposals from the public and from the industry. In practice, the input comes more from the industry than from the public and this should come as no surprise. For one thing, the outcome of a particular piece of regulation may have a significant impact on a firm or a sector of the industry, and on occasion firms have been put out of business by changes to rules large and small. In contrast, the change may be of small immediate concern to the average member of the public, who has a million other things to worry about before he gets around to whether short sales should be allowed only after an uptick. Consequently, there is a tendency for the industry to be better organized and far better funded. In just

Summaries of Regulatory Concepts and Issues ■ **171**

the first six months of 2009, the financial industry spent nearly $225 million lobbying Congress to change proposed regulatory reform measures,[1] and the total for the year almost certainly exceeded half a billion dollars. And that does not even include campaign contributions as Congress swung into the 2010 election year. It would be unfair, though, to characterize this full-court press merely as an attempt to buy a particular outcome. Firms also educate regulators and legislators, pointing out the practical problems, the costs, and the unintended consequences. More often than many observers would believe, they actually support regulation in some form. Lawmakers and regulators actually seek this input, and they balance the industry commentary with that provided by consumer groups, regulatory officials, and academics.

Benign though this education and consultation process is meant to be, it does present the possibility for a form of regulatory capture. Lawmakers and regulators become dependent on the potential targets of regulation, not only for their opinions but also for data on which to base putatively objective analysis. As argued in Chapter 13 (Cost-Benefit Analysis), any attempt to estimate the cost of implementing particular regulatory measures must be based in part or in whole on data provided by the regulated firms. The same holds true of other information requirements, and so policy is developed to a significant degree on the basis of information from the industry. In the worst of scenarios, this is like asking the bank robber to design the vault.

The reality is less malevolent, partly because the policymakers know that their information comes from sources of less-than-pristine objectivity, and partly because the industry rarely speaks with one voice. They often take different views or diametrically opposed positions, and so the consultation process is rarely if ever a financial industry steamroller rolling down the halls of the Rayburn House Office Building.

There will always be potential for regulatory capture, just as there will always be the potential for similar phenomena in other sectors of public service. One important step to reduce the threat is the professionalization of the regulatory sector, as detailed in Chapter 15, but the best antidote to regulatory capture will be to recognize the potential in the course of the regulatory process.

Informational disadvantages do not appear solely in the process of drafting regulation. They are also a part of the market—a common one if not a natural one. These so-called *information asymmetries* present regulatory challenges of their own, from a fairness and an efficiency point of view.

---

[1] Rachel Beck, "Lobbyists Influence Financial Reform," Associated Press, October 17, 2009.

INFORMATION ASYMMETRIES

"Information asymmetry" is simply an impressive way to say that one party to a deal knows more about the thing being bought or sold than the other (so impressive that it won three economists the Nobel Prize in 2001). If you have ever bought anything on eBay, you have been on the receiving end of an information asymmetry (hopefully without an unhappy ending). The clearest embodiment of asymmetric information is insider trading. Someone knows that ABC Corporation is going to acquire XYZ, Inc. for a share price nicely above the current price, so he goes in with both feet and rakes it in with both hands (hands that, we would hope, will end up in cuffs). There are some wonks who would assert that this should not be illegal, since it is simply a manifestation of an efficient market reflecting all known information in the market price, even if that information is not known by the whole market. Pay no attention to them; good markets are fair as well as efficient.

Beyond the obvious example of insider trading, there are more insidious manifestations of asymmetric information that concern regulators. A trader who has received a large order to buy a particular stock, perhaps from a pension fund or other institution, knows that this order will send the price of the stock higher. The rest of the market does not know it yet, and he could take advantage (illegally) of this knowledge by placing orders for his own account or the accounts of favored customers before he sends the price skyward by executing the institutional order.

It is important to distinguish between knowledge and beliefs when thinking about asymmetric information. As the term *information* implies, it really pertains only to things that are known (such as that big institutional order or the takeover of XYZ Inc.). If a firm's research department concludes that ABC shares will go down based on its own analysis but then recommends purchasing the shares to its customers, the practice is better termed a *conflict of interest* (also onerous) rather than an information asymmetry.

It should be stressed that an act is not always illegal or unethical simply because it is based on information asymmetry. Financial markets are the same as the markets for puppies or houses or life insurance: One side has a better understanding of the quality of the products or the risk to the insurer than the other. But since it is harder to return a toxic asset than a refrigerator whose light will not turn on, regulators seek to identify those that cross the line into unfair transactions, and to level the field.

One lesson learned from the financial crisis is that information asymmetries may be two or more steps removed from the ultimate victim. Consider our old friend, the residential mortgage-backed security (RMBS). The bank that originates the mortgage is the only party that really has any idea of the homeowner's ability and intention of paying the mortgage. The bank knows it is a bad loan but makes the loan anyway because it already knows that the mortgage will be sold on to an RMBS (not on every occasion, but just often enough to threaten the economic wellbeing of the world). The bank does not volunteer information on the mortgage's shaky foundation to the RMBS arranger, but then the arranger does not really ask, anyway, since it will not be stuck with the bill, either. A few steps down the line is the RMBS holder or the firm that wrote default insurance to cover its potential default; the information asymmetry worked its way right through the system to the last person in line.

CONFLICTS OF INTEREST

Lurking beneath most of the issues that plague the market is one fundamental issue that will never go away: conflicts of interest. The market is all about interactions between parties and that leads to a complicated web of trust and dependency. A customer trusts her broker or investment adviser to provide good advice and best execution regardless of how the outcome affects the broker's paycheck. Brokers trust each other to carry through on the deals they make in the market and to do so fairly. Research analysts are supposed to be objective in their analysis, rating agencies are supposed to be indifferent to the fact that the issuer is paying for the rating, regulators are supposed to focus on their current job and not what goes on their resume, lawmakers are supposed to do what is good for the market and not what is likely to get the electorate all in a lather before the next election.

The story of the financial crisis is by all accounts one of conflicts of interest gone unattended, and perverse incentives overriding the market mechanism as short-term personal gains trumped longer-term benefits and the common good. Market purists may argue that self-interest balances out and makes the market tick, but many of the lessons learned in the past few years are about identifying and managing conflicts of interest just as a firm would manage any other type of risk. And *management* is the key word, since elimination is impossible. The critical question then is how a conflict of interest is best managed, and the answer will vary from one instance to another. A popular approach has been simply to make the conflict "transparent"—the idea being that being forewarned of the conflict allows the other party to do something about it. The problems with this approach are that not everyone will see or understand the disclosure (how far did you get into your last prospectus, and did you have your legal dictionary with you when you read it?), and that there may not always be a viable alternative. For example, if there is already a relationship with the conflicted firm, it may be prohibitively expensive to end the relationship and go elsewhere, especially when the conflict is a common practice and there may not be a better choice. And what if the conflicted person takes advantage of his or her position anyway? If the stock analyst on TV recommends that viewers buy shares of ABC like there is no tomorrow, and does the requisite disclosure that he or she owns the stock but then dumps the stock after it has been pumped up, what recourse is there now? Another approach is for regulators to ban a particularly obnoxious practice outright, such as recommending that your customers buy a stock you are trying to unload from your own inventory. This is often more effective, but hard to put into effect for practices that are sometimes ethical and sometimes not (you cannot ban stock analysts from telling people on TV to buy any stock that they own; otherwise, they cannot talk about the stocks they really like).

So, understanding conflicts of interest is a key to considering many of the issues that are faced in the reform of financial regulation. Recognizing that they are an inescapable element of markets and that no single solution will address each one equally well is a good first step.

In a market as big and complicated as the financial market, there rarely is such a one-size-fits-all solution. This argument aptly describes the problem of conflicts of interest, but it is wheeled out in many other regulatory debates, especially when there are big firms and little firms (and little investors) involved.

ONE SIZE FITS ALL

Although we speak in general of "the market," there are in a sense two markets operating parallel to each other for most securities—one for the big institutions and one for individuals and other "retail" investors. In an ideal world and your Econ 101 textbook, the distinction is not important since there is one supply curve, one demand curve, and one point where they meet. But in the markets as they actually exist, it is impractical or even impossible to have the same rules apply for both: You do not make the Yankees conform to the Little League "everyone plays in every game" rule, and you do not require cars in the Indy 500 to signal when switching lanes. Attempts to govern the institutions retail firms would likely be met with the same level of success.

There are three basic reasons why this is so. One has to do with logistics. There have been in the past well-intentioned proposals to require firms, for instance, to contact their customers and give them the option to opt out of a particular regulatory requirement, such as receiving a paper copy of their statements in the mail. That may sound perfectly reasonable, and may be achievable for a small investment advisory firm. But if you tell Morgan Stanley that they need to do that for each and every one of their customers, you are unlikely to receive a positive response. Similar considerations arise for banks dealing with a large volume of transactions (whether actual banking transactions or even call center operations) or other firms with either a high volume of activity or a large number of customers and counterparties.

A second reason has to do with the dynamics of the market. A trade for a very large number of shares will overwhelm and flatten the market, distorting the price for retail and investors alike. For this reason, most markets accommodate a lower or slower level of transparency for the display of large orders and execution of large trades. The principle is particularly true in stock markets, but holds true in most other markets as well.

Finally, some firms really do not deal with small customers who are unsophisticated in the ways of the market. Indeed, there are entire sectors of the industry based on dealing only with so-called sophisticated customers such as institutions or individuals who meet certain minimum asset requirements. The idea behind this is that regulation is really meant to protect those investors who are not in a position to defend themselves against asymmetry of information. With the assumption that the rich and the big got rich and big by knowing their way around the market, the argument goes, there is need to constrain with burdensome regulations those firms that deal only with the rich and big.

This concept has long been embedded in the law, in the United States and elsewhere. Requirements concerning registration of securities, transparency, and other measures have been specifically "disapplied" to institutions and individuals who meet the asset and other requirements. The problem is that this makes a few too many assumptions. No point in naming names, but we could all name a few celebrities who have more celebrity than intellectual firepower, and though they may have the resources to absorb a larger loss in the market than the rest of us, they are not known for their iron self-restraint, either. This is not to say that the laws should be changed to protect the famous, but rather that there is a certain logical fallacy in assuming that the wealthy are necessarily sophisticated investors.

Of greater concern is the fate of the not-so-sophisticated institution. In many cases, institutions are investing the funds for individuals. In fact, most

176 ■ Appendix 1

small investors put their investments in professionally managed mutual funds and the retirement funds for many are in the hands of pension funds. Universities and state and local governments are also institutional investors in whose success the average citizen has a stake. And yet institutions may on occasion be less sophisticated than the investments they invest in. This is not a new phenomenon; Orange County, California, faced a particularly dire financial situation after it had been sold investments that it later alleged had been misrepresented to it. In the recent financial crisis, billions of dollars have been wiped from the accounts of universities, state and local governments, and financial institutions themselves because of bad investments. And that is not even counting Bernie Madoff, who made a career of duping the rich and the big, whether they were individuals or institutions.

One problem with the one-size-does-not-fit-all argument is that it shows up a bit too often in regulatory debates, and can sometimes be a spurious argument. When the debate about reforming best execution was underway in Europe, many large institutions objected to any regulation that would define best execution as the *best price*, on the grounds that really big trades were impacted by other factors like whether the exchange showing the best price could execute the trade quickly. As a result, a counterproposal was made to let the trader decide what constituted best execution (and depending on how the trader is compensated, this could create a conflict of interest), regardless of whether the trade was for 100 shares or 100,000. In making this proposal, they still wanted a one-size-fits-all policy; they just wanted it to be their size.

When writing regulation, the devil is in the details, and in the implementation. Often, any attempt to make a rule that will cover all people in all instances will collapse under its own weight. There is a school of thought that says rules should not be detailed at all, but should set forth the goals or principles to be achieved: that we should in fact aim for "principles-based" rather than "rules-based" regimes. This approach gained traction throughout the past decade, but fell quickly out of fashion with the financial crisis and the subsequent desire to write rules that are detailed and consequently more easily enforced.

Appendix 2: Excerpt from Obama Administration's Reform Proposal, "Financial Regulatory Reform: A New Foundation"*

SUMMARY OF RECOMMENDATIONS

Please refer to the main text for further details

I. **Promote Robust Supervision and Regulation of Financial Firms**
   A. Create a Financial Services Oversight Council
      1. *We propose the creation of a Financial Services Oversight Council to facilitate information sharing and coordination, identify emerging risks, advise the Federal Reserve on the identification of firms whose failure could pose a threat to financial stability due to their combination of size, leverage, and interconnectedness (hereafter referred to as a Tier 1FHC), and provide a forum for resolving jurisdictional disputes between regulators.*
         a. *The membership of the Council should include (i) the Secretary of the Treasury, who shall serve as the Chairman; (ii) the Chairman of the Board of Governors of the Federal Reserve System; (iii) the Director of the National Bank Supervisor; (iv) the Director of the Consumer*

---

*http://www.financialstability.gov/docs/regs/FinalReport_web.pdf

Financial Protection Agency; (v) the Chairman of the SEC; (vi) the Chairman of the CFTC; (vii) the Chairman of the FDIC; and (viii) the Director of the Federal Housing Finance Agency (FHFA).

    b. *The Council should be supported by a permanent, full-time expert staff at Treasury. The staff should be responsible for providing the Council with the information and resources it needs to fulfill its responsibilities.*

2. *Our legislation will propose to give the Council the authority to gather information from any financial firm and the responsibility for referring emerging risks to the attention of regulators with the authority to respond.*

B. Implement Heightened Consolidated Supervision and Regulation of All Large, Interconnected Financial Firms

1. *Any financial firm whose combination of size, leverage, and interconnectedness could pose a threat to financial stability if it failed (Tier 1 FHC) should be subject to robust consolidated supervision and regulation, regardless of whether the firm owns an insured depository institution.*

2. *The Federal Reserve Board should have the authority and accountability for consolidated supervision and regulation of Tier 1 FHCs.*

3. *Our legislation will propose criteria that the Federal Reserve must consider in identifying Tier 1 FHCs.*

4. *The prudential standards for Tier 1 FHCs—including capital, liquidity and risk management standards—should be stricter and more conservative than those applicable to other financial firms to account for the greater risks that their potential failure would impose on the financial system.*

5. *Consolidated supervision of a Tier 1 FHC should extend to the parent company and to all of its subsidiaries—regulated and unregulated, U.S. and foreign. Functionally regulated and depository institution subsidiaries of a Tier 1 FHC should continue to be supervised and regulated primarily by their functional or bank regulator, as the case may be. The constraints that the Gramm-Leach-Bliley Act (GLB Act) introduced on the Federal Reserve's ability to require reports from, examine, or impose higher prudential requirements or more stringent activity restrictions on the functionally regulated or depository institution subsidiaries of FHCs should be removed.*

6. *Consolidated supervision of a Tier 1 FHC should be macroprudential in focus. That is, it should consider risk to the system as a whole.*

7. *The Federal Reserve, in consultation with Treasury and external experts, should propose recommendations by October 1, 2009 to better align its structure and governance with its authorities and responsibilities.*

C. Strengthen Capital and Other Prudential Standards for All Banks and BHCs

1. *Treasury will lead a working group, with participation by federal financial regulatory agencies and outside experts that will conduct a fundamental reassessment of existing regulatory capital requirements for banks and BHCs, including new Tier 1 FHCs. The working group will issue a report with its conclusions by December 31, 2009.*

2. *Treasury will lead a working group, with participation by federal financial regulatory agencies and outside experts, that will conduct a fundamental reassessment of the supervision of banks and BHCs. The working group will issue a report with its conclusions by October 1, 2009.*

3. *Federal regulators should issue standards and guidelines to better align executive compensation practices of financial firms with long-term shareholder value and to prevent compensation practices from providing incentives that could threaten the safety and soundness of supervised institutions. In addition, we will support legislation requiring all public companies to hold non-binding shareholder resolutions on the compensation packages of senior executive officers, as well as new requirements to make compensation committees more independent.*

4. *Capital and management requirements for FHC status should not be limited to the subsidiary depository institution. All FHCs should be required to meet the capital and management requirements on a consolidated basis as well.*

5. *The accounting standard setters (the FASB, the IASB, and the SEC) should review accounting standards to determine how financial firms should be required to employ more forward-looking loan loss provisioning practices that incorporate a broader range of available credit information. Fair value accounting rules also should be reviewed with the goal of identifying changes that could provide users of financial reports with both fair value information and greater transparency regarding the cash flows management expects to receive by holding investments.*

6. *Firewalls between banks and their affiliates should be strengthened to protect the federal safety net that supports banks and to better prevent spread of the subsidy inherent in the federal safety net to bank affiliates.*

D. Close Loopholes in Bank Regulation

1. *We propose the creation of a new federal government agency, the National Bank Supervisor (NBS), to conduct prudential supervision and regulation of all federally chartered depository institutions, and all federal branches and agencies of foreign banks.*

2. *We propose to eliminate the federal thrift charter, but to preserve its interstate branching rules and apply them to state and national banks.*

3. *All companies that control an insured depository institution, however organized, should be subject to robust consolidated supervision and regulation at the federal level by the Federal Reserve and should be subject to the nonbanking activity restrictions of the BHC Act. The policy of separating banking from commerce should be re-affirmed and strengthened. We must close loopholes in the BHC Act for thrift holding companies, industrial loan companies, credit card banks, trust companies, and grandfathered "nonbank" banks.*

E. Eliminate the SEC's Programs for Consolidated Supervision

The SEC has ended its Consolidated Supervised Entity Program, under which it had been the holding company supervisor for companies such as Lehman Brothers and Bear Stearns. We propose also eliminating the SEC's Supervised Investment Bank Holding Company program. Investment banking firms that seek consolidated supervision by a U.S. regulator should be subject to supervision and regulation by the Federal Reserve.

F. Require Hedge Funds and Other Private Pools of Capital to Register

All advisers to hedge funds (and other private pools of capital, including private equity funds and venture capital funds) whose assets under management exceed some modest threshold should be required to register with the SEC under the Investment Advisers Act. The advisers should be required to report information on the funds they manage that is sufficient to assess whether any fund poses a threat to financial stability.

G. Reduce the Susceptibility of Money Market Mutual Funds (MMFs) to Runs

The SEC should move forward with its plans to strengthen the regulatory framework around MMFs to reduce the credit and liquidity risk profile of individual MMFs and to make the MMF industry as a whole less susceptible to runs. The President's Working Group on Financial Markets should prepare a report assessing whether more fundamental changes are necessary to further reduce the MMF industry's susceptibility to runs, such as eliminating the ability of a MMF to use a stable net asset value or requiring MMFs to obtain access to reliable emergency liquidity facilities from private sources.

H. Enhance Oversight of the Insurance Sector

Our legislation will propose the establishment of the Office of National Insurance within Treasury to gather information, develop expertise, negotiate international agreements, and coordinate policy in the insurance sector.

Excerpt from Obama Administration's ■ **181**

Treasury will support proposals to modernize and improve our system of insurance regulation in accordance with six principles outlined in the body of the report.

I. Determine the Future Role of the Government Sponsored Enterprises (GSEs)

> *Treasury and the Department of Housing and Urban Development, in consultation with other government agencies, will engage in a wide-ranging initiative to develop recommendations on the future of Fannie Mae and Freddie Mac, and the Federal Home Loan Bank system. We need to maintain the continued stability and strength of the GSEs during these difficult financial times. We will report to the Congress and the American public at the time of the President's 2011 Budget release.*

II. **Establish Comprehensive Regulation of Financial Markets**

A. Strengthen Supervision and Regulation of Securitization Markets

1. *Federal banking agencies should promulgate regulations that require originators or sponsors to retain an economic interest in a material portion of the credit risk of securitized credit exposures.*

2. *Regulators should promulgate additional regulations to align compensation of market participants with longer term performance of the underlying loans.*

3. *The SEC should continue its efforts to increase the transparency and standardization of securitization markets and be given clear authority to require robust reporting by issuers of asset backed securities (ABS).*

4. *The SEC should continue its efforts to strengthen the regulation of credit rating agencies, including measures to promote robust policies and procedures that manage and disclose conflicts of interest, differentiate between structured and other products, and otherwise strengthen the integrity of the ratings process.*

5. *Regulators should reduce their use of credit ratings in regulations and supervisory practices, wherever possible.*

B. Create Comprehensive Regulation of All OTC Derivatives, Including Credit Default Swaps (CDS)

> *All OTC derivatives markets, including CDS markets, should be subject to comprehensive regulation that addresses relevant public policy objectives: (1) preventing activities in those markets from posing risk to the financial system; (2) promoting the efficiency and transparency of those markets; (3) preventing market manipulation, fraud, and other market abuses; and (4) ensuring that OTC derivatives are not marketed inappropriately to unsophisticated parties.*

182 ◼ Appendix 2

C. Harmonize Futures and Securities Regulation
The CFTC and the SEC should make recommendations to Congress for changes to statutes and regulations that would harmonize regulation of futures and securities.

D. Strengthen Oversight of Systemically Important Payment Clearing, and Settlement Systems and Related Activities
We propose that the Federal Reserve have the responsibility and authority to conduct oversight of systemically important payment, clearing and settlement systems, and activities of financial firms.

E. Strengthen Settlement Capabilities and Liquidity Resources of Systemically Important Payment, Clearing, and Settlement Systems
We propose that the Federal Reserve have authority to provide systemically important payment, clearing, and settlement systems access to Reserve Bank accounts, financial services, and the discount window.

III. **Protect Consumers and Investors from Financial Abuse**

A. Create a New Consumer Financial Protection Agency

1. *We propose to create a single primary federal consumer protection supervisor to protect consumers of credit, savings, payment, and other consumer financial products and services, and to regulate providers of such products and services.*

2. *The CFPA should have broad jurisdiction to protect consumers in consumer financial products and services such as credit, savings, and payment products.*

3. *The CFPA should be an independent agency with stable, robust funding.*

4. *The CFPA should have sole rule-making authority for consumer financial protection statutes, as well as the ability to fill gaps through rule-making.*

5. *The CFPA should have supervisory and enforcement authority and jurisdiction over all persons covered by the statutes that it implements, including both insured depositories and the range of other firms not previously subject to comprehensive federal supervision, and it should work with the Department of Justice to enforce the statutes under its jurisdiction in federal court.*

6. *The CFPA should pursue measures to promote effective regulation, including conducting periodic reviews of regulations, an outside advisory council, and coordination with the Council.*

7. *The CFPA's strong rules would serve as a floor, not a ceiling. The states should have the ability to adopt and enforce stricter laws for institutions of all types, regardless of charter, and to enforce federal law*

concurrently with respect to institutions of all types, also regardless of charter.

8. *The CFPA should coordinate enforcement efforts with the states.*
9. *The CFPA should have a wide variety of tools to enable it to perform its functions effectively.*
10. *The Federal Trade Commission should also be given better tools and additional resources to protect consumers.*

B. Reform Consumer Protection

1. *Transparency. We propose a new proactive approach to disclosure. The CFPA will be authorized to require that all disclosures and other communications with consumers be reasonable: balanced in their presentation of benefits, and clear and conspicuous in their identification of costs, penalties, and risks.*

2. *Simplicity. We propose that the regulator be authorized to define standards for "plain vanilla" products that are simpler and have straightforward pricing. The CFPA should be authorized to require all providers and intermediaries to offer these products prominently, alongside whatever other lawful products they choose to offer.*

3. *Fairness. Where efforts to improve transparency and simplicity prove inadequate to prevent unfair treatment and abuse, we propose that the CFPA be authorized to place tailored restrictions on product terms and provider practices, if the benefits outweigh the costs. Moreover, we propose to authorize the Agency to impose appropriate duties of care on financial intermediaries.*

4. *Access. The Agency should enforce fair lending laws and the Community Reinvestment Act and otherwise seek to ensure that underserved consumers and communities have access to prudent financial services, lending, and investment.*

C. Strengthen Investor Protection

1. *The SEC should be given expanded authority to promote transparency in investor disclosures.*

2. *The SEC should be given new tools to increase fairness for investors by establishing a fiduciary duty for broker-dealers offering investment advice and harmonizing the regulation of investment advisers and broker-dealers.*

3. *Financial firms and public companies should be accountable to their clients and investors by expanding protections for whistleblowers, expanding sanctions available for enforcement, and requiring non-binding shareholder votes on executive pay plans.*

4. *Under the leadership of the Financial Services Oversight Council, we propose the establishment of a Financial Consumer Coordinating Council with a broad membership of federal and state consumer protection agencies, and a permanent role for the SEC's Investor Advisory Committee.*

5. *Promote retirement security for all Americans by strengthening employment-based and private retirement plans and encouraging adequate savings.*

IV. Provide the Government with the Tools It Needs to Manage Financial Crises

A. Create a Resolution Regime for Failing BHCs, Including Tier 1 FHCs

We recommend the creation of a resolution regime to avoid the disorderly resolution of failing BHCs, including Tier 1 FHCs, if a disorderly resolution would have serious adverse effects on the financial system or the economy. The regime would supplement (rather than replace) and be modeled on to the existing resolution regime for insured depository institutions under the Federal Deposit Insurance Act.

B. Amend the Federal Reserve's Emergency Lending Authority

We will propose legislation to amend Section 13(3) of the Federal Reserve Act to require the prior written approval of the Secretary of the Treasury for any extensions of credit by the Federal Reserve to individuals, partnerships, or corporations in "unusual and exigent circumstances."

V. Raise International Regulatory Standards and Improve International Cooperation

A. Strengthen the International Capital Framework

We recommend that the Basel Committee on Banking Supervision (BCBS) continue to modify and improve Basel II by refining the risk weights applicable to the trading book and securitized products, introducing a supplemental leverage ratio, and improving the definition of capital by the end of 2009. We also urge the BCBS to complete an in-depth review of the Basel II framework to mitigate its procyclical effects.

B. Improve the Oversight of Global Financial Markets

We urge national authorities to promote the standardization and improved oversight of credit derivative and other OTC derivative markets, in particular through the use of central counterparties, along the lines of the G-20 commitment, and to advance these goals through international coordination and cooperation.

C. Enhance Supervision of Internationally Active Financial Firms

We recommend that the Financial Stability Board (FSB) and national authorities implement G-20 commitments to strengthen arrangements for

international cooperation on supervision of global financial firms through establishment and continued operational development of supervisory colleges.

D. Reform Crisis Prevention and Management Authorities and Procedures

We recommend that the BCBS expedite its work to improve cross-border resolution of global financial firms and develop recommendations by the end of 2009. We further urge national authorities to improve information-sharing arrangements and implement the FSB principles for cross-border crisis management.

E. Strengthen the Financial Stability Board

We recommend that the FSB complete its restructuring and institutionalize its new mandate to promote global financial stability by September 2009.

F. Strengthen Prudential Regulations

We recommend that the BCBS take steps to improve liquidity risk management standards for financial firms and that the FSB work with the Bank for International Settlements (BIS) and standard setters to develop macroprudential tools.

G. Expand the Scope of Regulation

1. *Determine the appropriate Tier 1 FHC definition and application of requirements for foreign financial firms.*
2. *We urge national authorities to implement by the end of 2009 the G-20 commitment to require hedge funds or their managers to register and disclose appropriate information necessary to assess the systemic risk they pose individually or collectively*

H. Introduce Better Compensation Practices

In line with G-20 commitments, we urge each national authority to put guidelines in place to align compensation with long-term shareholder value and to promote compensation structures do not provide incentives for excessive risk taking. We recommend that the BCBS expediently integrate the FSB principles on compensation into its risk management guidance by the end of 2009.

I. Promote Stronger Standards in the Prudential Regulation, Money Laundering/Terrorist Financing, and Tax Information Exchange Areas

1. *We urge the FSB to expeditiously establish and coordinate peer reviews to assess compliance and implementation of international regulatory standards, with priority attention on the international cooperation elements of prudential regulatory standards.*

2. *The United States will work to implement the updated International Cooperation Review Group (ICRG) peer review process and work with partners in the Financial Action Task Force (FATF) to address jurisdictions not complying with international anti-money laundering/terrorist financing (AML/CFT) standards.*

J. Improve Accounting Standards

1. *We recommend that the accounting standard setters clarify and make consistent the application of fair value accounting standards, including the impairment of financial instruments, by the end of 2009.*

2. *We recommend that the accounting standard setters improve accounting standards for loan loss provisioning by the end of 2009 that would make it more forward looking, as long as the transparency of financial statements is not compromised.*

3. *We recommend that the accounting standard setters make substantial progress by the end of 2009 toward development of a single set of high quality global accounting standards.*

K. Tighten Oversight of Credit Rating Agencies

We urge national authorities to enhance their regulatory regimes to effectively oversee credit rating agencies (CRAs), consistent with international standards and the G-20 Leaders' recommendations.

Index

A
AARP. *See* American Association of Retired Persons (AARP)

ABSs. *See* asset backed securities (ABSs)

AIG
- CDS exposure and insufficient collateral, 39
- credit default swaps, 5
- Federal Reserve, 29, 39
- government bailout of, 25
- liquidity crisis was tipping point for, 39
- performance pay, government bailout money for, 48
- taxpayers' funds collateralized, 39

American Association of Retired Persons (AARP), 105

American Bankers Association, 58, 61–62

Anti-Trust Division of Justice, 17–18

Asian financial crisis, 16

asset backed securities (ABSs), 32–33, 36, 181

Associated Press, 87, 171

Australia, 97, 136

B
Bank for International Settlements, 38, 43, 185

Bank of America, 16–17, 77

Basel Committee for Banking Supervision (BCBS), 140

BCBS. *See* Basel Committee for Banking Supervision (BCBS)

Bear Stearns
- collapse of, 21, 38
- government bailout of, 25, 134
- investment banks and bad asset classes, 14
- J.P. Morgan, force fed by, 77
- rating agency downgrade and tipping point, 5, 92

repos, 13–14

residential mortgage-backed securities (RMBSs), 3, 13–14

SEC as holding company for, 180

systemic risk, 2–6, 10, 13–14

toxic assets, difficult-to-price, 6

Berkshire Hathaway, 89

Bernanke, Chairman Benjamin, 29, 60, 78–79

Bernie Madoff scandal, xxi, xxiii, 110, 112, 147, 176

British East India Company, xvi

brokerage firms, 107, 116

Buffet, Warren, 89

C
CCO. *See* Chief Compliance Officer (CCO)

CDOs. *See* collateralized debt obligations (CDOs)

CDSs. *See* credit default swaps (CDSs)

Center for Capital Markets Competitiveness of the U.S. Chamber of Commerce, 130

Center for Economic and Policy Research (CEPR), 87–88

CEPR. *See* Center for Economic and Policy Research (CEPR)

Certified Regulatory and Compliance Professional [FINRA], 151

CFPA. *See* Consumer Financial Protection Agency (CFPA)

CFTC. *See* Commodity Futures Trading Commission (CFTC)

Chief Compliance Officer (CCO), 110, 114, 151–52

civil liability, 27–28, 30, 92

CMBSs. *See* commercial mortgage-backed securities (CMBSs)

Code of Conduct Fundamentals for Credit Rating Agencies, 140

collateralized debt obligations (CDOs), 11, 31, 42, 95–96

187

188 ■ Index

commercial mortgage-backed securities (CMBSs), 31–32, 37, 40, 42. *See also* residential mortgage-backed securities (RMBSs)

Commodity Futures Trading Commission (CFTC), xvi, 38–39, 64, 75, 80, 129, 149, 178, 182

Community Reinvestment Act (1977), 60, 183

conclusions and recommendations

about, 142, 154–55

capital requirements for risky activities, higher, 144

chief compliance officer reporting to Board of Directors, 152

clawbacks and other malus provisions, 153

compliance profession, elevating the, 151–52

crisis, planning for the next, 144–46

decisions are made by individuals not organizations, 152–53

failing firms should be left to their own fate, 144

federal regulatory service, creating a, 148–51

Financial Regulation Service Institute, 149

firms receiving government support to repay every penny, 145

Foreign Service Institute, 148, 150

Foreign Service Officers (FSOs), 148

haircut for firms holding failing securities, 145

Inspector General (OIG), 112, 116, 147, 151

modern markets and self-regulation, 143–44

penalties for senior managers, 145

performance goals as part of regulatory examinations, 153

performance goals for analysts, 153

pitchforks, put down the, 154

power to dismiss senior managers and board of directors, 146

pre-funding the pool, 145–46

rating organizations, keep them on a short leash, 153–54

regulation to bolster oversight of markets, 143

regulatory service, need for a professionalized, 146–48

salary capping to prevent another crisis, 153

SEC, staff reforms by, 148

systemic risk and complexity of the market, 143

systemic risk regulator for failing firms, 146

Volcker Rule on size of firms, 144

conflict of interest, 63, 72, 89, 97, 173–74

Congressional Oversight Panel for the TARP program, 68

Consumer Financial Protection Agency (CFPA), 57, 62, 64–65, 182–83

consumer protection

about, 57–58

agency, politically sensitive issue, 64

agency powers, what are they?, 65–67

American Bankers objection to, 61–62

bad loans and regulation of financial service providers, 67

Community Reinvestment Act (1977), 60, 183

conclusion, 68

conflict of interest, 63

Congressional Oversight Panel for the TARP program, 68

Consumer Financial Protection Agency (CFPA), 57, 62, 64–66, 182–83

consumer regulator for consumer financial products, 61–65

credit card industry, xxviii, 32, 59, 61, 64, 70, 91, 161, 180, 6459

federal regulators to coordinate, 61

Federal Reserve, 63

"for protection from unfair and deceptive practices," 65

Government Accountability Office (GAO), 57–58

non-banks, 61, 63–64, 66

Office of the Comptroller of the Currency, 63, 75–76, 79, 149

Office of Thrift Supervision, 63, 75–76, 79, 149

regulations, effectiveness of existing, 59–61

regulations are overly burdensome, 60–61

self-interest on part of lender, 67

sub-prime securitization problem and rise in interest rates, 67

systemic risk and, 67–68

three arguments for, 62

transparency, 68
über-regulator for consumer protection, 58
cost-benefit analysis
  about, 121–22
  assumptions, variable/wide ranging, 124
  backward looking data for future projections, 126
  basics of, 122–27
  bell curve, fallacy of using middle of, 127
  benefits of, 128–29
  conclusion, 132
  Federal agencies and, 129
  government use of, 129–30
  Homeland Security regulations, 122
  illusion of accuracy, 125
  as imprecise estimate, 124
  measurement, problems in, 124–25
  monetizing costs and benefits, 123, 125
  as negotiating tactic, 130–31
  political factors prevent regulation, 127
  problems, other, 125–27
  third party not necessarily an independent party, 131
  time-horizon of, 126
  as tool for ultimate decisions, 127
CRA. *See Credit Rating Agency Reform Act (CRA)*
CRA Reform Act, 84–85, 89, 95
credit card industry, xxviii, 32, 59, 61, 64, 70, 91, 161, 180
credit default swaps (CDSs), xxiv, 5, 37–39, 42–44, 73, 181–82
credit derivatives, 70–71, 102, 140, 158–59, 184
credit rating agencies
  AAA, diluting the meaning of, xxi
  AAA mortgage securities, defaulting, 84
  AAA ratings slashed to junk levels, 86
  about, 83–84
  bell curve for agency models, 9, 35, 38, 86, 96, 126–27
  bond ratings, corporate and municipal, 89–91
  capital adequacy rules, 94
  civil liability, 27–28, 30, 92
  collateralized debt obligations (CDOs), 11, 31, 42, 95–96
  conclusion, 98–99
  CRA Reform Act, 84–85, 89, 95
  Credit Rating Agency Reform Act (CRA), 84, 140

federal bailout of mortgage market, 87–88
First Amendment, 93, 154
issuer-pays model, 85, 88, 97–98, 154
maximizing profits by management, 88
mortgage-backed securities deals, 98
Nationally Recognized Statistical Rating Organization (NRSRO), 84–89, 94–97, 154
point-in-time ratings, 96
rating blunders, 93
ratings, how they are made, 89–92
ratings and bankruptcy, 90
ratings distorted by conflict of interest or outright greed, 89
residential mortgage-backed securities (RMBSs), 13–14, 31–34, 36–37, 39, 49, 84–85, 88, 93, 95
Sarbanes-Oxley Act, 83, 100–101, 107
SEC to study, 83
special-purpose vehicle (SPV), 32–33, 35, 91
structured finance products, 35–37
structured finance ratings, 91–92
subprime mortgage ratings, downgrading, xvii–xix, 88, 93
tighten oversight of, 186
toxic assets, role played by, 34
user-pays model and conflict of interest, 97
as utilities, 97–98
"voluntary regulation does not work," 95
what keeps them up at night?, 92–93
Credit Rating Agency Reform Act (CRA), 84, 140
customer complaints, 107, 110–11, 116

D
Depository Trust Clearing Corporation (DTCC), 5
disclosure, 68, 71–73, 117, 141, 159, 174, 183
Dodd, Senator Chris, 78
DTCC. *See* Depository Trust Clearing Corporation (DTCC)
Dutch East India Company, xvi

E
Efficient Market Hypothesis, xix, 70
Enron, 83–84, 93, 98
European Union, 92, 97, 135–39

F

Fannie Mae, 25, 181
Federal Deposit Insurance Act, 184
Federal Deposit Insurance Corporation (FDIC), 75–76
Federal Reserve, 29, 39, 53–56, 63, 75–79, 184
Federal Savings and Loan Insurance Corporation, 76
Federal Trade Commission (FTC), 75, 183
financial crisis, xxiii, 9, 11, 16, 50, 150–52, 156, 163, 172–76
Financial Industry Regulatory Authority (FINRA), 106, 109, 111–13, 138, 151–52, 168–69
   Certified Regulatory and Compliance Professional, 151
financial institutions, 8, 16, 24, 53, 78, 87, 91, 94, 140, 144
Financial Service Authority (UK), 121
Financial Services Committee, 68, 70, 78, 101–2
Financial Stability Board (FSB), 54, 139, 184–85
FINRA. *See* Financial Industry Regulatory Authority (FINRA)
First Amendment, 93, 154
Fitch, 84, 86, 88
foreign regulators, 133
Foreign Service Institute, 148, 150
Foreign Service Officers (FSOs), 148
Freddie Mac, 25, 181
FSOs. *See* Foreign Service Officers (FSOs)
FTC. *See* Federal Trade Commission (FTC)

G

G-20. *See* Group of 20 (G-20)
Glass-Steagall Act, 18–19, 76–77
GLB Act. *See Gramm-Leach-Bliley Act (GLB Act)*
Goldman Sachs, 4, 17, 77, 87, 104, 160
Government Accountability Office (GAO), 57–58
government-sponsored enterprises (GSEs), 25
Gramm-Leach-Bliley Act (GLB Act), 77–78, 178
Great Crash, 76, 112
Great Recession, 3
Greece, 134–35
Greenberg, Chairman Ace, 4, 10
Greenspan, Alan, 42, 62, 64, 70
Group of 20 (G-20), 139–40, 184–86

GSEs. *See* government-sponsored enterprises (GSEs)

H

hedge funds, 6, 102, 105, 157–58, 180, 185
Homeland Security regulations, 122
Home Ownership and Equity Protection Act (HOEP), 62
House Committee on Energy and Commerce, 57
House Committee on Oversight and Government Reform, 88, 101
House Financial Services Committee, 68, 70, 101–2

I

IAIS. *See* International Association of Insurance Supervisors (IAIS)
Icelandic banks, 93
incentives and compensation
   about, 46–47
   Adam Smith, what he right?, 56
   AIG performance pay, government bailout money for, 48
   bank's program, three principles for assessing, 55–56
   bonus calculations, 51
   clawback of incentive pay, 50, 52
   compensation at TARP institutions, 53
   compensation reform, 47
   compliance and risk management staff, 56
   disincentives to discourage excessive risky behavior, 50
   executives and huge pay packages, 47
   Federal Reserve guidance (2009), 53–56
   financial services restructuring debate, 46
   Financial Stability Board and "sound compensation practices," 54
   government regulation of financial services industry, 47
   incentive compensation, 29, 48–51, 55–56, 153
   incentives encourage inordinate risk, 50, 53
   Keynesian stimulus packages and nationalization of U.S. automaker, 47
   long-term policy, 47
   malus schemes, 50, 52–53
   mortgage environment as first domino of financial crisis, 50
   non-cash compensation for executives, vesting of, 51

pay packages, 47–48, 53
performance goals and risk, 49–50, 153
performance management and bonus
  programs, 56
rating agency analysts and bank's senior
  management, 49
regulators and issues of justice and
  revenge, 46
revised compensation for individual
  traders, research or credit analysts, 53
revised compensation for officers and
  employees, 53
revised compensation for top
  management, 53
reward with risk, aligning, 50–52
RMBS shares and performance goals,
  49–50
self-interest, competing, 56
Senate bill on financial reform (2009) and
  excessive compensation plans, 47
TARP-based guidance for groups creating
  risk for the firm, 54
insider trading, 107, 113, 116, 137, 157,
  172
Inspector General (OIG), 112, 116, 147, 151
institutions are "too big to fail." *See also*
  Troubled Asset Relief Program (TARP)
accountability of senior management and
  boards, 22
Anti-Trust Division of Justice and phone
  market, 17–18
anti-trust powers/legislation, 18
assets weighted by level of risk, 16
banks, keep them small, 17–18
bonds, arbitrage between prices of, 16
capital cushion requirements, 17
capital requirements, increase, 19–20
commercial *vs.* investment banking
  activities, 18
conclusion, 22–23
do nothing, 22
financial disclosures, mandatory, 19
Glass-Steagall Act, bring back, 18–19
government intervention *vs.* free market
  principles, 17, 21
government support is swiftest, 23
hedge funds, 16, 19, 102, 105, 157–58
highly leveraged firm, 16
Long Term Capital Management, 16
market capitalization, 16
moral hazard encourages inordinate risks,
  22
pay limits for officers, 20

Plan B, 10, 20, 22, 30, 81, 144
policy options, 17–22
proprietary trading by commercial banks,
  19
Resolution Authority, 20–22
risk of unknown loss, 21
Sherman Anti-Trust Act, 18
systemic risk, identify, 22
too-big-to-fail concept, 15–17
Volcker, Fed Chairman Paul, 18–19
Volcker Rule, 19
Insurance Core Principles, 140
International Association of Insurance
  Supervisors (IAIS), 140–41
International Organization of Securities
  Commissioners (IOSCO), 140
international regulations
  Asia, regulatory initiatives in, 136
  Basel Committee for Banking Supervision
    (BCBS), 140
  Code of Conduct Fundamentals for Credit
    Rating Agencies, 140
  conclusion, 141
  EU privacy laws, 137, 141
  Europe, stock exchanges in, 135
  The European Union, 136–38
  Financial Stability Board (FSB), 54, 139–
    40, 184–85
  FSA's Handbook of regulations, 138
  global markets, interconnectedness of,
    134
  herd mentality (short-term market
    movements), 134
  Insurance Core Principles, 140
  International Association of Insurance
    Supervisors (IAIS), 140–41
  International Organization of Securities
    Commissioners (IOSCO), 140
  international organizations, 139–41
  Markets in Financial Instruments
    Directive (MiFID), 136
  overseas regulators, 135–39
  privacy laws, 134–35, 137, 141
  Prospectus Directive governs filing
    requirements, 137
  regulation, principles based *vs.* rules-
    based, 138–39
  SEC and shift toward principles-based
    regulation, 138
  Sunday is the new Monday, 133–35
  U.S. Credit Rating Reform Act, 140
investment advisers, 107, 109, 115, 131,
  160, 173, 180, 183

192 ▪ Index

investment banking, 4, 18–19, 47, 76–77, 180
Investment Company Act of 1940, 107
IOSCO. *See* International Organization of Securities Commissioners (IOSCO)
issuer-pays model, 85, 88, 97–98, 154

J
Joint (House and Senate) Economic Committee, 101

K
Kanjorski, Paul, 98–99
King, Governor Mervyn, 19

L
Lehman Brothers, 8, 22, 25, 38, 77, 87, 134
leverage, 6, 16, 147, 159, 177–78, 184
lobbying, 92, 99–100, 104, 126, 131, 171
Long Term Capital hedge fund collapse, 11
Long Term Capital Management (LTCM), 16

M
Madoff Investment Securities, 109
Malthus, Ricardo, xvii
malus schemes, 50, 52, 153
margin call, 6
market abuse, 107, 113, 181
Markets in Financial Instruments Directive (MiFID), 136
Merrill Lynch, 4, 77, 87
MMFs. *See* Money Market Mutual Funds (MMFs)
money laundering activity, 119, 151, 185–86
money market fund, 7–9, 11, 92
Money Market Mutual Funds (MMFs), 180
Moody's, xi, 84, 86, 88–89, 94, 98
moral hazard
  AAA ratings of riskiest assets, 26
  about, xxiv, 24–25
  of businesses associated with the irresponsible firms, 28
  clawback of previous compensation, 29
  conclusion, 30
  creditors as the other, 28–30
  creditors should not be made whole, 30
  as deciding factor in risk decisions, 26
  emergency pool of funds trigger clawback in compensation and civil liability, 28
  emergency pool of funds trigger government to dismiss any or all senior management or Board, 27

failures, provisions for, 29–30
federally insured deposits of individuals, 24
firms extending credit to irresponsible firms stand to lose their investment, 28
government bailout of AIG and Bear Stearns, 25
government bailout of financial institutions, 24
government can create, 27
government-sponsored enterprises (GSEs), 25
government support of failing banks prevents uncertainty, 28
government support of important institutions, 30
as life insurance, 26
moral suasion alone will not carry the day, 29
Plan B, 30
practice of, 26
punish or reward firm *vs.* the individual, 27
"punish the leaders, not the organization," 27–28
regulatory debate on, 30
"risks are fully understood to be risky," 26
risky behavior by firms too big to fail, 26
salary and incentive compensation, forfeiture of, 29
sanctions against senior management, 29–30
sanctions for individuals making risk-taking decisions, 27
self-interest, 30
short-term funding contracts and exemption from haircuts, 28–29
systemic risk, need for new rules for, 25
theory of, 25–26
third-party, 28, 30
Morgan Stanley, 17, 78, 92, 104, 160, 175

N
NASDAQ stock market, 113, 160, 168
National Bank Supervisor (NBS), 179
Nationally Recognized Statistical Rating Organization (NRSRO), 84–89, 94–97, 154
NBS. *See* National Bank Supervisor (NBS)
New York Stock Exchange (NYSE), 113, 168
New York Times, 27, 89, 98–99, 104, 138
Nightly Business Report, 43
non-banks, 61, 63–64, 66

NRSRO. *See* Nationally Recognized
    Statistical Rating Organization
NYSE. *See* New York Stock Exchange (NYSE)

O

Obama's Financial Regulatory Reform
  accounting standards, improve, 186
  asset backed securities (ABS), 32, 36, 181
  bank regulation, close loopholes in,
    179–80
  banks and BHCs, strengthen capital and
    other prudential standards for, 179
  BHCs including Tier 1 FHCs, create
    resolution regime for failing, 184
  compensation practices, introduce better,
    185
  Consumer Financial Protection Agency
    (CFPA), 57, 62, 64–65, 182–83
  consumer protection, reform, 183
  credit rating agencies, tighten oversight
    of, 186
  crisis management and management
    authorities and procedures, reform,
    185
  Federal Reserve's Emergency Lending
    Authority, 184
  financial abuse, protect consumers and
    investors from, 182–84
  financial crisis, provide government with
    tools to manage, 184
  financial firms, promote robust
    supervision and regulation of,
    177–81
  financial markets, establish regulation of,
    181–82
  Financial Services Oversight Council,
    177–78
  Financial Stability Board, 184–85
  futures and securities regulation,
    harmonize, 182
  global financial markets, improve
    oversight of, 184
  government sponsored enterprises (GSEs),
    181
  Gramm-Leach-Bliley Act (GLB Act),
    77–78, 178
  hedge funds and other private pools of
    capital, 180
  insurance sector, enhance oversight of,
    180–81
  interconnected financial firms,
    heightened supervision and regulation
    of all large, 178

international capital framework,
    strengthen, 184
international cooperation, improve,
    184–86
international financial firms, enhance
    supervision of, 184–85
International Regulatory Standards, raise,
    184–86
investor protection, strengthen, 183
Money Market Mutual funds (MMEs), 180
National Bank Supervisor (NBS), 179
OTC Derivatives including Credit Default
    Swaps (CDS), comprehensive
    regulation of, 181–82
payment clearing and settlement systems,
    strengthen, 182
prudential regulation and money
    laundering/terrorist financing,
    stronger standards for, 185
Prudential regulations, strengthen, 185
recommendations, summary of,
    177–86
regulation, expand scope of, 185
SEC programs for consolidated
    supervision, eliminate, 180
securitization markets, strengthen
    supervision and regulation of, 181
tax information exchange, stronger
    standards in, 185
OCC. *See* Office of the Comptroller of the
    Currency (OCC)
Office of Compliance Inspections and
    Examinations (OCIE), 108–9
Office of Information and Regulatory Affairs
    (OIRA), 130
Office of Management and Budget, 130
Office of the Comptroller of the Currency
    (OCC), 75–76
Office of Thrift Supervision (OTS), 63,
    75–76, 79, 149
OIG. *See* Inspector General (OIG)
OIRA. *See* Office of Information and
    Regulatory Affairs (OIRA)
over-the-counter market, 39, 71, 168

P

Parmalat, 84
Petrou, Karen, 43
Plan B, 10, 20, 22, 30, 81, 144
point-in-time ratings, 96
political capture, 104
privacy laws, 134–35, 137, 141
private equity funds, 105, 180

194 ■ Index

R
Regan administration, xv
regulation and innovation
  about, 41–44
  conclusions, 45
  credit default swaps (CDSs), 42–44
  financial innovation and risk
    management, 42
  financial innovation pushes boundary of
    complexity further, 43
  financial regulators and regulatory lag on
    innovations, 43
  internal risk controls, 44
  legislation to reform markets after
    near-collapse of financial system, 41
  market complexity, 44
  mortgage-backed securities, 42
  policy implications, 44
  regulation could stifle all innovation, 42
  residential mortgage-backed securities, 44
  transparency as regulatory tool, 44
regulation of free markets
  about, xv–xvi
  Bernie Madoff scandal, xxi
  Commodities Future Trading Commission
    and transparency to credit derivatives
    market, xvi
  conclusion, xx–xxi
  credit rating agencies and subprime-loan
    pools, xvii–xix, 88, 93
  credit rating agencies diluted meaning of
    AAA, xxi
  Efficient Market Theory, xix
  market collapse is 2008, xx
  markets, inefficiencies and imbalances of
    distorted, xvii
  market self-regulation, xix–xx
  perfect markets regulate themselves, xx
  philosophy to math, the shift from,
    xvii–xix
  regulation, ideological legitimacy of,
    xv
  regulation is not separate from market,
    xv
  regulation *vs.* justice, xx
  regulation *vs.* retribution, xx
  self interest and free trade, xvii
  selfish interest drives irresponsible,
    inordinate risk-taking and fraud, xxi
  Smith, Adam, xvi–xvii
  subprime mortgages, xxi
  transparency and market self-regulation,
    xix

regulations
  are there other ways to achieve the same
    aim?, 158
  conclusion, 161
  do the exemptions make sense?, 158
  is the goal of regulation worthwhile?,
    156–57
  is the regulation likely to attain the goal?,
    157
  is the right agency responsible?, 159–60
  transparency provisions, do the rules have
    the right level?, 159
  unintended consequences, are there any?,
    157
  what exemptions exist?, 158
regulations, the politics of
  about, 100–101
  American Association of Retired Persons
    (AARP), 105
  Black Caucus, 103–4
  Center for Responsive Politics, 104
  credit derivatives, 70–71, 102, 140,
    158–59, 184
  "Deficiency Letter," 111
  Enforcement Division, 111
  government's role in markets, ideological
    struggle over, 103
  hedge funds, 6, 102, 105, 157–58, 180,
    185
  House committee, 100–101
  House Committee on Oversight and
    Government Reform, 88, 101
  House Financial Services Committee, 68,
    70, 101–2
  Joint (House and Senate) Economic
    Committee, 101
  lobbying, 92, 99–100, 104, 126, 131,
    171
  political capture, 104
  political process, 101–5
  Ponzi scheme, multi-million dollar, 111
  private equity funds and lobbying, 105
  regulatory capture, 104, 169–71
  Securities and Investments industry and
    lobbying, 104
  Senate Banking Committee, 29, 58, 62,
    77–79, 101–2
regulators and compliance officers
  about, 106
  advertising and marketing review,
    117–18
  anti-money laundering, 151
  brokerage firms, 107, 116

Index ■ **195**

business unity compliance officers,
  114–15
Chief Compliance Officer (CCO), 110, 114,
  151–52
compliance departments, 113–19
compliance systems, 118–19
conclusions, 119–20
conduct of examinations, 110–12
customer complaints, 107, 110–11, 116
due diligence process, 119
examination, cause, 109
examination, cyclical, 109
examination, risk-focused, 109
examination and reporting, 117
examinations and inspections, 108–9
Financial Industry Regulatory Authority
  (FINRA), 106, 109, 111–13, 138,
  151–52, 168–69
functions, other, 119
insider trading, 107, 113, 116, 137, 157,
  172
Internet complicates marketing review
  process, 118
investment advisers, 107, 109, 115, 131,
  160, 173, 180, 183
Investment Company Act of 1940, 107
market abuse, 107, 113, 181
money laundering activity, 119, 151,
  185–86
monitoring, 115–16
Office of Compliance Inspections and
  Examinations, 108–9
risk identification and risk assessment
  methodology, 108
SEC examination program, 108–9
SEC rule making process, 107–8
Securities Act of 1933, 107
Securities and Exchange Commission
  (SEC), 106–16
Securities Exchange Act of 1934, 107
Self-Regulatory Organizations, 109, 111–
  12, 116, 138, 152, 160, 168–69
trading activity, surveillance of, 118
trading floor compliance officer, 115
regulatory capture, 104, 169–71
regulatory concepts and issues
  conflict of interest, 173–74
  consequences, unintended, 166–68
  information asymmetries, 172–73
  moral hazard, 163–65
  one size fits all, 174–76
  playing fields, unlevel, 165–66
  regulatory capture, 169–71

self-regulation, 168–69
  systemic risk, 163–65
  too big to fail, 163–65
regulatory reform matters, xxiii–xxv
regulatory structure rebuilding
  fifty 50 state-level regulators for securities
    for banking, 75
  Commodity Futures Trading Commission
    (CFTC), 38–39, 64, 75, 80, 129, 149,
    178, 182
  Consolidated Supervised Entity (CSE)
    program, 77
  consumer protection, 80
  consumer protection issues, consolidated
    body to handle, 79
  FDIC for safety of deposits, 76
  Federal Deposit Insurance Corporation
    (FDIC), 75–76
  federal regulator for insurance industry,
    79
  Federal Reserve, 75–76, 78–79
  Federal Savings and Loan Insurance
    Corporation, 76
  Federal Trade Commission (FTC), 75
  Financial Services Committee, 68, 70, 78,
    101–2
  Glass-Steagall Act, 76–77
  the Great Crash, 76
  Municipal Securities Rulemaking Board,
    76
  National Credit Union Administration, 76
  New Deal reforms of 1930s, 76
  Office of the Comptroller of the Currency
    (OCC), 63, 75–76, 79, 149
  Office of Thrift Supervision (OTS), 63,
    75–76, 79, 149
  Ponzi scheme, 81
  proposed changes, other, 79–80
  regulatory agencies, why so many?,
    76–77
  Savings and Loan crisis, 76
  SEC and the investment banks,
    77–78
  SEC regulated big banks, 77
  systemic regulator, do we need,
    80–81
  systemic responsibility, Feds *vs.* state, 82
  "to concentrate or not to concentrate,"
    81–82
  voluntary regulation doesn't work, 77
repos. *See* repurchase agreements (repos)
Republican lawmakers, 58
Republicans, Senate, 61

196 ■ Index

repurchase agreements (repos)
  agreements, 7–8
  Bear Stearns, 13–14
  Lehman, 8
  market, 6, 13
Reserve Primary Fund, 8
residential mortgage-backed securities
  (RMBSs), 13–14, 31–34, 36–37, 39,
  49, 84–85, 88, 93, 95. *See also*
  commercial mortgage-backed
  securities (CMBSs)
RMBSs. *See* residential mortgage-backed
  securities (RMBSs)
Russian financial crisis, 16

S
salary capping, 153
Sarbanes-Oxley Act, 83, 100–101, 107
Savings and Loan crisis, 9, 11
Securities Act of 1933, 107
Securities and Exchange Commission (SEC),
  106–16
Securities Exchange Act of 1934, 107
self-interest, xvii, xxi, 30, 56, 67, 157, 173
self-regulation, xix–xx, 73, 143–44, 168–69
Self-Regulatory Organizations (SROs), 109,
  111–12, 116, 138, 152, 160, 168–69
Senate Banking Committee, 29, 58, 62,
  77–79, 101–2
Sherman Anti-Trust Act, 18
six degrees of separation, 11
Smith, Adam, xvi–xvii, 56
Society of Corporate Compliance and Ethics'
  Certified Compliance and Ethics
  Professional, 151
special-purpose vehicle (SPV), 32–33, 35,
  91
spoiler alert, 15
SPV. *See* special-purpose vehicle (SPV)
SROs. *See* Self-Regulatory Organizations
  (SROs)
Standard & Poor (S&P), 84, 88, 94
structured finance products, 32, 34–36, 73,
  84, 88
Stuart, John, xvii–xviii
subprime mortgages
  AAA rating for, 33–34
  interest rates, rising, 86
  investment bankers, xxi
  mortgage payments and, 34
  pooled risk, 33
  ratings, downgrading, xvii–xix, 88, 93
  structured investments backed by, 37

as toxic assets, 32–34, 37
systemic risk and market meltdown
  about, 1
  AIG and credit default swaps, 5
  Bear Stearns, 2–6, 10, 13–14
  borrowed money, short *vs.* long-term, 2
  "breaking the buck," 8
  collateral damage, 6–7
  conclusion, 12
  economy is about connections, 1
  economy is not the sum of its parts, 1
  funding, day-to-day, 2–3
  government intervention, 9–10, 12
  hedge fund redemption, 6
  investment practice, legal covenants
    governing, 4
  Lehman repos, 8
  leverage, 6
  Long Term Capital hedge fund collapse,
    11
  loss of confidence, 3
  margin call, 6
  money market fund, 7–9, 11, 92
  regulation to focus on firms *vs.* system as a
    whole, 12
  regulatory reform proposals, 2, 12
  repurchase agreement (repo), 3, 6–8, 13
  risk of fluctuation in the overnight price of
    an asset, 3
  rumor control and market psychology, 4
  rumors, at the mercy of, 4–6
  rumors, self-fulfilling nature of, 9
  rumors and bank runs, 4
  rumors cause a crisis, 4
  run on the bank, institutional, 6
  SEC regulations restricting what money
    market fund for investment, 7
  six degrees of separation, 11
  speculative (junk) bond status, 4
  system collapse, why not before?, 10–12
  systemic, how a problems goes, 3–10
  systemic risk, how it works, 2–9
  systemic risk, macro/micro, 2
  systemic risk and Bear Stearns, 13–14
  system is complex and prone to
    uncertainty and rumor, 12
  toxic assets, difficult-to-price, 6

T
TARP. *See* Troubled Asset Relief Program
  (TARP)
Theory of Moral Sentiments (Stuart), xvii–xviii
Tier 1FHC, 177–79, 184–85

Index ■ **197**

too-big-to-fail concept, 15–17
toxic assets
  AAA rating for housing market, 34
  AAA rating for senior tranches, 34
  AAA rating for subprime mortgages, 33–34
  AAA rating for tranches, 34, 36
  AAA rating for U.S. Treasury bonds, 34
  about, 31
  asset-backed securities (ABSs), 32–33, 36
  Bank for International Settlements, 38, 43, 185
  cash reserves and firms selling CDSs, 38
  CDS and 'over the counter' exchange of money, 38
  CLO, 31
  collateralized debt obligations (CDOs), 11, 31, 42, 95–96
  commercial mortgage-backed securities (CMBSs), 31–32, 37, 40, 42
  conclusion, 40
  credit default swaps (CDSs), 31, 37–39
  credit rating agencies, role played by, 34
  credit rating agencies and structured finance products, 35–37
  credit rating and conflicts of interest, 35
  derivative products, 31
  housing market and market for securitized products, 36
  low-risk assets out of high-risk assets, building, 33–34
  mortgage-backed securities, securitization concentrated the risk into, 40
  mortgage-backed securities and credit default, 40
  mortgage back securities, creditworthiness of, 33
  PBS's *Nightly Business Report*, 38
  rating process as an advisory service, 36
  residential mortgage-backed securities (RMBSs), 13–14, 31–34, 36–37, 39, 49
  special-purpose vehicle (SPV), 32–33, 35, 91
  structured finance and pool of very large income stream, 32
  structured finance products, 32, 34–36, 73, 84, 88
  structured or securitized products, 31
  subprime loans, senior trance composed entirely of, 33–34
  subprime mortgage, 32–34, 37
  tranches, 33–37, 51
  Volcker, Fed Chairman Paul, 42, 45
  what are they?, 32–33
  why are they toxic, 32–33
trading floor compliance officer, 115
tranches, 33–37, 51
transparency
  about, xv–xvi, xix, 39, 42, 44, 69–74, 98
  conflict of interest within firms, 72
  credit default swaps (CDSs), 73
  credit derivatives, 70–71, 102, 140, 158–59
  "default position" for information disclosure, 74
  degrees of, 71–73
  disclosure, 68, 71–73, 117, 141, 159, 174, 183
  Efficient Market Hypothesis, 70
  markets, growing complexity of, 70
  market self-regulation, xix, 73
  over-the-counter market, 39, 71, 168
  as regulation, 69–71
  regulatory filings, 73–74
  as the remedy, what to consider, 73–74
  reporting, 71–72, 74, 88, 115, 117, 119, 152
Treasury bonds, 25, 34–35, 49
Troubled Asset Relief Program (TARP)
  Congressional Oversight Panel, 68
  financial institutions, 53
  firms, capping salaries in, 153
  funded firms, 53
  guidance and relative compensation, 54
  money, 20
  money paid back, 54
  program money went in one door and out the other to influence legislation, 105
  recipients, 20, 54

U
über-regulator for consumer protection, 58
U.S. Chamber of Commerce, 58, 105, 130–31

198 ■ Index

U.S. Credit Rating Reform Act, 140
U.S. Treasury bonds, 25, 34–35, 49

V
Volcker, Fed Chairman Paul, 18–19, 42, 45
Volcker Rule, 19

W
Wall Street Journal, 42, 52, 65, 93–94, 98–99
Warren, Elizabeth, 68
The Wealth of Nations (Smith), xvi–xvii
WorldCom, 84